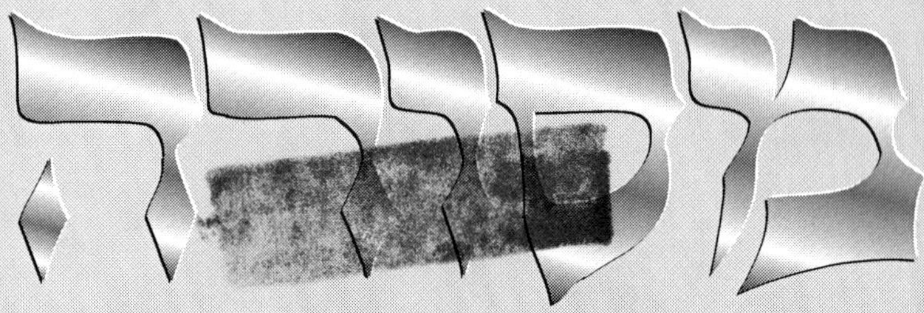

ArtScroll Mesorah Series®

Rabbi Nosson Scherman / Rabbi Meir Zlotowitz

General Editors

מגילת רות

עם פירוש ויאמר לקוצרים

OF KINGS

Commentary and insights on

THE BOOK OF RUTH

RABBI ELIEZER GINSBURG

Translated by

Rabbi Shmuel Himmelstein

[redacted]

MOTHER

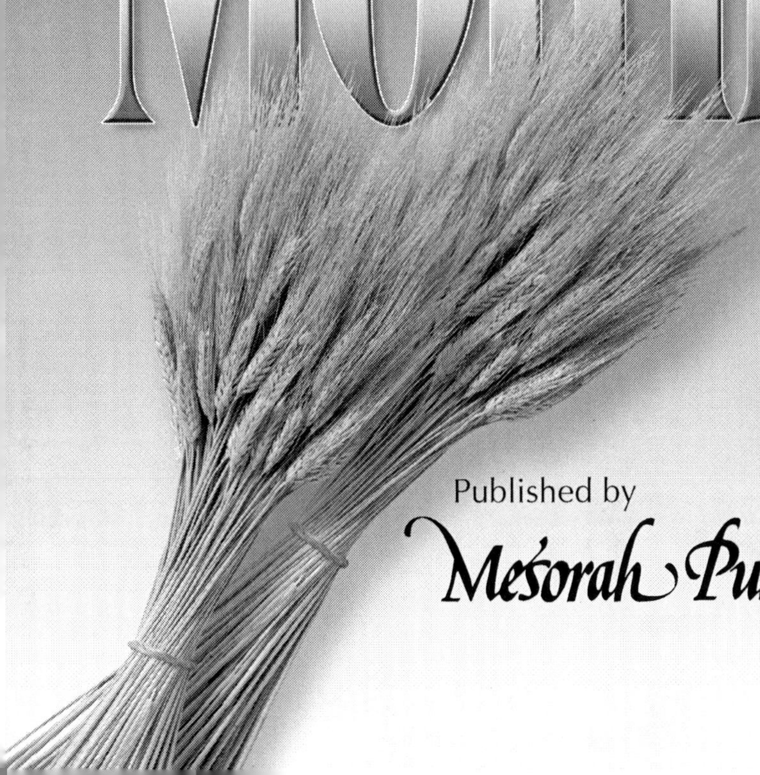

Published by

Mesorah Publications, ltd

FIRST EDITION
First Impression . . . April 2002
Second Impression . . . April 2010

Published and Distributed by
MESORAH PUBLICATIONS, Ltd.
4401 Second Avenue
Brooklyn, New York 11232

Distributed in Europe by
LEHMANNS
Unit E, Viking Business Park
Rolling Mill Road
Jarrow, Tyne & Wear NE32 3DP
England

Distributed in Australia & New Zealand by
GOLDS WORLD OF JUDAICA
3-13 William Street
Balaclava, Melbourne 3183
Victoria Australia

Distributed in Israel by
SIFRIATI / A. GITLER — BOOKS
6 Hayarkon Street
Bnei Brak 51127

Distributed in South Africa by
KOLLEL BOOKSHOP
Ivy Common 105 William Road
Norwood 2192, Johannesburg, South Africa

ARTSCROLL MESORAH SERIES®
MOTHER OF KINGS

ISBN 10: 1-57819-774-0
ISBN 13: 978-1-57819-774-3

Typography by Compuscribe at ArtScroll Studios, Ltd.

Printed in the United States of America by Noble Book Press
Bound by Sefercraft, Quality Bookbinders, Ltd. Brooklyn, N.Y.

We lovingly dedicate this sefer to our parents,
who, through their wisdom and by their example,
inspire and guide us in everything we do.

In memory of

***Mr. Joseph Straus* ע"ה**

and in honor of

***Mrs. Gwen Straus* תחי'**

and

***Mr. And Mrs. Aaron Rubin* שיחיו**

Dr. and Mrs. Jeffrey Rubin

◆§ Author's Preface

I write these words with gratitude to the *Ribbono Shel Olam,* Who has granted me the privilege of presenting this work to the English-speaking public.

I am indeed fortunate to have such close friends as Rabbi Meir Zlotowitz and Rabbi Nosson Scherman. Under their guidance and supervision, ArtScroll's talented staff presented this *sefer* to the English-speaking public in a concise and appealing manner. My sincere thanks to Rabbi Shmuel Himelstein, the gifted *talmid chacham* who translated, adapted, and edited the *sefer.*

In just a few words, I would like to express my gratitude to Dr. Yoseph Rubin and family for their continuous support of my literary efforts in Torah. He and his family have always said yes to my requests. May the *Ribbono Shel Olam* grant them הצלחה וברכה and שמחות.

Finally, I would like to express my deep appreciation for the constant support and assistance I have always received from my wife תחי', who has played a major role in all aspects of the publication of my *sefarim.*

May we merit to see the fulfillment of all the promises made by our prophets, and meet at the time of redemption with the "Mother of Kings."

Eliezer Ginsburg
Iyar 5762

◆§ Introduction to Megillas Ruth

Many reasons have been given as to why *Megillas Ruth* is read on Shavuos, and with the help of Hashem, I would like to share a reason that occurred to me. As Shavuos is the festival of the Giving of the Torah, we have to be worthy to receive the Torah. What a person must do to be worthy of this we can learn from Ruth the Moabite, who was worthy of a true receiving of the Torah and of being the mother of the Davidic monarchy line. R' Yitzchak Ze'ev HaLevi Soloveitchik, the "Brisker Rav," commented on the verse, "May Hashem make the woman who is coming into your house like Rachel and like Leah, both of whom built up the House of Israel" (*Ruth* 4:11), that just as Rachel and Leah became the mothers of the Jewish people, so did Ruth become the mother of the monarchy. And what motivated her? It was her fine qualities and humane nature, as she stated (1:16), "Do not urge me to leave you, to turn back and not follow you," for how could she leave Naomi all alone after all the troubles she had already suffered? This was Ruth's primary concern in this regard. That concern affected her deeply and took root within her until she ultimately came to recognize Hashem and to understand the truth, and wanted "Your God to be my God."

Thus, in order to be worthy of the Torah one needs fine qualities and a humane nature. These qualities refer specifically to one's relationship with one's fellow man, for only then can one have "Israel camped before the mountain" (*Shemos* 19:2), which, as *Chazal* tell us, was "as a single person, with a single heart," without any quarrels, and, on the contrary, with love and friendship, with each concerned for the other's welfare. That, indeed, is why they were worthy of receiving the Torah (*Or HaChaim,* ibid.).

Since Ruth's heart was totally devoted to caring for Naomi, and since she was willing to forsake all the pleasures of this world which she had had in her father's home and instead chose to become a poor woman who gathered grain in the fields, she was worthy of having the Kingdom of the House of David come from her, and that House, as *Rambam* writes (*Hilchos Melachim* 5:6) is "the heart of all of Israel." After all, every person is a microcosm of the entire world, and if a person carries within his heart the burden of a single other person, he has the privilege of carrying the burden of all of Israel in his heart. Thus we find in the Midrash on *Megillas Esther,* on the verse (*Esther* 2:11), "Every day Mordechai used to walk about . . . to find out about Esther's well-being and what would become of her," that one who is concerned about the well-being of a single person will be given the privilege of being concerned with the well-being of all of Israel, as it states at the end of *Esther* (10:3), "he sought the good of his people."

The same was true for all Jewish leaders who were privileged to attain that rank purely because of the character trait of shouldering the burden of the Jewish people. We can see this in the first *Ra'aya Mehemna* — "Faithful Shepherd" — Moshe Rabbeinu (*Shemos* 2:11): "It happened in those days that Moshe grew up and went out to his brethren and observed their burdens." *Rashi* comments, "He cast his eyes and his heart to grieve for them." Harav Simcha Zissel Zeeve, the *Alter* of Kelm, in his *Chochmah U'Mussar* (1:99), states that Moshe did not let nature take its course, where one grieves at the distress of another and as time goes by forgets about it, but Moshe "cast his eyes," in other words his power of envisioning things — that being the power of the mind — and thought continuously of their grief, until his heart grieved as much for them as he would have grieved for himself. That is what is meant by "and observed their burdens," meaning that he envisioned them in his mind as if they were in front of him, and grieved as if he himself were undergoing the same suffering.

Midrash Rabbah states on the verse (ibid. 3:4), "Hashem saw that he turned aside to see," that Hashem said, "Since he turned and was angry as he saw the suffering of Israel in Egypt, he is worthy of being a shepherd over them." Immediately "Hashem called out to him from amid the bush." Thus we see that it was because Moshe was aroused to suffer along with their suffering that he was privileged to bring them close to their Father in Heaven, to bring them to Mount Sinai, to receive the Torah from Heaven, to lead them in the desert for forty years, to have them sustained by the manna due to his merit — and all of this because he was moved by their suffering. One can see from this the greatness of carrying the burden of one's fellow, and the reward the person will earn for this great attribute. And just as Moshe became the first shepherd of Israel because of this attribute, Ruth was privileged to become the mother of the monarchy because of this same attribute, and the same is true for every individual who is truly concerned about the troubles of Israel. He is then privileged to attain the Crown of Torah and to become a leader and shepherd of the Holy Flock of Hashem.

MOTHER OF KINGS

א וַיְהִי בִּימֵי שְׁפֹט הַשֹּׁפְטִים וַיְהִי רָעָב בָּאָרֶץ

I

1. וַיְהִי בִּימֵי שְׁפֹט הַשֹּׁפְטִים — And it was in the days when the Judges judged.

We are told in *Bava Basra* 15b, "It was a generation that judged its judges. If (a judge) said to a person, 'Take out the splinter between your teeth,' he would reply, 'Take out the beam between your eyes.' " In other words it was a generation that rebuked its judges. This is the opposite of what should be the normal order of things, with the judges rebuking the people. After all, it is the judge who is the one to influence his generation positively or negatively. For a judge to influence people for the good is obviously what we expect, but it is also possible for a judge to influence people negatively. Indeed, I once heard a comment from R' Shmuel Rozofsky on the verse (*Bamidbar* 11:4), "The rabble that was among them cultivated a craving, and the Children of Israel also wept once more, and said: 'Who will feed us meat?" R' Shmuel noted that there are two interpretations of who the rabble were. *Rashi* states that they were the mixed multitude that left Egypt with the Jewish people, while a Midrash says that these were the Jewish elders, who had a craving for meat, and this influenced the Children of Israel to cry and ask for meat. So too were the people in this generation influenced negatively to rebuke its judges.

We may also add another interpretation of a generation that "judged its judges" namely that the people of that generation influenced the judges. As the generation was corrupt and involved in theft, they tried to influence the judges to also become involved in theft.[1]

וַיְהִי בִּימֵי שְׁפֹט הַשֹּׁפְטִים — And it was in the days when the Judges judged.

Rashi explains that this was before Shaul ruled in Israel, where the generations were supported by the merits of the judges. We need to explain what this verse is trying to teach us when it tells us that Elimelech lived before there was a king in Israel.

In *Bava Basra* (15b) it states, "It was a generation that judged its judges. If (a judge) said to a person, 'Take out the splinter between your teeth,' he would reply, 'Take out the beam between your eyes.' " In other words, as we explained above, the generation would rebuke its judges, and was not willing to be influenced by them. This is the reverse of the natural order, where the judge is the one to rebuke people and to influence the

1. See *Sefas Emes, Parshas Devarim,* 5635, beginning "*Mutav hadavar.*"

1 *And it was in the days when the Judges*
judged, and there was a famine in the land,

---

generation. Therefore, since they did not accept the influence of the judges, the generation was not supported by the merits of the judges, and there was a famine in the land. This we see in the continuation of the verse, "And it was in the days when the Judges judged, and there was a famine in the land."

Now we can understand the words of *Rashi* who wrote that this was before Shaul ruled (i.e., before there was a king). The generations of the kings were different than those of the judges, for in the days of the judges, when the generations refused to accept the rebukes and the influence of the judges, they were not privileged to be supported through the virtue of the judges. The generations of the kings, though, were different, for the ability of the king to be a favorable influence on his generation is not dependent on the behavior of the generation. Thus, just as the rule of the monarchs was whether people wanted it or not, as we can see when *Rambam* writes (*Hilchos Melachim* 3:3) that if anyone revolts against a king of Israel the king has the right to put him to death, so too is the influence of the king for the people's benefit whether they want it or not, whether they are worthy or not, for the merits of the king benefit the people.

That is also the explanation of the *gemara* regarding David HaMelech's morning schedule, as stated in *Berachos* 3b: "Rav Abba bar Biana said in the name of R' Shimon bar Chasida: A harp hung over David's bed, and when midnight came . . . he would immediately get up and study Torah until dawn. As soon as dawn arose, the Sages of Israel would come in to him and would say, 'Our master, the king, your people Israel need sustenance,' " etc. The *gemara* there ends with the verse in *Tehillim* (86:2), "Guard my soul, for I am devout." Thus did David say to the Holy One, Blessed is He, "Lord of the Universe, am I not pious? All the kings of East and West sleep until (the end of) the third hour (of the day), while I arise at midnight to praise You." *Maharsha* explains that David acted like a poor man who gets up early to work and earn his sustenance. Thus did David rise early — in the middle of the night — to thank Hashem, because it was through his merit that the generation received sustenance when the people went out to work, whether its individuals were worthy or not. This behavior was requested by Moshe Rabbeinu (*Bamidbar* 27:16-17), "May Hashem, God of the Spirits of all flesh, appoint a man over the assembly, who shall go out before them and come in before them"; and *Rashi* comments that this "going out" and "coming in" are all due to the leader's merits. He sustains the generation, and the entire generation is dependent on his merit.

א/ב וַיֵּלֶךְ אִישׁ מִבֵּית לֶחֶם יְהוּדָה לָגוּר בִּשְׂדֵי
ב מוֹאָב הוּא וְאִשְׁתּוֹ וּשְׁנֵי בָנָיו: וְשֵׁם הָאִישׁ

וַיְהִי בִּימֵי שְׁפֹט הַשֹּׁפְטִים וַיְהִי רָעָב בָּאָרֶץ וַיֵּלֶךְ אִישׁ מִבֵּית לֶחֶם יְהוּדָה לָגוּר בִּשְׂדֵי מוֹאָב הוּא וְאִשְׁתּוֹ וּשְׁנֵי בָנָיו — And it was in the days when the Judges judged, and there was a famine in the land, and a man went from Bethlehem in Yehudah to sojourn in the fields of Moab, he, his wife, and his two sons.

There are various deductions which we can make from this verse, from which we will see that the sin of Elimelech was not the one which people customarily assume.

Rashi states that this occurred in the days of Ivtzan, and *Chazal* say that Ivtzan was Boaz. Why then did the verse not say, "And it happened in the days of Ivtzan," as we see in *Esther* (1:1), "And it happened in the days of Ahasuerus"? Why does *Ruth* begin with "And it was in the days when the Judges judged"? Also, why does the verse state twice, "*vayehi* — And it was"? [*Yalkut* Section 597 discusses why this is stated twice.]

It appears from this verse that Elimelech never had any intention to stay in the fields of Moab for any length of time, for the verse does not state, "A man went from Bethlehem in Yehudah to *live* (*leisheiv*) in the fields of Moab," but says only "to *sojourn* (*lagur*) in the fields of Moab" — for he planned to be there for but a short time. As we see in the interpretation of the *Haggadah* on the verse (*Bereishis* 47:4), "We have come to sojourn in the land," the tribes had not come to live there but only to sojourn there. Similarly, Elimelech planned to remain there for a short time. Only after his death are we told that (*Ruth* 1:4) "they *lived* there about ten years." This, indeed, was the sin of Naomi's sons, Machlon and Kilion. As *Rambam* (*Hilchos Melachim* 5:9) puts it, even though one is permitted to leave Eretz Yisrael during a drought, this is not the way a pious person should act. That was why Machlon and Kilion — who were the greatest Torah scholars of their generation and left the country only because of great distress — deserved to be destroyed. *Rambam* only states that Machlon and Kilion deserved to be destroyed but does not say the same about Elimelech, because Elimelech only went to Moab to sojourn there, as the verse concludes, "They came to the field of Moab and there they remained," hoping to stay for but a short time.

The reason why Elimelech left Eretz Yisrael is hinted at in the verse, for it was "in the days when the Judges judged." On this we are told (*Bava Basra* 15b) that they would judge their judges, and people would not listen to their words or rebukes. This, of course, was a terrible transgression of the Jewish people, for they had great sages but did not learn from them *and a man went from Bethlehem in Yehudah to sojourn in the fields of Moab, he, his wife, and his two sons.*

---

and did not heed their rebuke.[1] Therefore, when Elimelech saw that the people refused to listen to the judges, he decided to leave Bethlehem so as to remove this sin from them, and possibly to cause the people to repent as a result.

Another reason for Elimelech's leaving is hinted at in the words, "and there was a famine in the land," which is the second time we find "and there was" in the same first verse of *Ruth.* This hints to us that the famine was a separate reason in itself for Elimelech's leaving, for he saw that even though there was a famine in the land, the people were still not praying to "the Provider of All," namely Hashem, but rather relied on Elimelech as being able to end the famine. This, too, was a reason why Elimelech thought it necessary — for the welfare of the generation — to leave Eretz Yisrael for a short time. Once the people saw that Elimelech was not with them and would realize that they could not rely on him, they would turn to Hashem — which is what they did.[2] [3] Indeed, these considerations of Elimelech were valid ones, except that they caused Hashem to deal with the *tzaddik* in accordance with the strict provisions of the law (*middas hadin*). This is because Hashem treats people measure for measure, and if a person acts with mercy and lovingkindness (*middas harachamim*) to others, Hashem acts toward him in the same way, and if the person acts in accordance with strict justice, Hashem acts with him in accordance with strict justice. Strict justice demands that the person should act — according to his own level — in every way perfectly. Now, since Elimelech acted in accordance with the provisions of strict justice, where any considerations of mercy don't count (unlike those who work according to the provisions of mercy where such considerations would indeed count), he was treated according to strict justice. Thus, when Elimelech's book was opened on Rosh Hashanah (as we see in *Yalkut* 599), the attribute of strict justice demanded accountability from Elimelech for his miserliness, in that he was miserly when dealing with the poor who came to disturb him (see *Rashi* there). As a result, he was punished.

---

1. I also heard that R' Shmuel Brudny said that if there is a generation with very few Torah sages and the very few keep diminishing in number, you should know that the generation does not need them, either because people do not listen to them or because they do not learn from their deeds.

2. So too do we find in *Megillah* 15b that one of the reasons Esther invited Haman to the feast was so that the Jews would not say that they had one of their people in the king's household to take care of their problem, and would not rely on Hashem to deliver them.

3. This idea is found in *Midrash Ruth* 1:4.

This also explains why Elimelech was punished immediately, without any prior warning, whereas this was not the case with his sons. *Rashi* on the verse (1:5), "The two of them, Machlon and Kilion, also died," notes that "also" implies that first they were stricken with loss of their money, in that their camels and flocks died, and only afterwards did they also die. As far as the sons were concerned, Hashem's complaint against them was that they lived outside Eretz Yisrael, and using His attribute of mercy He first had their animals die. The complaint against Elimelech, on the other hand, was about a much finer point: the way he dealt with the poor. But since he had dealt with the Jewish people strictly according to justice and without any mercy, he was punished strictly according to justice, and was not given the opportunity to repent. Such an opportunity is part of Hashem's mercy, as stated in *Mesillas Yesharim (*Ch. 4).

That was what Naomi meant when she said (1:21-22), "I was full when I went away, but Hashem has brought me back empty . . . Hashem has testified against me, the Almighty has brought misfortune upon me." *Rashi* remarks there that "Hashem has testified against me" refers to the attribute of strict justice, as in (*Hoshea* 5:5), "The pride of Israel will be humbled before Him." This refers to the death of Elimelech, which occurred without Hashem's first being slow to anger, but rather with the immediate anger of the attribute of strict justice. "The Almighty has brought misfortune upon me" refers to the deaths of Machlon and Kilion, where there was mercy in Hashem's justice, as we see in the words of Yaakov (*Bereishis* 43:14), "And may Almighty God grant you mercy before the man." Even though Hashem is a King and (*Mishlei* 29:4), "Through justice a king establishes a land," nevertheless there is mercy in His justice. That was why the two sons did not die immediately but only ten years later, and even then first they lost their possessions and then their lives.

It states in the Midrash (*Yalkut* 600) that the name "Elimelech" indicates "From me (*eilai*) will come the monarchy (*malchus*)," for he thought that from him would come the Davidic monarchy. In this he erred, because to be eligible for the monarchy one needs to be concerned for all of Israel. Even though his words were accurate, in that the monarchy eventually resulted from his daughter-in-law, he himself was excluded, for someone who makes calculations such as he did indicates that he was not concerned about the troubles of the Jewish people. As such, he could have no connection to the monarchy.

וַיֵּלֶךְ אִישׁ מִבֵּית לֶחֶם יְהוּדָה לָגוּר בִּשְׂדֵי מוֹאָב הוּא וְאִשְׁתּוֹ וּשְׁנֵי בָנָיו — A man went from Bethlehem in Yehudah to sojourn in the fields of Moab, he, his wife, and his two sons.

The verse does not say that "a man and his wife and his two sons went from Bethlehem in Yehudah." Instead, there is a break between the man on the one hand and his wife and two sons on the other. This break is significant; it indicates that the others did not want to leave, and only Elimelech wanted to. The others only went because that was what Elimelech wanted. On the other hand, when he died they did not return to Eretz Yisrael, because that is the way the *yetzer hara* (Evil Inclination) works. At first it comes as a guest, but in the end it takes over as the owner, and the three of them eventually wanted to remain in Moab.

וַיֵּלֶךְ אִישׁ מִבֵּית לֶחֶם יְהוּדָה לָגוּר בִּשְׂדֵי מוֹאָב הוּא וְאִשְׁתּוֹ וּשְׁנֵי בָנָיו — A man went from Bethlehem in Yehudah to sojourn in the fields of Moab.

Shlomo HaMelech states (*Mishlei* 20:24), "A man's steps are from Hashem, but what does a man understand of His way?" The reason that Elimelech went to the fields of Moab was because of miserliness, but this was part of Hashem's plan, so that the souls of David and of the *Mashiach* would be brought forth from the fields of Moab, as in the verse (*Tehillim* 89:21), "I have found David, My servant, with My holy oil I have anointed him." On this *Chazal* comment, "Where was he found? In the fields of Moab."

We find in *Berachos* 35b that R' Shimon bar Yochai says: "If a person plows during the plowing season and sows during the sowing season and harvests during the harvest season and threshes at the threshing season and winnows when it is windy, what will become of Torah study? Rather, at a time when people do Hashem's will their work is carried out by others, as it states (*Yeshayahu* 61:5), 'Foreigners will stand and tend your flocks and the sons of the stranger will be your plowmen and your vineyard workers.' On the other hand, when Israel do not do Hashem's will their work is done by themselves, as it states (*Bamidbar* 11:14), 'You will gather your grain, your wine, and your oil.' " This, indeed, was fulfilled in the case of Elimelech and of Boaz, as I will explain based on the *Sefas Emes* (*Shavuos* 5659), who quotes the *Or HaChaim* on the verse in *Parshas Yisro* (*Shemos* 19:5), "And now, if you will hearken well to Me and observe My covenant, you shall be to Me the most beloved treasure of all peoples": The Jewish people were created to bring forth the holy sparks from the entire world. If they merit it, they are able to do so based on the power of the Torah, which is like a rock which attracts its sparks from wherever they are. On the other hand, if they are unable to do so, the Jewish people have to be dispersed into *galus* (Diaspora). The *Sefas Emes* added that this was the meaning of the words of the prophet Yirmiyahu (16:19), "Hashem, my Strength, my Stronghold and my Refuge on the day of distress," where "my Strength, my Stronghold and my Refuge" refers to Torah and "the day of distress" refers to *galus.* Through these two — Torah and *galus* — the gentiles will come to you from the ends of the earth.

אֱלִימֶלֶךְ וְשֵׁם אִשְׁתּוֹ נָעֳמִי וְשֵׁם שְׁנֵי־בָנָיו ׀ מַחְלוֹן
וְכִלְיוֹן אֶפְרָתִים מִבֵּית לֶחֶם יְהוּדָה וַיָּבֹאוּ שְׂדֵי־מוֹאָב
ג וַיִּהְיוּ־שָׁם׃ וַיָּמָת אֱלִימֶלֶךְ אִישׁ נָעֳמִי וַתִּשָּׁאֵר הִיא
ד וּשְׁנֵי בָנֶיהָ׃ וַיִּשְׂאוּ לָהֶם נָשִׁים מֹאֲבִיּוֹת שֵׁם הָאַחַת
עָרְפָּה וְשֵׁם הַשֵּׁנִית רוּת וַיֵּשְׁבוּ שָׁם כְּעֶשֶׂר שָׁנִים׃

Thus, the mission of Elimelech, which required that he leave for the fields of Moab, was to bring forth the souls of David and the *Mashiach;* but it was Boaz who merited having Ruth come to his home on her own, due to the power of the Torah within him. We see this meaning in the way *Chazal* interpret the name "Boaz," which they interpret as "*Bo oz shel Torah*" ("in him is the strength of the Torah"). Elimelech, though, was on a lower spiritual level, where he had to take care of matters on his own. That was why he himself had to leave for the fields of Moab to bring forth the souls of David and the *Mashiach.* In the case of Boaz, though, who was very great in Torah, Hashem treated him as he would later treat R' Shimon bar Yochai, and all his needs were taken care of by others, and Ruth came to his threshing floor on her own.

This may also be hinted at in the verse (*Michah* 7:20), "Grant truth to Yaakov, kindness to Avraham": When the children of Yaakov strengthen themselves in the truth, i.e., in the Torah, kindness is done to them, to draw close those who are far away as well — the converts, *gerim* — for converts are called Sons of Avraham. This was indeed fulfilled in the case of Boaz and Ruth; because Boaz strengthened himself in Torah, he merited to have Ruth the Moabite draw close to him.

וַיֵּלֶךְ אִישׁ מִבֵּית לֶחֶם יְהוּדָה לָגוּר בִּשְׂדֵי מוֹאָב הוּא וְאִשְׁתּוֹ וּשְׁנֵי בָנָיו — A man went from Bethlehem in Yehudah to sojourn in the fields of Moab, he, his wife, and his two sons.

A question may be asked: Why does the first verse just mention a man, his wife, and his two sons, without mentioning their names, and only in the second verse are we told their names?

It appears that Elimelech certainly was aware of the ruling (later formulated by *Rambam* in *Hilchos Melachim* 5:9) that even though one is permitted to leave Eretz Yisrael when there is a famine in the land, it is not the way a pious person should act, and great sages who do so are held accountable for having left the country. Elimelech's humility, though, was such that he did not consider himself as the greatest sage of the generation, and therefore he felt he was permitted to leave. Thus, when

[2] *The name of the man was Elimelech, the name of his wife Naomi, and his two sons were named Machlon and Kilion, Ephrathites of Bethlehem in Yehudah. They came to the field of Moab and there they remained.*

[3] *Elimelech, Naomi's husband, died; and she was left with her two sons.* [4] *They married Moabite women, the name of the one was Orpah, and the name of the second Ruth, and they lived there about ten years.*

---

the verse states, "a man went from Bethlehem in Yehudah," it is because Elimelech did not consider himself a great man. Similarly (*Bamidbar* 12:3), "The man Moshe was exceedingly humble." However, Elimelech's humility was not authentic. Rather, he had miserliness deeply embedded in his heart, which caused him to think was not the greatest sage of his generation and therefore did not need to act with great piety and refrain from leaving Eretz Yisrael even at a time of famine. Thus, when the second verse mentions their names, it is to tell us that "the man" was Elimelech, a great Torah scholar, and that his wife was the famed woman Naomi, and their two sons were Machlon and Kilion, who were renowned throughout the world. How then did they dare to leave Eretz Yisrael to live in the fields of Moab?

2. וְשֵׁם שְׁנֵי בָנָיו מַחְלוֹן וְכִלְיוֹן — And his two sons were named Machlon and Kilion.

The verse should simply have that "his sons were named Machlon and Kilion." Why does it mention his "two" sons? This is to teach us that the two were equal, as we find in *Yoma* 62b regarding the two he-goats of Yom Kippur, where the Torah states (*Vayikra* 16:5), "he shall take two he-goats" — and we learn that both must be alike. Here, too, the two were alike, in that they lived together in love and harmony. They were like Moshe and Aharon, about whom we are told (*Tehillim* 133:1), "How good and how pleasant is the dwelling of brothers in unity," for this is one of the greatest of attributes.[1] This verse thus teaches us: Even though they lived together in love and in harmony, that did not help them against Hashem's anger, for "The two of them, Machlon and Kilion, also died" (1:5).

---

1. I also heard that the reason we mention Menasheh and Ephraim when we bless our children is because they lived together in perfect harmony, and neither had any complaints against the other. Thus we see that even when Yaakov gave the rights of the firstborn to Ephraim over Menasheh, who was the actual firstborn, he was in no way offended.

ה וַיָּמֻתוּ גַם־שְׁנֵיהֶם מַחְלוֹן וְכִלְיוֹן וַתִּשָּׁאֵר הָאִשָּׁה
ו מִשְּׁנֵי יְלָדֶיהָ וּמֵאִישָׁהּ׃ וַתָּקָם הִיא וְכַלֹּתֶיהָ
וַתָּשָׁב מִשְּׂדֵי מוֹאָב כִּי שָׁמְעָה בִּשְׂדֵה מוֹאָב
ז כִּי־פָקַד יהוה אֶת־עַמּוֹ לָתֵת לָהֶם לָחֶם׃ וַתֵּצֵא

---

5. וַיָּמֻתוּ גַם שְׁנֵיהֶם מַחְלוֹן וְכִלְיוֹן וַתִּשָּׁאֵר הָאִשָּׁה מִשְּׁנֵי יְלָדֶיהָ וּמֵאִישָׁהּ — The two of them, Machlon and Kilion, also died; and the woman was bereft of her two children and of her husband.

Why are they referred to as "children" — *yeladim* — and not as sons — *banim* — when they were grown, married men? The reason for this is that Naomi blamed herself for their deaths. Similarly (*Bava Basra* 22), when Rav Adda bar Ahavah died, all the Amoraim present blamed themselves for his death, and claimed, "I punished him." So too are we told (*Berachos* 5b) that when children die, it is because of the sins of their parents. Here, too, Naomi blamed herself for the deaths of her two sons, considering them as children who die because of their parents' sins.

One can also say that the word "*banim*" ("sons") comes from the word "*binyan*" ("a building"), for the parents are the foundations upon which the *banim* stand, like a *binyan*. Once the *banim* died Naomi remained without her *binyan* and therefore her children are not called "*banim,*" but "*yeladim.*"[1]

וַתִּשָּׁאֵר הָאִשָּׁה מִשְּׁנֵי יְלָדֶיהָ וּמֵאִישָׁהּ — And the woman was bereft of her two children and of her husband.

Tosefes Berachah notes that in Verse 3 it states, "she was left with her two sons," whereas in the present verse it refers to them as "her two children." We also need to explain why the verse tells us that her husband died, when it already stated so in Verse 3.

It appears to me that we may draw a comparison between the deaths of her sons and the death of her husband: Just as Naomi was held responsible for the death of her husband in that she did not protest[2] when her husband wanted to leave Eretz Yisrael, as stated in *Yalkut* 599, so too was she held responsible for not protesting against her sons when they married foreign women. Even though they did so without asking her for permission, as it states, "They married Moabite women," and does not state, "She took for them wives" — as was the case with Yishmael (*Bereishis* 21:21): "His mother took him a wife from the land of Egypt" — Naomi was nevertheless

---

1. I heard this from my friend, R' Avraham Greenberg.

2. See *Avodah Zarah* 18a, where we are told that the wife of R' Chanina ben Tradyon was punished because she should have protested what her husband was doing.

5 The two of them, Machlon and Kilion, also died; and
the woman was bereft of her two children and of her
husband.
6 She then arose along with her daughters-in-law
to return from the fields of Moab, for she had heard
in the fields of Moab that HASHEM had remembered
His people by giving them food. 7 She left the place

---

punished for not protesting. Indeed, the Midrash there states that if one person protests an evil deed the evil decree is annulled, whereas if no one protests, the evil decree goes into effect.

Now we understand why it states "her children" rather than "her sons," for even though they were already adults, the fact that she never protested — even though she could have done so, for they were "her children" — caused her to be punished and to be left without her husband and children.

6. וַתָּקָם הִיא וְכַלֹּתֶיהָ וַתָּשָׁב מִשְּׂדֵי מוֹאָב כִּי שָׁמְעָה בִּשְׂדֵה מוֹאָב כִּי פָקַד יהוה אֶת עַמּוֹ לָתֵת לָהֶם לָחֶם — She then arose along with her daughters-in-law to return from the fields of Moab, for she had heard in the fields of Moab that Hashem had remembered His people by giving them food.

It would appear that when the verse goes to the trouble of saying "she arose" ("*vatakom*") it implies that there was a rejuvenation ("*tekumah*"), as we see in the verse (*Bereishis* 23:17), "And the field was confirmed" ("*vayakom*"), on which *Rashi* comments, "it had a rejuvenation ("*tekumah*"), in that it passed from the hands of a common person into those of a king." Similarly, by the deaths of Machlon and Kilion there was a rejuvenation, in that Naomi was aroused to return to Eretz Yisrael, and her two daughters-in-law were aroused to convert. As the Midrash says later, on the verse (1:7), "they set out on the road": They were studying the laws of conversion, after seeing the terrible punishment of the deaths of these two righteous men. In fact, it was out of great fear that they sought to turn to the God of Israel. The same is true of the men who were on the ship with Yonah, as it states (*Yonah* 1:16), "Then the men felt a great fear of Hashem; they slaughtered a sacrifice to Hashem and took vows." On this, *Rashi* comments that they converted and became Jews.

וַתָּקָם הִיא וְכַלֹּתֶיהָ וַתָּשָׁב מִשְּׂדֵי מוֹאָב כִּי שָׁמְעָה בִּשְׂדֵה מוֹאָב כִּי פָקַד יהוה אֶת עַמּוֹ לָתֵת לָהֶם לָחֶם — She then arose along with her daughters-in-law to return from the fields of Moab, for she had heard in the fields of Moab that Hashem had remembered His people by giving them food.

Since the punishments meted out to the three men by Hashem had roused the women to repent and to return to Eretz Yisrael, why does this

א/ח מִן־הַמָּקוֹם֙ אֲשֶׁ֣ר הָֽיְתָה־שָׁ֔מָּה וּשְׁתֵּ֥י כַלֹּתֶ֖יהָ עִמָּ֑הּ
ח וַתֵּלַ֣כְנָה בַדֶּ֔רֶךְ לָשׁ֖וּב אֶל־אֶ֥רֶץ יְהוּדָֽה׃ וַתֹּ֤אמֶר

---

verse add, as a second reason, that "she had heard in the fields of Moab that Hashem had remembered His people by giving them food"? Indeed, a simple reading of the text would seem to imply that if Naomi had not heard that the famine was over in Eretz Yisrael, she would not have returned. How can that be?

The answer to this question is to be found in the *Targum* of the verse which states that Hashem had remembered His people, the House of Israel, to give them food because of their leader's prayers before Hashem, their leader being Boaz the Righteous One.[1] The prayers of the righteous have the power to transform Hashem's attribute of strict justice to that of mercy, as we see in *Rashi* on the verse (*Bereishis* 8:1), "Hashem remembered Noah," and as we see on the verse (ibid. 21:6), "Sarah said, 'Hashem has made laughter of me; whoever hears will laugh for me.' " *Rashi,* quoting the Midrash, states that on that very day many barren women conceived, many ill people were cured, and many prayers were answered, and there was much rejoicing in the world.

Now, Naomi was afraid to return to Eretz Yisrael, because since she felt that her leaving it had meant she had spurned it, it might not now accept her return, in accordance with the verse (*Vayikra* 18:25), "The land disgorged its inhabitants." She prayed that she would be able to return but was afraid that her prayer would not be accepted. However, once she heard that Hashem had ended the famine, due to the prayers of Boaz — and we know that through the prayers of the righteous Hashem's attribute of strict justice is transformed to mercy and many prayers are answered along with that of the righteous person — she felt sure that her prayer had also been accepted, and she was thus able to return to Eretz Yisrael, to the inheritance of her forefathers.

7. וַתֵּצֵא מִן הַמָּקוֹם אֲשֶׁר הָיְתָה שָׁמָּה וּשְׁתֵּי כַלֹּתֶיהָ עִמָּהּ וַתֵּלַכְנָה בַדֶּרֶךְ לָשׁוּב אֶל אֶרֶץ יְהוּדָה — She left the place where she had been, accompanied by her two daughters-in-law, and they set out on the road to return to the land of Yehudah.

We find in *Sotah* 42b that Rava learned: "Because of the four tears that Orpah cried for her mother-in-law, she had the merit of having four great warriors come from her, as it states (1:14), 'They raised their voice and wept

---

1. The author of *Chelek B'nei Yehudah* explained that the *Targum* relies on the fact that the verse states, "by giving them" ("*laseis lahem*") rather than "He gave them" ("*nasan lahem*"), implying that the decree of famine had not yet been annulled, but Naomi had heard from actual angels that Hashem had decreed that the famine would be over because of the prayers of Boaz, and that fact she could only find out from actual angels.

1/7 *where she had been, accompanied by her two daughters-in-law, and they set out on the road to return to the land of Yehudah.*

---

again.' " Thus, we see that according to Rava, Orpah's reward was for the tears she had shed rather than for the steps she took as she accompanied Naomi, the righteous woman, on the way to Eretz Yisrael. In *Yalkut,* though, we find that Rav Yitzchak said, "Because of the four steps that Orpah walked with Naomi her mother-in-law, she merited to have four great warriors," in opposition to the *gemara* that states it was because of her tears.

One can explain this with the words of the *Alter* of Kelm, in his *Chochmah U'Mussar* (p. 428): In truth, Orpah had a wicked heart but an intelligent mind, and went with Naomi only because Naomi was an intelligent woman. Orpah was very impressed with her and felt comfortable with her and was willing to suffer poverty as long as she could be with Naomi and enjoy Naomi's intellect. Thus, according to this view, when she accompanied Naomi it was for her own personal enjoyment and therefore she did not deserve any reward for walking with her.

However, once Naomi persuaded her to go back to her people and convinced her that it was not worthwhile to convert and she decided on her own that it would be better for her to return, in keeping with her wicked heart and mind, the fact that she nevertheless cried four tears when leaving Naomi merited a reward, and four great warriors came from her.

We still have to reconcile the fact that Orpah, an intelligent woman willing to endure poverty just to enjoy the intellectual side of Naomi, nevertheless engaged in all types of despicable, immoral acts on the night she left Naomi, as *Chazal* tell us (*Midrash Rabbah* there). *Chazal* also tell us (*Sotah* 3a), "A person does not commit a sin unless a spirit of folly enters into him." How did Orpah fall so low that very night?

It would appear that this was a fulfillment of the words of Shlomo HaMelech in *Mishlei* (14:33), "Wisdom will reside in an understanding heart," which the *Alter* of Kelm explained as follows: Even if it sometimes does good, an evil heart does not stay good for any length of time. Therefore, immediately after she decided to return to her nation all her wisdom left her and she was left empty. This emptiness was then filled with animal lusts, which is why she acted as she did that night.

וַתֵּצֵא מִן הַמָּקוֹם אֲשֶׁר הָיְתָה שָׁמָּה וּשְׁתֵּי כַלֹּתֶיהָ עִמָּהּ וַתֵּלַכְנָה בַדֶּרֶךְ לָשׁוּב אֶל אֶרֶץ יְהוּדָה — She left the place where she had been, accompanied by her two daughters-in-law, and they set out on the road to return to the land of Yehudah.

Midrash Lekach Tov states that "they set out on the road to return" means that they were discussing the laws of converting to Judaism. *Gishmei Berachah* says that this is learned from the extra words in the verse, because the verse could simply have said, "to return to Bethlehem." The fact that the verse says, "to return to the land of Yehudah" is a hint that they were discussing a return to the religion of the Jewish people.

We may add that what was being discussed is also alluded to in this verse. *Rambam* (*Hilchos Issurei Bi'ah* 14:34), regarding the acceptance of converts, writes, "One tells him: You should know that the World to Come is only for the righteous, and these are Israel, and when you see that Israel are in distress in this world, they have good reserved for them in the World to Come, for they cannot receive most of their good in this world like the other nations, lest they become conceited and go astray and lose the reward of the World to Come, as it states (*Devarim* 32:15), 'Yeshurun became fat and kicked.' " *Rambam* (*Hilchos Teshuvah* 1:35) on the verse (*Yeshayahu* 60:21), "Your people will all be righteous; they will inherit the land forever," states that "the land" refers to "the land of life," i.e., the World to Come. That, too, is the meaning of the extra words of this verse, "the land of Yehudah," namely the World to Come which is reserved for the righteous, who are the Jewish people.

"They set out on the road to return" (1:7). Naomi had been telling them of the way to Eternal Life, where there is no death and where there is only good and no evil (as *Rambam* phrases it in *Hilchos Teshuvah* 8:1), and that is the reward which is unsurpassed by any other, and bliss beyond any other, when the soul returns to the World to Come, where the righteous, who are called the Jews, are.

Even though *Rambam* writes at the end of 1:5 that the righteous of the other nations also have a place in the World to Come, this is as explained by *Ramchal* (*Derech Hashem* 3:4), that in the World to Come one will find the Jewish people, while the souls of the righteous of other nations will be attached in some way to that of the Jews.

וַתֵּלַכְנָה בַדֶּרֶךְ לָשׁוּב אֶל אֶרֶץ יְהוּדָה — They set out on the road to return to the land of Yehudah.

Yalkut (601) explains why the text states, "they set out on the road," instead of being more concise. According to *Yalkut,* this teaches us that they walked barefoot, with their feet touching the ground. It appears that the reason they did so was because they were repenting, and this is accordance with the eighth principle of Rabbeinu Yonah in *Sha'ar HaTeshuvah,* who wrote: "The eighth principle is submission in one's actions, to answer placatingly . . . and not to concern oneself with pretty clothes and jewelry. And we are told about Achav (*I Melachim* 21:27), 'He fasted, slept with the sackcloth, and walked about slowly,' and Hashem, may He be praised, said (ibid. v. 29), 'Have you seen that Achav has humbled himself before Me?' By walking slowly, doing the opposite of what kings do, for they march swiftly with their troops, he showed that he had repented."

Naomi also fulfilled the tenth principle of the *ba'al teshuvah* (the penitent): "to rectify whatever one has done wrong. If one was guilt of a wanton glance, one should keep one's eyes downcast, and if one was guilty of *lashon hara* (speaking evil of others) he should study Torah, and with all those organs with which he sinned, he should endeavor to do *mitzvos* with them . . . if his legs used to run to do evil, they should run to perform a *mitzvah* . . . if the eyes were haughty, he should look down." Now, the sin of which Naomi was guilty was that she did not rebuke her husband when he sought to leave Eretz Yisrael and she left with him, wearing her splendid clothes and attractive shoes, and therefore when they returned to Eretz Yisrael she walked barefoot without the attractive shoes and splendid clothes she had worn when they left Eretz Yisrael to go to Moab.

Shoresh Yishai (by the *tzaddik* and *chassid* R' Shlomo Alkabetz) writes that the reason they walked barefoot was because of their love of Eretz Yisrael, so that their bodies would touch the land. It would appear that that, too, is part of being a *ba'al teshuvah,* as we saw in *Rabbeinu Yonah* above. Since they had sinned with their feet in not showing the importance of Eretz Yisrael, when leaving Moab they tried to fulfill the *mitzvah* of loving Eretz Yisrael with their feet by walking barefoot, so that their bodies would touch Eretz Yisrael, thereby showing its importance.

It might seem that this contradicts what *Mishnah Berurah* says (301:62), that it is a matter of *tznius* (modesty) not to walk barefoot. Indeed, we know that Naomi and Ruth were very observant of the laws of *tznius,* as we are told in the Midrash (beginning of Ch. 2) as quoted by *Yalkut* there. If so, how did they walk barefoot? From here, though, we have proof to the words of *Shelah,* quoted in *Mishnah Berurah* (2:14), that if one wishes to walk barefoot as part of his repentance for his sins, it is permitted. That, indeed, is what David HaMelech did in his repentance. Thus, if we say that they were barefoot because of their repentance, we have an answer to this seeming contradiction.

There is a *gemara* in *Taanis* (23b), which tells of Abba Chilkiyah, who did not wear shoes except when he had to cross a stream, at which time he put on his shoes. How did he go barefoot if this is not considered to be *tzanu'a* (modest)? *Ben Yehoyada* discusses this and writes: "When he (i.e., Abba Chilkiyah) said that 'What was on the road I could see but not what was in the water,' this does not mean that elsewhere he walked barefoot, *chas veshalom.* Rather, he would wrap a thin, old piece of cloth around his feet in order to serve as a divider between his feet and the ground, like slippers, but that does not protect one from being bitten by a snake or scorpion."

Based on what we said earlier, we can say that he walked barefoot as *ba'alei teshuvah* do. Abba Chilkiyah felt he had to do *teshuvah* because once there was a drought and both he and his wife prayed for rain. Clouds appeared first in the corner where his wife stood and prayed and only afterwards in his corner. He saw from this that his wife was more worthy, and he felt that it was because when there were robbers in the neighborhood he had prayed that they should die, whereas his wife had prayed that they should repent, and they did indeed repent.

We find in the *Zohar Midrash Ne'elam* on *Parshas Vayeira* that it is a *mitzvah* to pray that the wicked should repent and not enter into *Gehinnom* for their sins, as it states (*Tehillim* 35:13), "As for me, when they were ill (i.e., when they were wicked), my clothing was sackcloth." That was why Abba Chilkiyah repented and acted like a *baal teshuvah* and walked barefoot — in order to feel the pain of earth and stones which the robbers would have suffered if they had died and were buried without *teshuvah,* and would have been punished after death.

וַתֵּלַכְנָה בַדֶּרֶךְ לָשׁוּב אֶל אֶרֶץ יְהוּדָה — They set out on the road to return to the land of Yehudah.

We can understand that Naomi, who had come from Yehudah, was returning to it, but how can we use the word "return" in regard to Ruth and Orpah, who were from Moab and who had never lived there before?

It would appear that there is a hint to their ancestor Lot here, because Moab came from Lot, and in regard to Lot it states (*Bereishis* 12:4), "And Lot went with him," i.e., Lot went with Avraham. We are told there (12:9), "Avraham journeyed on, journeying steadily toward the south." *Rashi* states that all of his journeys to the south of Eretz Yisrael were in the direction of Jerusalem, which is in the portion of Yehudah — to Mount Moriah, which is his inheritance. Thus they were returning to the land of Yehudah, to the place where their ancestor Lot had lived before he separated from Avraham.

וַתֵּלַכְנָה בַדֶּרֶךְ לָשׁוּב אֶל אֶרֶץ יְהוּדָה — They set out on the road to return to the land of Yehudah.

Another explanation for why the verse contains extra words, "They set out on the road," is in accordance with what we learn in *Berachos* (5b): "R' Shimon bar Yochai states: Hashem gave Israel three precious gifts, and all of them are acquired through suffering: Torah, Eretz Yisrael, and the World to Come." Now that Naomi had been out of Eretz Yisrael for ten years, she needed to undergo new suffering in order to be worthy of returning to live in Eretz Yisrael. Therefore, when she was on her way back she prayed that the suffering of traveling should count toward the suffering one needs in order to gain Eretz Yisrael. Indeed, the Midrash says that they walked barefoot, so that this suffering

[8] *Then Naomi said to her two daughters-in-law, "Go, return, each of you to her mother's house.*

would enable them to be worthy of Eretz Yisrael.

There is still another aspect we need to explain. As we know (from v. 19 below — "The two of them went on until they came to Bethlehem"), Naomi returned to Bethlehem in the land of Yehudah. Why, then, does the verse not state, "They set out on the road to return to Bethlehem in the land of Yehudah," the place from which Naomi had set out? It is possible that Naomi was afraid that she would not be able to live in Bethlehem anymore as part of her punishment for having left it, in fulfillment of the verse (*Vayikra* 18:25), "The land disgorged its inhabitants." She therefore only planned to live in the land of Yehudah, in whichever place Hashem would allow her to live.

8. וַתֹּאמֶר נָעֳמִי לִשְׁתֵּי כַלֹּתֶיהָ לֵכְנָה שֹּׁבְנָה אִשָּׁה לְבֵית אִמָּהּ — Then Naomi said to her two daughters-in-law, "Go, return, each of you to her mother's house."

Shoresh Yishai asks how the verse can have two verbs next to one another — "go" and "return" — which have the exact opposite meaning of one another, for "go" implies moving forward, while "return" means going back.

It would appear that they had already arrived in Eretz Yisrael, because the Midrash states that "They set out on the road to return to the land of Yehudah" (1:7), which means that they walked barefoot because of their love of Eretz Yisrael, so their feet could touch its soil. Thus we must say that they had already come into Eretz Yisrael. With this in mind, we may be able to answer the question.

On the verse (*Devarim* 33:19), "The tribes will assemble at the mount, there they will slaughter offerings of righteousness," *Rashi* comments, "Through Zevulun's trading, the merchants of the nations of the world will come to his land, as [Zevulun] lives on the coast, and they will say, 'Since we have suffered to come this far, we will go to Jerusalem and see the God of this nation and how He acts.' When they see Israel worshiping one God and eating one type of food (i.e., kosher food), they will say, 'There is no nation as worthy as this one,' and they will convert there, as it states, 'There they will slaughter offerings of righteousness.' "

Now, Naomi really wanted the two of them to convert, but according to *halachah* one is required to reject a potential convert (as stated in *Yevamos* 47), but she nevertheless hinted to them to convert, and said to them, "Go, return," i.e., return to your own nation, but first go to the Tabernacle in Shilo in accordance with the verse, "The tribes will assemble at the mount"; for she was thinking that they would see that "there is no nation worthy as this one," and they would ultimately convert.

°יעשה [°יַעַשׂ ק׳] יהוה עִמָּכֶם חֶסֶד כַּאֲשֶׁר
ט עֲשִׂיתֶם עִם־הַמֵּתִים וְעִמָּדִי׃ יִתֵּן יהוה לָכֶם וּמְצֶאןָ
מְנוּחָה אִשָּׁה בֵּית אִישָׁהּ וַתִּשַּׁק לָהֶן וַתִּשֶּׂאנָה קוֹלָן
י וַתִּבְכֶּינָה׃ וַתֹּאמַרְנָה־לָּהּ כִּי־אִתָּךְ נָשׁוּב לְעַמֵּךְ׃
יא וַתֹּאמֶר נָעֳמִי שֹׁבְנָה בְנֹתַי לָמָּה תֵלַכְנָה עִמִּי
יב הַעוֹד־לִי בָנִים בְּמֵעַי וְהָיוּ לָכֶם לַאֲנָשִׁים׃ שֹׁבְנָה
בְנֹתַי לֵכְןָ כִּי זָקַנְתִּי מִהְיוֹת לְאִישׁ כִּי אָמַרְתִּי יֶשׁ־לִי
תִקְוָה גַּם הָיִיתִי הַלַּיְלָה לְאִישׁ וְגַם יָלַדְתִּי בָנִים׃
יג הֲלָהֵן ׀ תְּשַׂבֵּרְנָה עַד אֲשֶׁר יִגְדָּלוּ הֲלָהֵן תֵּעָגֵנָה
לְבִלְתִּי הֱיוֹת לְאִישׁ אַל בְּנֹתַי כִּי־מַר־לִי מְאֹד מִכֶּם
יד כִּי־יָצְאָה בִי יַד־יהוה׃ וַתִּשֶּׂנָה קוֹלָן וַתִּבְכֶּינָה
עוֹד וַתִּשַּׁק עָרְפָּה לַחֲמוֹתָהּ וְרוּת דָּבְקָה בָּהּ׃

---

10. וַתֹּאמַרְנָה לָּהּ כִּי אִתָּךְ נָשׁוּב לְעַמֵּךְ — And they said to her, "No, we will return with you to your people."

In verse 7 above, it states that Naomi was "accompanied" by her two daughters-in-law (*shtei kaloseha eema — ayin, mem, heh*), whereas in the present verse it states, "we will return with you" (*eetach — alef, tav, chaf — nashuv).* What is the difference in meaning between "*eema*" and "*eeta*"?

On the verse (*Bamidbar* 22:12), "Hashem said to Bilam, 'You shall not go with them' " (*eemahem — ayin, mem, heh, mem*), *Tzeil HaEidah* notes that later the Torah speaks of going "*eetam*" — *alef, tav, mem.* He states that there is a difference between the two words. The word "*eem*" applies when two people go together in perfect agreement, as far as their intentions are concerned, while *es* ("*eetam*") implies two people doing the same thing together, but without having the same intention behind their action.

One can thus say that when they left the fields of Moab, all three women had the same intention, with all wanting to return to the land of Yehudah, but when Naomi started entreating them to return to their land, even though both replied, "No, we will return with you" (1:10), Naomi's words affected Orpah, and she was no longer of the same view as Naomi and Ruth, and began to wonder whether it was wise for her to go to the land of Yehudah. That is why the verse states, "we will return with you" (*eetach*) rather than "*eemach,*" in that they did not all have the same view.

14. וַתִּשֶּׂנָה קוֹלָן וַתִּבְכֶּינָה עוֹד וַתִּשַּׁק עָרְפָּה לַחֲמוֹתָהּ וְרוּת דָּבְקָה בָּהּ — They raised their voice and wept again. Orpah kissed her mother-in-law, but

May HASHEM deal kindly with you, as you have dealt
kindly with the dead and with me! 9 *May HASHEM grant*
that you may find security, each in the home of her
husband." She kissed them, and they raised their voice
and wept. 10 *And they said to her, "No, we will return*
with you to your people." 11 *But Naomi said, "Turn*
back, my daughters. Why should you come with me?
Have I more sons in my womb who could become hus-
bands to you? 12 *Turn back, my daughters, go, for I am*
too old to have a husband. Even if I were to say, 'There
is hope for me!' and even if I were to have a husband
tonight — and even bear sons — 13 *would you wait for*
them until they were grown up? Would you tie your-
selves down for them, not to marry anyone else? No,
my daughters! I am very embittered on account of you,
for the hand of HASHEM has gone forth against me."
14 *They raised their voice and wept again. Orpah*
kissed her mother-in-law, but Ruth clung to her.

Ruth clung to her.

David HaMelech says in *Tehillim* (24:3), "Who may ascend the mountain of Hashem, and who may stand in the place of His sanctity?" I have heard it said that there are people who ascend the mountain of Hashem but then fall down again, but the purpose of ascending the mountain is to "stand in the place of His sanctity" steadfastly. The difference between Orpah and Ruth was that while Orpah ascended the mountain, she was unable to stand there, and one who falls from the high mountain falls into the deepest pit. Ruth, on the other hand, was able to "stand in the place of His sanctity."

This is hinted at in the verse (*Tehillim* 68:7), "He releases those bound in fetters" (*bakosharos*), upon which we are told in *Bamidbar Rabbah* (3:6), "If they are not worthy, they weep (*bochim*), and if they are worthy, they sing" (*meshorerim*). Thus, Orpah was not worthy and she wept, while Ruth was worthy and the Sweet Singer of Israel (*II Shmuel* 21:1), David HaMelech, came from her.

The way to achieve standing "in the place of His sanctity" is to perform the *mitzvos* in their entirety. Thus, on the verse (*Devarim* 8:1), "The entire commandment that I command you today you shall observe to perform," *Rashi* explains that if one starts a *mitzvah* he should complete it. Orpah began the *mitzvah* but did not complete it, and therefore *Chazal* say that on the night she left Naomi she committed all types of immoral, animalistic

טו וַתֹּאמֶר הִנֵּה שָׁבָה יְבִמְתֵּךְ אֶל־עַמָּהּ וְאֶל־
טז אֱלֹהֶיהָ שׁוּבִי אַחֲרֵי יְבִמְתֵּךְ׃ וַתֹּאמֶר רוּת אַל־

---

acts. Ruth, however, who fulfilled the *mitzvah* in its entirety, was elevated to the level of the monarchy.

וַתִּשֶּׂנָה קוֹלָן וַתִּבְכֶּינָה עוֹד — They raised their voice and wept again.

Both Ruth and Orpah cried. The question can be asked: We can understand that Orpah cried because she was leaving her mother-in-law, but Ruth was staying with her, so why did she cry?

It would appear that Ruth interpreted Naomi's words to mean that she was rejecting her and was not willing to accept her, when Naomi said, "Go, return, each of you to her mother's house" (1:8). This was especially true when both daughters-in-law had replied, "No, we will return with you to your people," and Naomi again asked them to leave with the words, "Turn back, my daughters" (1:12). Ruth felt that Naomi refused to accept her as a convert, and that was why she cried.

It also occurred to me that Ruth cried because of Orpah, for she realized how far Orpah would fall once she rejected what she had first accepted in going back to the land of Yehudah, as mentioned above.

15. וַתֹּאמֶר הִנֵּה שָׁבָה יְבִמְתֵּךְ אֶל עַמָּהּ וְאֶל אֱלֹהֶיהָ שׁוּבִי אַחֲרֵי יְבִמְתֵּךְ — So she said, "Look, your sister-in-law has returned to her people and to her god; go follow your sister-in-law."

The *gemara* (*Yevamos* 47a) deduces from his verse that a non-Jew in our times who wishes to convert is asked, "Why do you want to convert? Don't you know that Jews in our time are persecuted and oppressed?" etc.

Of course, what is required of a person who wishes to become a convert is his acceptance of the Torah, as stated in *Rambam* (*Hilchos Issurei Bi'ah* 13): "With three actions did Israel enter into the covenant: with *bris milah,* with immersion in a *mikveh* and with a *korban* (sacrifice) . . . So too, for future generations, when a non-Jew wishes to enter into the covenant (of Judaism) and to stand under the wings of the *Shechinah* and to accept upon himself the yoke of the *mitzvos,* he needs *milah,* immersion and a *korban.*" It is logical to assume that the convert's acceptance of *mitzvos* is deduced from the Jewish people's acceptance of the Torah. Just as the Jewish people accepted the Torah when they proclaimed (*Shemos* 24:7), "*na'aseh venishma*" ("we will do and we will heed"), i.e., with unconditional acceptance (the way the angels accepted Hashem), so too must the convert show unconditional acceptance. Just as there is nothing which can prevent an angel from fulfilling his mission, so there is nothing in the world which can prevent the Jewish people from fulfilling the Torah — neither fire nor

[15] *So she said, "Look, your sister-in-law has re-*
turned to her people and to her god; go follow
your sister-in-law." [16] *But Ruth said, "Do not*

---

water, rulers' decrees nor killings — that is the way a convert must accept his conversion. That is why one tells the prospective convert, "Why do you want to convert? Don't you know that Jews in our time are persecuted and oppressed?" etc. If he says, "I know this, and I am not worthy," he is accepted immediately (see *Rambam*, *Hilchos Issurei Bi'ah* 13:1).

However, what we still need to clarify is the source for the fact that we attempt to dissuade the person from converting, and we accept him only if he is insistent.

The *gemara* in *Avodah Zarah* 2b tells us that Hashem first went to all the different nations of the world and asked each if it was willing to accept the Torah. Each had its own reason for refusing. For example, Yishmael refused it because it forbids theft, and about Yishmael we are told, (*Bereishis* 16:12), "his hand [is] against everyone." Eisav rejected it because it forbids murder, and about him it says (ibid. 27:40), "by your sword you shall live." Now, it is human nature for a person to do what others are doing, but where others refrain from doing something, it is difficult to be the only person to do that action. Even though the Jewish people saw that no other nation was willing to receive the Torah, this did not cause them any doubts, and they very much wanted to accept the Torah, even stating, "*na'aseh venishma.*" From the fact that Hashem first went to the other nations we learn that at first we try to dissuade a person from converting, as Naomi did when she said, "Look, your sister-in-law has returned to her people and to her god; go follow your sister-in-law" (1:15) (and as the other nations of the world did at the time of the receiving of the Torah, in returning to their own gods). Ruth, though, answered, "Your people are my people, and your God is my God" (1:16). The greatness of their willingness to receive the Torah is expressed in Moshe's last words to the Jewish people, when he told them (*Devarim* 33:2), "Hashem came from Sinai — having shone forth to them from Seir." This indicates the separation of the Jewish people from the other nations. And Moshe continued: "You loved the tribes greatly, all its holy ones were in your hands," and nevertheless the Jewish people did not refrain from accepting the Torah.

וַתֹּאמֶר הִנֵּה שָׁבָה יְבִמְתֵּךְ אֶל עַמָּהּ וְאֶל אֱלֹהֶיהָ שׁוּבִי אַחֲרֵי יְבִמְתֵּךְ — So she said, "Look, your sister-in-law has returned to her people and to her god; go follow your sister-in-law."

In reality, this was ultimately not good advice, because we learned earlier that when Orpah returned to her family she returned to their debauched ways, whereas we also know what happened to Ruth, who stayed with Naomi. How, then, could Naomi have given Ruth such advice? We can see from this that there is no prohibition against giving adverse advice to a Ben Noach who wishes to convert in an effort to dissuade him from converting, because, as we are told in *Yevamos* (47b), "Converts are as hard for Israel (to endure) as leprosy." At the outset, then, when the prospective convert comes to ask to be converted, one tries to persuade him not to do so and says to him, "Don't you know that at present Israel are persecuted and oppressed, despised, harassed and afflicted?"

וַתֹּאמֶר הִנֵּה שָׁבָה יְבִמְתֵּךְ אֶל עַמָּהּ וְאֶל אֱלֹהֶיהָ שׁוּבִי אַחֲרֵי יְבִמְתֵּךְ — So she said, "Look, your sister-in-law has returned to her people and to her god; go follow your sister-in-law."

The reason the verse states, "So she said," rather than stating clearly, "So Naomi said," is that since the statement appears to be *lashon hara* — even though in this case it was permitted as it was meant to serve a specific purpose — the prophet did not want to attribute it to her directly.

The question which needs to be answered is how Naomi was sure that Orpah was going to return to her foreign gods, and would not became a *ger toshav* — a person who keeps the seven *mitzvos* of the Sons of Noach. After all, the commander of the army of the king of Aram, Na'aman, a leper cured by the prophet Elisha, became a *ger toshav,* as we see in *Sanhedrin* 74b. We also need to explain why the text earlier stresses, "but Ruth clung to her" (v. 14). What do these words add?

It appears that this verse hints to us as to the reason why Orpah changed her mind, even though she had at first planned to go back with Naomi and Ruth to Bethlehem. It would appear that what made her change her mind was not what Naomi said, because she had already known what Naomi now mentioned even before they had left Moab, but the fact that "they raised their voice and wept again," caused her to change her mind about accompanying Naomi. She simply was unable to bear Naomi's distress. Ruth, on the other hand, was the exact opposite — the very factor that made Orpah leave was the same one that made Ruth cling even more closely to Naomi.

The attribute of bearing a burden with another and suffering when another person suffers is one which is unique to the Jewish people because we are all one nation, so that when we are in distress we draw closer together. Among other nations, though, one does not find this, as they are not organically a single entity.[1] Thus, when Naomi saw that her crying caused Orpah to leave her and that Orpah was not ready to assume

---

1. I once heard the following from my older brother, R' Chaim Yerucham: At the receiving of the Torah, on the verse (*Shemos* 19:2), "And Israel encamped there, opposite the mountain," *Rashi* comments, "as one person, with one heart," whereas when the Egyptians

the burdens of another, she realized that "your sister-in-law has returned to her people and to her god," and that there was no connection between Orpah and the acceptance of the truth.

We find this idea in *Yevamos* (47), where we are told that a non-Jew in our times who wishes to convert is asked, "Why do you want to convert? Don't you know that Jews in our time are persecuted and oppressed, despised, harassed and afflicted?" If he replies that "I know and am not worthy," he is accepted immediately. On this, *Rashi* writes: "The convert must say, 'I am not worthy of partaking of their suffering, and I hope that I will be worthy of doing so.' " This is exactly what we said earlier: that a condition for conversion is for the person to be willing to suffer with the Jewish people, and one who is not ready to do so is not worthy of entering under the wings of the *Shechinah.*

I heard another explanation for how Naomi knew that Orpah would return to her former gods, quoted in the name of R' Chaim Shmulevitz. Naomi knew the danger of the environment, and once she saw that Orpah wanted to return to her home in Moab, Naomi realized that the environment there would influence her until she would totally return to her gods.[1]

So too did I find in the *sefer Lev Eliyahu* by Harav Eliyahu Lopian (*Bereishis* p. 32) which brings a *Chazal* regarding the angels sent to overturn S'dom, who were wrong in saying, "we will destroy," as if they — rather than Hashem — would be the ones to destroy the cities. The reason they sinned was because once they had gone down to S'dom they were infected by the evil of the Sodomites and thus they, too, did something improper. *Chazal* tell us that they were exiled from their place for 158 years, namely that for 158 years they were not purified from their *tumah* (ritual uncleanliness) and were therefore unable to go up to their place. With this we can understand what R' Chama bar Chanina said (*Bereishis Rabbah* 50:9): When the angels said, "*we* will destroy," they were

---

pursued the Jewish people *Rashi* reverses the order and says about the Egyptians that they were "with one heart, as one person." The reason for the difference in order is that the Jewish people is by its nature one entity, whereas the Egyptians were not one but in this specific case they were united together in a single desire — to destroy the Jewish people, *chas veshalom.*

1. R' Gedalya Zupnik told me that when they lived in Shanghai all *the yeshivah bachurim* (students) were forbidden to sleep anywhere except in the "ghetto." The home of R' Chaim was outside the "ghetto," and one Friday night R' Mordechai Karpinshprung and R' Eliezer Horodzeiski learned with R' Chaim until a late hour. As it was very late, they did not return to the "ghetto" but instead slept in R' Chaim's home. The police found out about this, and on *Motza'ei Shabbos* in the middle of the night they arrested them along with two others, R' Gedalya and another student whom they suspected, and the four were left in prison overnight in a very cramped place. In the morning they were put together with thieves and murderers, and remained there a number of days. R' Chaim told the *bachurim* who were in prison: "Don't talk to anyone else there, so that they should not affect you spiritually, as we can see from the influence of the environment on Orpah."

א/טז תִּפְגְּעִי־בִי לְעָזְבֵךְ לָשׁוּב מֵאַחֲרָיִךְ כִּי אֶל־אֲשֶׁר תֵּלְכִי
אֵלֵךְ וּבַאֲשֶׁר תָּלִינִי אָלִין עַמֵּךְ עַמִּי וֵאלֹהַיִךְ אֱלֹהָי׃

---

boasting. Indeed, this was the sin of S'dom, as we see in *Yechezkel* (16:49), "Behold, this was the sin of S'dom, your sister: She and her daughters had pride, surfeit of bread."

I heard in the name of R' Levi Krupenia, that when my grandfather (the author of *Or Yechezkel*) was in the United States, a store across the road from the yeshivah was open on *Shabbos.* Much as my grandfather tried, he was unable to have the owner close the store on *Shabbos.* He then declared that that alone was reason enough to leave the United States, for he was afraid that the owner might influence him to lessen his concern for the holy *Shabbos.* What he meant by this was that the environment has such a strong influence that a person may not realize that a sin is being committed, and when a person does not realize that a sin was committed, it is quite possible for him, too, to commit the sin if there is an opportunity to do so. What differentiates a living person from a dead person is that a living person can feel pain, whereas a dead person does not, and one who does not feel the pain of a sin is liable to emulate the sinners.

16. וַתֹּאמֶר רוּת אַל תִּפְגְּעִי בִי לְעָזְבֵךְ לָשׁוּב מֵאַחֲרָיִךְ — But Ruth said, "Do not urge me to leave you, to turn back and not follow you."

We need to understand the repetition of "to leave you" and "not follow you." I noticed that *Meishiv Nefesh* by *Bach* explains the verse before this one, and by his explanation we can understand the present verse.

The previous verse states, "So she said, 'Look, your sister-in-law has returned to her people and to her god; go follow your sister-in-law' " (1:15). Why did Naomi say "go follow your sister-in-law" rather than simply, "go follow her"? Also, what did Naomi add when she stated, "to her god"? Wouldn't "follow her" be sufficient? What Naomi meant was that Ruth should follow Orpah in order to prevent her from sinning. Orpah planned to return to her god, and it would be a profanation of Hashem's Name if she would publicly practice idolatry. Thus Naomi requested that Ruth should go after Orpah to keep her from sinning. The reason Ruth should do so was because Orpah was the sister-in-law whom she loved, and it would be a good deed to bring this poor soul under the fold of the *Shechinah,* with the ultimate aim that both would come back and be converted to being full Jews. Ruth answered her, "Do not urge me to leave you, to turn back and not follow you," because if I turn back and follow Orpah I might wind up following in her ways, and rather than bringing her to the correct way, she might turn me completely into the wrong path.

1/16 *urge me to leave you, to turn back and not follow you. For*
wherever you go, I will go; where you lodge, I will lodge;
your people are my people, and your God is my God;

One can also explain the repetition of "to leave you . . . and not follow you" in that "to leave you" means a total break between the two, but "not follow you" means that even though there is a great distance between us, we will still have some contacts from time to time, where one will visit the other on occasion. Thus, Ruth asked that neither of these situations should develop — not a complete break, nor even a temporary one.

כִּי אֶל אֲשֶׁר תֵּלְכִי אֵלֵךְ וּבַאֲשֶׁר תָּלִינִי אָלִין עַמֵּךְ עַמִּי וֵאלֹהַיִךְ אֱלֹהָי — "For wherever you go, I will go; where you lodge, I will lodge; your people are my people, and your God is my God."

Even though Naomi asked her to return to her own people, Ruth wanted to cling to Naomi, to the extent of "wherever you go, I will go; where you lodge, I will lodge," etc. This would apply even after death, where each person returns to his rest and where the situation is indeed one of "leaving." This is in accordance with what we find in *Midrash Rabbah* (*Shemos Rabbah* 52:3), that the wife of R' Shimon Chalafta said to Rebbi, "Does one righteous man see another in the World to Come? Doesn't every righteous man have a [separate] world for himself? Doesn't it say (*Koheles* 12:5), 'Man goes to his world'? It does not say 'worlds' but 'world.' " That is what Ruth asked for when she said, "where you die, I will die, and there I will be buried . . . if anything but death separates me from you," namely that only death would separate them, where one might die before the other, but after the death of both of them, Ruth asked to be reunited with Naomi, in her place.

It appears that Ruth did not think that she was worthy of being in the same place as Naomi, her mother-in-law. As we see from *Ramchal* (R' Moshe Chaim Luzzatto) in his *Derech Hashem* 2:4 — in explanation of *Rambam* (*Hilchos Teshuvah* 3:5) who writes that the righteous of the nations of the world have a share in the World to Come — *Ramchal* says, "In the World to Come one will not find any other nations except for Israel, and the souls of the righteous of the nations will be given a different form which will be attached to Israel, and they will be to them as a garment to a person, and it is in that form that they will benefit from the good, and there is nothing in their law which will have them attain more than this." This was what Ruth asked — that in the World to Come she would not be separated from Naomi, but would be like a garment to the soul of Naomi.

Now we have to reconcile the words of *Rambam* in *Hilchos Issurei Bi'ah* (13:14), who writes that the proper way to act when a person comes to convert to Judaism is to check to see if there is some financial reason, etc., why the person wishes to convert. If one does not find any external reason, one tells the person about the burden of keeping the *mitzvos* and the great effort necessary in performing them, in order to dissuade him from converting. If one sees that he nevertheless did not leave one can assume that he is converting because of love of the Jewish religion and accepts him, as we see from the verse (*Ruth* 1:18), "When she saw that she was determined to go with her, she stopped arguing with her."

Thus we see that *Rambam* assumes simply that the acceptance of Ruth and her desire to convert were because of her love of Hashem, and not because of any reward[1] and as *Rambam* writes (*Hilchos Teshuvah* 10:1), "One who says, 'I will perform the *mitzvos* and will study the Torah's wisdom in order to obtain the blessings stated in it,' or that 'I will be able to attain the World to Come,' is not considered serving Hashem out of love, because one who does these out of love does not do them because of any motivation in the world and not because of fear of punishment or because of any reward in the World to Come, but only does what is right because it is right, with the reward coming on its own." Now, according to what we wrote, that Ruth wanted to be in Naomi's portion, that would seem to be a case of one who converts in order to receive a reward, and if so, how does *Rambam* bring proof from Ruth that one accepts converts only if one sees that the person came out of love of Hashem?

We are told (*Bava Kamma* 41b) that Shimon the Imsonite would expound on the word *es* each time it appeared in the Torah. When he reached the word *es* in *Devarim* 10:20, "*Es* Hashem, your God, you shall fear," he stopped his expositions. *Rashi* in the chapter *Ha'ish Mekadeish* (*Kiddushin*) explains that he stopped because he was afraid to include anyone else that one should fear as much as one must fear Hashem. In *Pesachim, Maharsha* explains that even though earlier on the same *parshah* R' Shimon did not stop his expositions when he reaches a previous verse which states, "You shall love *es* Hashem, your God," the reason is because there one can use the word *es* to compare one's love for a Torah scholar to one's love of Hashem, but one cannot compare the fear of Hashem — of Hashem's rewards and punishments — to that of a Torah scholar, because there are no rewards and punishments from a Torah scholar.

From this we see that loving a Torah scholar is a fulfillment of the *mitzvah* of loving Hashem, for the word *es* includes Torah scholars. Therefore we can conclude that Ruth's love of Naomi and her desire to convert were as a result of love of Hashem.

Furthermore, *Rambam* in his *Sefer HaMitzvos* (*Mitzvah* 6) states that

---

1. Which would mean that the conversion was not out of love of Hashem.

Hashem commanded us to attach ourselves to Torah scholars, to befriend them and to remain in their presence in every possible way: in food and drink and in business, so that we will learn to emulate their ways and acquiring true belief from their words. This is in accordance with Hashem's words (*Devarim* 10:20), "to Him you shall cleave." Thus Ruth's aim was to cleave to Naomi and thereby to fulfill the *mitzvah* of "to Him you shall cleave," and was clearly out of love of Hashem. For this reason, *Rambam* brings proof from Ruth that a convert is accepted if his decision to convert came out of love of Hashem.

עַמֵּךְ עַמִּי — "Your people are my people." We are told in *Yevamos* 47b that Naomi said, "We have been commanded 613 commandments," to which Ruth replied, "Your people are my people," namely that she was willing to accept upon herself the fulfillment of all the *mitzvos.* I find this difficult, because a woman is not obligated to perform *mitzvos* which are to be performed at a specific time, so why did she have to accept upon herself all 613 *mitzvos*?

From this we see that there are two separate aspects: acceptance of the yoke of the *mitzvos* on the one hand, and performance of the *mitzvos* on the other. Thus, even though women are exempt from performing time-related *mitzvos,* the acceptance of *na'aseh venishma* — "we will do and we will hear" — included all the men, women, and children, and referred to the entire Torah, including those *mitzvos* which they individually were not commanded.

Proof of the fact that acceptance and performance are separate can be found in the Midrash at the beginning of *Ruth,* which states, "R' Yochanan said: We are told (*Tehillim* 50:7), 'Hear O my people and I will speak' — 'Hear O my people' — in this world; 'and I will speak' — in the World to Come, in order that I might have a reply to the princes of the nations of the world, who will in the future act as prosecutors before Me, and say, 'Lord of the Universe! Both these (i.e., the other nations) and these (i.e., Israel) serve idolatry; these and these are guilty of immorality; these and these shed blood; yet these go to the Garden of Eden and the others go to *Gehinnom*?' At that time, the defense attorney of Israel will keep silent. The Holy One, Blessed is He, will say to him, 'Are you then silent without coming to the defense of My sons? By your life I will speak righteousness and save My people.' With what righteousness? R' Eliezer and R' Yochanan: One says: 'The righteousness which you brought to My world in that you accepted My Torah, for if you had not accepted My Torah I would have had the world revert to void and desolation.' "

The Midrash states clearly that even though you did not observe the Torah as it should have been observed, you nevertheless accepted it as it should have been accepted, and with the merit of that deed alone you will

א/יז **יז** בַּאֲשֶׁר תָּמוּתִי אָמוּת וְשָׁם אֶקָּבֵר כֹּה יַעֲשֶׂה
יְהוָה לִי וְכֹה יֹסִיף כִּי הַמָּוֶת יַפְרִיד בֵּינִי וּבֵינֶךָ׃

---

inherit *Gan Eden,* while the others will inherit *Gehinnom.* Thus we see clearly that acceptance and performance are two separate things, for even if you did not observe the Torah, you accepted it. The same is true for women, who — even though they are exempted from time-related *mitzvos* — nevertheless accepted the entire Torah upon themselves, for the Torah is a unified whole. We see a hint of this in the fact that the name *Ruth* totals 606 in *gematria,* and if we add to it the seven *mitzvos* that the non-Jews are required to observe we have a total of 613 *mitzvos.*

וַתֹּאמֶר רוּת אַל תִּפְגְּעִי בִי לְעָזְבֵךְ לָשׁוּב מֵאַחֲרָיִךְ כִּי אֶל אֲשֶׁר תֵּלְכִי אֵלֵךְ וּבַאֲשֶׁר תָּלִינִי אָלִין עַמֵּךְ עַמִּי וֵאלֹהַיִךְ אֱלֹהָי — But Ruth said, "Do not urge me to leave you, to turn back and not follow you. For wherever you go, I will go; where you lodge, I will lodge; your people are my people, and your God is my God."

The *Targum* tells us: "Naomi said, 'We are required to observe 613 commandments.' Ruth said, 'That which your nation observes, I will observe as if I had been required to observe it from ancient times.' " What was Ruth's answer when she stated that she would observe the commandments as if she had been required to from ancient times, and not only from this time on? Logically, the reference to ancient times meant the time of the giving of the Torah at Sinai through Moshe, because that was the only time that the Torah was given. Indeed, *Rambam* (*Hilchos Melachim* 8:11) writes that the definition of a *ger toshav* is a person who has accepted upon himself the observance of the seven Noahide laws, and who observes them because Hashem commanded this to be done through Moshe, even though all Noahides (i.e., all people except the Jewish people) were commanded earlier regarding this. However, if a Noahide observes these commandments only because he has come to these conclusions logically and not because he accepts them as having been given to Moshe at Sinai, he is not considered a *ger toshav,* and is not considered one of the righteous of the other nations or one of their wise men.

It appears that what Ruth wanted was to accept the Torah the same way the Jewish people had accepted it at Sinai, with (*Shemos* 24:7) "*na'aseh venishmah* — we will do and we will obey." We have shown in the essay "Regarding the Receiving of the Torah" that the condition which Hashem made with the Creation was that at the giving of the Torah, Israel must accept it: "If Israel accepts the Torah, you will continue to exist and if not, you will not exist." On this we are told in *Shabbos* 88a that it would have

[17] *where you die, I will die, and there I will be buried. Thus may* HASHEM *do to me — and more! — if anything but death separates me from you."*

---

been enough for Israel to accept it without saying, "We will do and we will obey." It was on their own volition that they added, "We will do and we will obey." At that time, a *bas kol* (a voice from On High) came forth and said, "Who revealed to My children this exalted secret, which is used by the Ministering Angels?" *Rashi* on *Shabbos* 88b explains that by this expression of the Jewish people, they were indicating that they were going with Hashem in full harmony as one does out of love, where they relied on him not to subject them to anything which they would be unable to withstand.

And that is what Ruth said to Naomi: "I will observe it as if I had been required to observe it from ancient times, the same way the Torah was accepted at Mount Sinai, with *na'aseh venishmah* out of love, and not only as one who accepts the Torah out of fear."

17. בַּאֲשֶׁר תָּמוּתִי אָמוּת וְשָׁם אֶקָּבֵר — "Where you die, I will die, and there I will be buried."

Rashi above brings the *gemara* in *Yevamos* 47b that from here we learn how a person who wishes to convert should be dealt with. One can add to this, for *Ben Yehoyada* asks: How is it that in all the other areas Ruth mentioned Naomi — "wherever you go, I will go; where you lodge, I will lodge; your people are my people; and your God is my god; where you die, I will die" — except that in regard to burial, she did not say, "where you are buried I will be buried."

It appears that in not mentioning this, Ruth showed her great modesty, for the *Alter* of Kelm (*Chochmah U'Mussar* I:367) said that just as one does not bury a righteous person next to a wicked one, one does not even bury a less righteous person next to a more righteous person, because we assume a person would prefer being buried near someone similar to him. Thus Ruth said, "there I will be buried," but not next to Naomi, because she could not attain Naomi's level in righteousness and greatness, and she could not hope to be buried next to her.

בַּאֲשֶׁר תָּמוּתִי אָמוּת וְשָׁם אֶקָּבֵר כֹּה יַעֲשֶׂה יהוה לִי וְכֹה יֹסִיף כִּי הַמָּוֶת יַפְרִיד בֵּינִי וּבֵינֵךְ — "Where you die, I will die, and there I will be buried. Thus may Hashem do to me — and more! — if anything but death separates me from you."

Rashi notes that this is the procedure for accepting converts, and so too does it state in *Yevamos* 47, and *Rashi* there explains the meaning of Ruth's words, "Thus may Hashem do to me — and more!" in the following way: Now that Hashem had begun to do harmful things to her, in that her husband had died and she had lost all her possessions, she was nevertheless willing to accept additional suffering, and only death would part between the two. If we read this superficially, it would seem that Ruth was cursing herself, that should she change her mind about joining the Jewish people and going with Naomi she should be afflicted with all types of misery. This is strange. After all, *Chazal* tell us that "one is forbidden to open one's mouth to Satan" by even mouthing a possibility of something bad befalling oneself.

To explain this, we need to understand that just as when Ruth said, "Where you die, I will die, and there I will be buried," that was part of the conversion procedure, so too was "Thus may Hashem do to me — and more" part of that procedure. Proof to this conclusion may be brought from *Yevamos* 47, which states that if a person asks to be converted, we say to him, "Why do you want to convert? Don't you know that Jews in our time are persecuted and oppressed?" etc. If he says, "I know this, and I am not even worthy," he is accepted immediately. We see that if a person wishes to convert we try to dissuade him and explain to him the difficulty of being a Jew, as we see how Naomi attempted to dissuade Ruth and told her how difficult it is to be Jewish.[1] *Rashi* there also adds that the prospective convert has to say, "I am not worthy of participating in the Jews' troubles, and only hope that I will become worthy of that." I heard from the author of *Pachad Yitzchak,* Harav Yitzchak Hutner, that what Rashi meant is that for a person to convert he must be willing to participate in all our troubles, and that was what Ruth meant when she said, "Thus may Hashem do to me — and more!"

It is also possible that *Rashi* meant something slightly different: that part of the conversion process is to be willing to accept suffering with love, for *Rambam* wrote (*Hilchos Issurei Bi'ah* 13:14): "One informs them about the burden of the Torah and the great effort needed to observe it, etc. If they accepted this and did not go away and we see that they came back out of love, one accepts them." We see from this that conversion must be something which comes out of love of Hashem and not out of fear, and part of accepting Hashem out of love is the willingness to accept suffering. That was what Ruth said when she declared, "Thus may Hashem do to me — and more!" Not only do I not spurn suffering, but I accept it in love. Even if Hashem causes me to suffer even more I will not go back on my conversion, and only death will separate you and me, for one who serves Hashem out of love can accept suffering.

According to what we just stated — that conversion must be only as a result of love of Hashem — we can answer a question asked by *Tosfos* on

1. As, for example, the prohibition of *yichud*.

a *beraisa* in *Yevamos* (48b), where we learned: "R' Chananiah, son of R' Rabban Gamliel says, 'Why is it that in our times converts are afflicted and suffer? It is because they do not convert out of love but rather out of fear.' " On this *Tosfos* asks: But we see in *Sotah* 31 that both are praiseworthy — one who serves Hashem out of love and one who does so out of fear. *Tosfos* leaves this question unanswered. However, according to what we stated, the question is answered. For a Jew, even serving Hashem out of fear is a positive action, as it states (*Tehillim* 31:20), "How abundant is Your goodness that You have stored away for those who fear You." However, in the case of a non-Jew who wishes to convert we require that this step be taken out of love, and if a person comes to convert and does not do so out of love but does so only out of fear, he will suffer pain.

The reason for this is that even though a person who converted to Judaism is considered as if he were a newly born infant, that only applies to his soul, in that all his sins are forgiven and he is considered like a new being. However, in terms of the blemishes he inflicted on the different worlds and on Creation in general, those are not erased. A convert must, then, always be a penitent to rectify the damage he did in the upper worlds. Thus *Sefas Emes* writes (*Parshas Naso* 5650, starting with the words "*Beparshas hateshuvah*"): "Even though there is such a thing as *teshuvah* among the other nations, as in Nineveh — they repented and changed their deeds to being good and then Hashem in His mercy forgave them — the ability to rectify the damage in the upper worlds caused by sin through repenting is something only available to the Jewish people, and that is through repentance out of love. Thus, one of the obligations of the convert is to repent for his whole life out of love for Hashem."

This might be hinted at in the words of Avraham, the father and the first of all converts who said, "I am but dust and ashes." "Dust" is explained by *Rashi* on the verse (*Bereishis* 2:7), "And Hashem God formed the man of dust from the ground," to mean that Hashem took the dust from the place where it states (*Shemos* 20:20), "An altar of earth (i.e., dust) you shall make me," in the hope that "[Man] will find atonement and be able to resist." "Ashes" refers to the nullification and total destruction of everything impure in Avraham that came to him from his forefathers. For *Chazal* tell us that throughout his life Avraham would afflict himself in order to uproot all the impurities in himself, and to remain pure, so that his ashes would atone for his past.

Based on this, we can explain the words of Boaz to Ruth (2:11-12), "I have been fully informed of all that you have done for your mother-in-law . . . and went to a people you had never known before. May Hashem reward your actions, and may your payment be full from Hashem, the God of Israel, under Whose wings you have come to seek refuge." The *Targum* there explains, "May Hashem give you a good reward in this world for your work and may your payment be full in the World to Come from Hashem in that you came to convert." We also see that on the verse (*Vayikra* 18:4), "Carry out My laws," *Ramban* states that a person who serves Hashem out of fear does not receive any reward in this world, but only in the World to Come, and only those who serve Hashem out of love receive a good life in this world and a full reward in the World to Come. Thus, what Boaz said to her was that since she had come to find refuge under Hashem's wings, which means converting out of love of Hashem, she would receive a reward both in this world and in the World to Come. We also see in *Sotah* 31, that one who serves Hashem out of love is hinted at in the verse (*Tehillim* 5:12), "All who take refuge in You will rejoice, they will sing joyously forever, You will shelter them." Thus their reward will be both in this world and in the World to Come.

Based on the above, we can understand why the true convert, Avraham ben Avraham, may Hashem avenge his blood, refused to be saved even after the Vilna Gaon sent him word that he was able to rescue him. He replied that he preferred to die *al kiddush Hashem* — for the sanctification of Hashem's Name — because only thus would there be proof that his worship of Hashem was out of love and not out of fear. It is possible that that is why he is referred to as the *ger tzedek* (the "righteous convert") who showed his righteousness and love in that he accepted upon himself to be burned alive in honor of Hashem.

כֹּה יַעֲשֶׂה יהוה לִי וְכֹה יֹסִיף — "Thus may Hashem do to me — and more."

As *Rashi* comments, "Just as He began to do bad things and His hand went against me to kill my husband and to have me lose my possessions." This is the sequence in conversion, for we see in *Yevamos* 47 that if a person in our times wishes to convert, one says to him, "Why do you wish to convert? Don't you know that at present Israel are persecuted and oppressed, despised, harassed and afflicted?" If he replies that "I know and am not worthy," he is accepted. *Rashi* there notes that "I am not worthy" means "I am not worthy of participating in the Jews' troubles, and only hope that I will become worthy of that." And that is what Ruth said: "I know that it was Hashem's justice that caused my husband to die and me to lose my possessions, for that is the way Hashem acts toward the Jewish people, 'and more' — I only hope that I will be worthy of it."

It would appear that the reason why this is expressed when one wishes to convert is that only through this does the *beis din* see that the person's decision to convert was an absolute one. Note also what Rabbeinu Yonah wrote (*Sha'ar* III, 49), regarding the Torah prohibition of *"Lo sonu es ha'ger* — You shall not afflict the convert": There are numerous occasions when Hashem warns us not to afflict the convert, because the convert has effectively forgotten his father's house and come to find protection under the *Shechinah.* This is like a deer which came to a flock and grazed with them. The shepherd took pity on the deer because it had left the wide expanses of the outdoors and had instead elected to live in a small area. The convert must feel that he has left a wide-open area and has elected to stand in a small, restricted area, namely the way Hashem treats the Jewish people, the children of Yaakov, according to the strict letter of the law — unlike the way He treats the other nations. Thus when Yitzchak blessed his son Yaakov, *Rashi* comments on the verse (*Bereishis* 27:28), "May God give you of the dew of the heavens," that this refers to Hashem's strict justice — if one is worthy of it, he will receive the dew, and if not, he will not; but in the case of Yitzchak's son Eisav it states (v. 39), "Of the fatness of the land will be your dwelling," whether he is righteous or not.

18. וַתֵּרֶא כִּי מִתְאַמֶּצֶת הִיא לָלֶכֶת אִתָּהּ וַתֶּחְדַּל לְדַבֵּר אֵלֶיהָ — When she saw that she was determined to go with her, she stopped arguing with her.

I saw in an old *sefer, Chelek Bnei Yehudah,* by R' Shimon Havilio, who quotes various commentaries on this verse, that we are told in *Bava Metzia* (84) that once Reish Lakish accepted upon himself the yoke of the Torah he was no longer able to leap across the river as he had previously, because the Torah weakens one physically. This is the same explanation here: When Naomi saw that at first Ruth walked with all her vigor, but at one point her strength weakened and she found it hard to keep up with Naomi even though she was young and Naomi was old — and in the normal course of things young people walk faster than old people — Naomi realized that since Ruth had accepted the Torah she had become weaker and therefore had to struggle to keep up with her, and that was why Naomi stopped arguing with her.

One can bring proof from here to what we wrote earlier on the verse, "Your people are my people" (1:16), that even though a woman is not commanded to fulfill a number of the commandments, nor is she commanded to study Torah as men are, nevertheless acceptance of the yoke of the Torah and the *mitzvos* is the same for men and women. Thus women, too, said, "We will do and we will listen," in regard to the whole Torah at Sinai, and that is why it is possible for women as well, when they accept upon themselves the yoke of the Torah, to have that acceptance weaken their strength. That was why Ruth became physically weaker and had to struggle to keep up with Naomi, even though Ruth was much younger.

❧ ❧ ❧

I heard in the name of the Gaon and the Chasam Sofer that only a person who accepts the Torah not for its own sake is weakened thereby. This explains why we find that in the case of Yaakov, even though he had spent fourteen years studying in the *beis midrash* of Shem and Ever,[1] he was nevertheless not weak and was able to roll away the rock from the well. *Rashi* there writes that this teaches us that he was very strong. Yet in the case of Reish Lakish, he did become weaker. The answer to this is that Reish Lakish agreed to accept upon himself the yoke of the Torah because R' Yochanan promised his sister as a wife, and thus his acceptance was not for its own sake. However, acceptance of the yoke of the Torah for its own sake does not weaken a person. This still leaves us with a question in terms of Ruth: In which way was Ruth's acceptance of the Torah not for its own sake, that it weakened her?

We see that Ruth performed great deeds of loving-kindness for Naomi, and converted and returned with her. However, since what had aroused her to convert was her compassion for Naomi when she said, "Do not urge me to leave you," this type of acceptance is also considered to be not for its own sake. She did not accept the Torah for its own sake, that being the desire of Hashem, but because of her feelings of compassion for Naomi. That is not the highest level of acceptance for its own sake, which would not result in weakening the person.

We see from this what is considered truly "for its own sake," and that even though Ruth's intentions were to help Naomi, that is not considered "for its own sake," and that is indeed a point one should think of carefully.

וַתֵּרֶא כִּי מִתְאַמֶּצֶת הִיא לָלֶכֶת אִתָּהּ וַתֶּחְדַּל לְדַבֵּר אֵלֶיהָ — When she saw that she was determined to go with her, she stopped arguing with her.

I saw that *Shoresh Yishai* explains "she stopped arguing with her" in accordance with *Yevamos* 47, that just as one tells the prospective convert about the punishment for sins, one informs him of the reward for *mitzvos*: "One tells him, 'You must know that the World to Come is only for the righteous,' " etc. Thus, the present verse tells us that Naomi told her about the punishment but not about the reward for *mitzvos.* "She told her, 'We are forbidden to go outside the *techum* on *Shabbos,*' [Ruth replied],

1. See *Megillah* 17a.

she stopped arguing with her, 19 *and the two of them*
went on until they came to Bethlehem.

'Wherever you go, I will go.' 'There are four types of death penalties,' [Ruth replied], 'Where you die, I will die.' " Then, when Naomi saw that Ruth was nevertheless insistent on coming with her, she did not go on to tell her the rewards for performing the *mitzvos,* and that is what is meant by, "she stopped arguing with her."

However we still have to explain how it was that Naomi did not tell Ruth about the rewards, if that is a requirement before accepting a convert. It appears from this that this procedure, of mentioning both the punishments and the rewards, is only meant to make it easier for the prospective convert to make up his mind at this trying time, as *Rambam* states in *Hilchos Teshuvah* (10:1), "A person should not say, 'I will perform the *mitzvos* of the Torah and study its wisdom so that I will receive all the blessings written in it, or so that I will earn the World to Come; and I will refrain from the sins against which the Torah warned us so that I will be saved from the curses written in the Torah or so that I will not be cut off from the life of the World to Come.' It is not proper to serve Hashem in this way, for one who serves in this way serves out of fear and this is not something praised by the prophets or by the Sages, and the only ones who serve Hashem in this way are ignoramuses and women and children, who are educated to serve out of fear until their intellect expands and they serve out of love." In the next paragraph (10:2), *Rambam* writes, "One who serves Hashem out of love is involved in the Torah and *mitzvos* and works in the path of wisdom, not because of anything (to be gained) in the world and not because of fear of punishment and not in order to inherit the good, but does what is true because it is true. The good (i.e., the person's reward) will then [incidentally] come because of it."

Since Naomi saw that Ruth was insistent on going with her, not because of fear of punishment or in order to inherit the good, but did what is true because it is true, she did not discuss with her the reward for *mitzvos,* so that her conversion would be because of love and not because of fear.

19. וַתֵּלַכְנָה שְׁתֵּיהֶם עַד בּוֹאָנָה בֵּית לָחֶם — And the two of them went on until they came to Bethlehem.

Rashi quotes Rav Avahu: "See how precious converts are to the Holy One, Blessed is He, that as soon as she decided to convert the verse made her equal to Naomi." This statement requires examination, for if indeed Ruth, by her action, became equal to Naomi — as we know that it is possible for a person to acquire his entire World to Come in but a

וַיְהִי כְּבוֹאָנָה בֵּית לֶחֶם וַתֵּהֹם כָּל־הָעִיר עֲלֵיהֶן
כ וַתֹּאמַרְנָה הֲזֹאת נָעֳמִי: וַתֹּאמֶר אֲלֵיהֶן אַל־

---

moment[1] — why should there be any special consideration toward converts? She should have enjoyed this status simply because of her actions! On the other hand, if her actions were not up to the level of Naomi's, why does this verse equate her to Naomi? After all, the Torah which Hashem gave us is a Torah of truth, and where only the truth is written, why should this consideration be a reason to write something about her which she might not deserve and might not be truthful?

It would appear, though, that one of these questions answers the other, as follows: The reason why Ruth was equated to Naomi was only because converts are considered precious by Hashem, and enjoy a special status before Hashem, receiving entirely different aid from Above, as we find in *Or HaChaim* on the verse (*Bereishis* 6:8), "Noach found grace in the eyes of Hashem." So too is this the case with Ruth, whose actions found grace in the eyes of Hashem, to the extent that the verse equates her with Naomi.

So too do we see today that *ba'alei teshuvah* are able to ascend to the highest levels of the Torah in a very short time, whereas others require a great deal of time and effort to reach such heights, whether in Torah knowledge or in *yiras shamayim* (fear of Heaven). And that is because of the special love Hashem has for converts and for *ba'alei teshuvah.* The source of the special aid from Above for converts and *ba'alei teshuvah* enables them to ascend the rungs of Torah knowledge speedily. This was also the case of the Jewish people when they left Egypt, where the people received the Torah at Sinai and all became converts (as we find in *Rambam*, *Hilchos Issurei Bi'ah* 11), and were able, within the space of fifty days, to ascend from the forty-ninth level of impurity, to the extent that they all became prophets at the time of the giving of the Torah at Sinai. This help from Above always exists, and works to this very day for converts and *ba'alei teshuvah.*

❦ ❦ ❦

One can explain the words of the Midrash differently, in accordance with the words of Rabbeinu Yonah (*Sha'ar* 2; *Derech* 3), who writes, "When a person heeds the reproofs of sages and of those who rebuke the community . . . and on the day he hears it accepts their rebuke . . . his repentance is accepted . . . and he acquires for his soul merits and a reward for all the *mitzvos* and rebukes, and happy is he because his soul

---

1. *Avodah Zarah* 10b.

1/19 *And it came to pass, when they arrived in Bethlehem, the entire city was tumultuous over them, and the women said, "Could this be Naomi?"*

---

has become saintly in but a short while, and *Chazal* said that (*Avos d'Rebbi Nasan* 23) one whose deeds exceed his wisdom — his wisdom endures, as it states (*Shemos* 24:7), 'We will do and we will listen.' " The explanation of the matter is that any person who accepts upon himself full-heartedly to observe and perform everything according to the Torah in which he is instructed and in accordance with the law which those in charge instruct him, from that day on he has a reward for all the *mitzvos,* because his ears hearkened to the words of the Torah and understood them, and is rewarded as well for those matters which he has not yet heard. According to this, we can understand how the verse here equated Ruth to Naomi from this time on, and it states, "And the two of them went."

וַתֵּלַכְנָה שְׁתֵּיהֶם עַד בּוֹאָנָה בֵּית לָחֶם — And the two of them went on until they came to Bethlehem.

Shoresh Yishai notes that the Hebrew word for "they" in this verse is given as "*shteihem*" with the letter *mem* as the last letter, rather than "*shteihen,*" which would have the letter *nun* as the last letter. Grammatically, words ending with the suffix *mem* are masculine, while those ending with the suffix *nun* are feminine. Why, then, does the verse use the word "*shteihem*" with a masculine suffix, when it refers to Naomi and Ruth? *Shoresh Yishai* answers that the reason for this use might be that the two women moved with the greater speed that is generally that of men rather than at the more sedate pace of women.

It is possible that they did so because of their love of Eretz Yisrael and their fear of whether they were worthy of living there. That was why they went as swiftly as men rather than more slowly, as women would do.

Now, for a woman to go so fast is not modest, so they did so only when there were no men to see them. Once they reached Bethlehem they slowed their pace to that of women. Thus the word *shteihem,* which is basically a feminine word (from the word *shtayim* — the feminine of "two") with a masculine suffix shows how at different times they moved as fast as men and at others times they move as sedately as women.

וַתֵּלַכְנָה שְׁתֵּיהֶם עַד בּוֹאָנָה בֵּית לָחֶם וַיְהִי כְּבוֹאָנָה בֵּית לֶחֶם וַתֵּהֹם כָּל הָעִיר עֲלֵיהֶן וַתֹּאמַרְנָה הֲזֹאת נָעֳמִי — And the two of them went on until they came to Bethlehem, and the entire city was tumultuous over them, and the women said, "Could this be Naomi?"

Why is it that Naomi wanted to return specifically to Bethlehem, where she knew she would suffer indignity in that she had left her home full and was returning empty? In fact, that was exactly what happened to her, as it states, "The entire city was tumultuous over them, and the women said, 'Could this be Naomi?' " Furthermore, there is no doubt that she suffered further indignity for having brought Ruth the Moabite with her, for the Moabites were scorned by the Jewish people, as the Torah states (*Devarim* 23:4), "An Ammonite or Moabite shall not enter the congregation of Hashem." Similarly, the young man standing by the harvesters said (2:6), "She is a Moabite girl . . . the one who returned with Naomi from the fields of Moab." If we can take as an example, if an honored person walks along the street with someone who is despicable, he will certainly be scorned as a result. And that was how it appeared to the crowds who saw Naomi with Ruth — and yet she returned to Bethlehem.

The best way to understand this is with a story told in the sefer *Or Elchanan.* R' Elchanan Wasserman asked someone to accompany him in going out to raise money for his yeshivah, and the person replied that he did not want to go because of the insults he might have to endure. R' Elchanan told him that whatever insults a person receives are decreed from Heaven, and there are different ways that a person can be insulted. The best way to receive these insults is through the Torah, and that is something to be happy about. Naomi knew that whatever insults she received would be decreed from Heaven and there was no way to flee from them if they had been decreed, and how much more are these insults worth if they come about when she is performing the *mitzvah* to love a convert.

וַתֵּלַכְנָה שְׁתֵּיהֶם עַד בּוֹאָנָה בֵּית לָחֶם וַיְהִי כְּבוֹאָנָה בֵּית לֶחֶם וַתֵּהֹם כָּל הָעִיר עֲלֵיהֶן וַתֹּאמַרְנָה הֲזֹאת נָעֳמִי — And the entire city was tumultuous over them, and the women said, "Could this be Naomi?"

See *Rashi* who notes that the vowelization under the letter *heh* in the words, *hazos Naomi* ("Could this be Naomi?") is a *chataf patach,* because it expresses a question: "Is this the Naomi who used to go out with covered wagons and mules? Did you see what happened to her because she left Eretz Yisrael?"

It appears that there was a special complaint against the descendants of Yehudah for leaving Eretz Yisrael, and that was why Elimelech and his sons were punished. This was what David HaMelech said to Shaul (*I Shmuel* 26:19), "They have driven me away this day from attaching myself to the heritage of Hashem, [as if] to say, 'Go worship the gods of others!' " Indeed, David was punished for the sin of leaving Eretz Yisrael, as we are told in *Midrash Rabbah* on *Naso,*[1] that when David fled from Shaul and brought his mother and father to the king of Moab because he was afraid

1. 14, *Bayom Hashevi'i.*

of Shaul, he trusted the Moabites because he was a descendant of Ruth the Moabite. Yet the king of Moab nevertheless killed them all, except for a single brother who managed to escape and to reach Nachas, king of Ammon. The king of Moab then sent troops to seize the brother. Ammon, though, did not give him over, and that is the good deed which Nachash did for David. That was why David later attacked Moab. All of this happened because they left Eretz Yisrael and went to Moab.

I saw something astounding in *Midrash Talpi'os* (Section "David," beginning "*Mizbe'ach*"). First, we can ask why David HaMelech did not kill Shimi at the time that Shimi cursed him, even though one who rebels against the monarchy is liable to the death penalty, and the king is forbidden to forgo any infringement on his honor. Furthermore, what wisdom did Shlomo HaMelech display after having been told by David (*I Melachim* 2:6), "You shall act according to your wisdom"? One can answer this by saying that David was not sure whether Shimi had cursed him for the sake of Heaven, in that Shimi felt that David should have trusted Hashem and not left Eretz Yisrael, for one who leaves Eretz Yisrael is compared as if he has no God; or perhaps he had cursed David as part of a revolt and as a display of insubordination. It was because of this doubt that David did not kill him, and instead commanded Shlomo, with his great wisdom, to ascertain what Shimi's motivation had been. Shlomo then commanded Shimi not to leave Eretz Yisrael. Then, when Shimi's slave disappeared, Shimi followed the slave to Gath, which was outside Eretz Yisrael. Shlomo then realized that what Shimi had said was not meant for the sake of Heaven, because he himself had also left Eretz Yisrael, and his cursing was indeed a revolt against David. That was why Shlomo had Shimi put to death.

It is possible that there is a greater requirement for those of the tribe of Yehudah to remain in Eretz Yisrael because this tribe's land included the most holy parts, the *Beis HaMikdash,* the place to which the whole world turns with its prayers, and whoever is closer to the holy places and the sacrifices is held to be more accountable if he leaves them. That was the complaint which Yirmiyahu had against the Jewish people (*Yirmiyahu* 2:13): "They have forsaken Me, the Source of living waters, to dig for themselves cisterns, broken cisterns that cannot hold water."

וַתֵּהֹם כָּל הָעִיר עֲלֵיהֶן וַתֹּאמַרְנָה הֲזֹאת נָעֳמִי — And the entire city was tumultuous over them, and the women said, "Could this be Naomi?"

In *Bava Basra* 91, the *gemara* asks, "What is meant by 'Could this be Naomi?' R' Yitzchak said: They exclaimed, 'Did you see Naomi who left Eretz Yisrael for another country and what became of her?' " This requires clarification, because by returning to Eretz Yisrael Naomi had done *teshuvah* — had repented her sin of leaving Eretz Yisrael, and returned to

Eretz Yisrael very speedily because of her love of the land, as mentioned earlier. Why, then, did she have to suffer the embarrassment of people saying, "Could this be Naomi?" when they saw what had happened to her?

We are told in *Berachos* 5 that Eretz Yisrael is one of Hashem's great gifts, and it is acquired only through suffering. Now that Naomi had left it, she needed to reacquire it. Thus she suffered this way when she returned to Bethlehem, thereby once again acquiring it. The very fact that people said, "Could this be Naomi?" and her embarrassment at being singled out this way was her suffering, and it led to her acquisition of Eretz Yisrael anew.

וַתֵּהֹם כָּל הָעִיר עֲלֵיהֶן וַתֹּאמַרְנָה הֲזֹאת נָעֳמִי — And the entire city was tumultuous over them, and the women said, "Could this be Naomi?"

See *Rashi* who notes that the vowelization under the letter *heh* in the words, *hazos Naomi* ("Could this be Naomi?") is a *chataf patach,* because it expresses a question: "Is this the Naomi who used to go out with covered wagons and mules? Did you see what happened to her because she left Eretz Yisrael?"

One must clarify how the women were permitted to say this, for we are told in the Torah (*Vayikra* 25:17), "Each of you shall not aggrieve his fellow, and you shall fear your God," which is a prohibition against aggrieving anyone through what one says. And *Rambam* writes (*Hilchos Mechirah* 14:13) "How is this? If a person is a *ba'al teshuvah* one may not say to him, 'Your earlier deeds were terrible and one receives pain as punishment for them.' Or if a person is burying his child, one may not say to him as Iyov's friends said to him (*Iyov* 4:6-7), 'Behold, was your fear [of God] not your foolishness . . . Remember, please, which innocent person perished?' " How, then, were the people of Bethlehem permitted to make such a statement, which embarrassed Naomi?

From this we can see the source and a proof to the words of the *Alter* of Kelm, in his *Chochmah U'Mussar* (I:332), "In the sin of *lashon hara* we find two seeming contradictions. *Devarim* 24:9 states, 'Remember what Hashem, your God, did to Miriam on the way,' on which *Ramban* commented, 'This is a commandment to teach Hashem's nation that one must be careful not to speak *lashon hara.*' But this is problematic, because we see that the Torah did not want to publicize which kind of tree the Tree of Knowledge was (*Rashi* on *Bereishis* 3:7), and yet the Torah did not do the same regarding the sin of Miriam. We must thus say that where there is a constructive purpose in doing so, this is permitted. Once the Torah wrote about her (i.e., Miriam's) sin, we learn that where it is constructive there is a *mitzvah* to tell *lashon hara* and one is indeed obligated to do so. So too did I hear in the name of R' Chaim of Volozhin on the verse (*Vayikra* 19:16), 'You shall not be a gossipmonger among your people, you shall not stand aside while your brother's blood is being shed,' that in those places where one is obligated to tell *lashon hara* and does not do so, he violates the prohibition of 'you shall not stand aside while your brother's blood is being shed.' From this we see how difficult it is to align our own thoughts in accordance with the Torah, for the sin of *lashon hara* is a very grievous one, which might suggest that a person should just act as if he is mute and never say anything, but even by doing so he might be guilty in a place where he is required to tell *lashon hara.* On this we are told (*Koheles* 7:16), 'Do not be overly righteous,' whereas the next two verses say, 'Be not overly wicked . . . he who fears Hashem performs them all.' Who among us is able to evaluate his actions in accordance with the Torah in order not to be guilty of either extreme, for both extremes are very dangerous, and only 'he who fears Hashem performs them all.' "

Now we understand better the connection between the two parts of the verse (*Vayikra* 19:16), "You shall not be a gossipmonger among your people, you shall not stand aside while your brother's blood is being shed," in that there may be occasions when there is a *mitzvah* to tell one's friend something which he needs to know in order to arouse him to do *teshuvah* and to accept his judgment, just as the people of Bethlehem did with Naomi. Their comments aroused Naomi to do *teshuvah* and to accept the judgment against her. We must, then, be able to evaluate properly what is needed in fear of Hashem, and not be guilty of either extreme in this.

We can also deduce from *Rashi's* language that the intent of the people of Bethlehem was only to strengthen themselves and to learn from Naomi how severe a sin it is to leave Eretz Yisrael and to live outside it, for *Rashi* states, "Is this the Naomi who used to go out with covered wagons and mules? Did you see what happened to her because she left Eretz Yisrael?" Thus, they did not say this to her but spoke among themselves, except that they spoke loudly enough for Naomi to hear. Their whole intention, though, was to strengthen themselves and to realize how serious a sin it is to leave Eretz Yisrael in order to live abroad.

וַתֵּהֹם כָּל הָעִיר עֲלֵיהֶן — And the entire city was tumultuous over them.

Midrash Ruth (3:6), states, "R' Tanchum said in the name of R' Azariah: It states (*Tehillim* 89:9), 'Hashem, God of Legions, who is like You, O Strong One, God,' Who brings about things in their due time. The wife of Boaz died that day, and all of Israel came to pay their respects, and Ruth, too, entered with Naomi. Thus, as one went out, the other came in." It appears that this fulfilled what *Chazal* tell us in *Kiddushin* 72b, on the verse (*Koheles* 1:5), "The sun rises and the sun sets": "A righteous person does not depart from the world until another righteous person like himself has been created." Now that the righteous wife of Boaz had died, Ruth was

תִּקְרֶאנָה לִי נָעֳמִי קְרֶאןָ לִי מָרָא כִּי־הֵמַר שַׁדַּי לִי
כא מְאֹד: אֲנִי מְלֵאָה הָלַכְתִּי וְרֵיקָם הֱשִׁיבַנִי יהוה לָמָּה
תִקְרֶאנָה לִי נָעֳמִי וַיהוה עָנָה בִי וְשַׁדַּי הֵרַע־לִי:

---

immediately there to replace her, as the *gemara* there states, "When Rav Yehudah died Rava was born, and when Rava died Rav Ashi was born."

The Chasam Sofer in his *chiddushim* on *Avodah Zarah* (63b) wrote that his whole life he could not understand from where *Chazal* derived the idea that a person who converts is considered like a newborn.[1] The source of this statement of *Chazal,* though, can be learned from *Ruth,* where we are told that when the wife of Boaz died Ruth arrived as if she had just been born. From this we see that someone who converts is considered exactly as if he were a newborn, and thus both events here occurred at the same time, as if to say that when the wife of Boaz died, Ruth was born.

19-20. וַתֹּאמַרְנָה הֲזֹאת נָעֳמִי וַתֹּאמֶר אֲלֵיהֶן אַל תִּקְרֶאנָה לִי נָעֳמִי קְרֶאןָ לִי מָרָא — The women said, "Could this be Naomi?" "Do not call me Naomi," she replied, "call me Mara . . ."

It appears that Naomi fulfilled that which Rabbeinu Yonah wrote in *Sha'arei Teshuvah* (*Sha'ar* I, 7th Principle), that every *ba'al teshuvah* must be humble and must accept upon himself to act in the way that *Chazal* stated in *Avos* (4:10), "Be humble before every person." From this, Rabbeinu Yonah concludes that one must not become angry or stubborn with others, and should not be affected by what he hears . . . as it states (*Eichah* 3:29), "Let him put his mouth to the dust — there may be hope. Let one offer his cheek to his smiter, let him be filled with disgrace."

20. וַתֹּאמֶר אֲלֵיהֶן אַל תִּקְרֶאנָה לִי נָעֳמִי קְרֶאןָ לִי מָרָא כִּי הֵמַר שַׁדַּי לִי מְאֹד — "Do not call me Naomi," she replied, "call me Mara, for the Almighty has dealt very bitterly with me."

The word "Mara" is written with an *alef* as its last letter, rather than with the more customary *heh.* Why this change? It occurred to me that this might be a hint at what we are told in *Shabbos* (104a), that the letter *alef* implies that one must learn something, and Naomi told the women of the city, "'Call me Mara' and learn from what happened to me because I left Eretz Yisrael and because my husband did not pity the poor, and maybe by the fact that you learn this from me I will be able to earn a place in the World to Come."

---

1. Note in *Meshech Chochmah* on *Parshas Va'eschanan* what he wrote to answer this.

[20] *"Do not call me Naomi [pleasant one]," she replied, "call me Mara [embittered one], for the Almighty has dealt very bitterly with me.* [21] *I was full when I went away, but* HASHEM *has brought me back empty. Why shall you call me Naomi; and* HASHEM *has testified against me, and the Almighty has brought misfortune upon me."*

כִּי הֵמַר שַׁדַּי לִי מְאֹד — "Has dealt very bitterly with me."

The meaning of word *"me'od,"* which we translated as "very," may be in accordance with the way *Chazal* explain it in the verse (*Devarim* 6:5), "with all your resources" (*me'odecha*), that with whatever measure (*middah*) Hashem measures (*moded*) you, be thankful (*modeh*) to Him. Thus, Naomi's acceptance of Hashem's verdict ended with the word *me'od,* to indicate that under no circumstances did she feel that she was upset with Hashem's verdict against her, but on the contrary she was thankful to Him, as she knew that everything was for her own good.

21. וַיהוה עָנָה בִי וְשַׁדַּי הֵרַע לִי — "And Hashem (*vaShem*) has testified against me, and the Almighty (*veShaddai*) has brought misfortune upon me."

We need to understand the seeming redundancy here. On the phrase "has testified against me," *Rashi* says that "Hashem's attribute of strict justice (*middas hadin*) testified against me," as in *Hoshea* 5, "The pride of Israel will testify before Him." In other words, even though the name "Hashem" is generally associated with Hashem's attribute of mercy (*middas harachamim*), when it is preceded by the letter *vav,* as it is in the present verse, that refers to *middas hadin.* This we see in *Ramban's* comments in *Parshas Beshalach,* where the verse states (*Shemos* 13:21), "And Hashem (*vaShem*) went before them," for *Ramban* states that wherever there is a reference to *"vaShem,"* it refers to Hashem and his *beis din.* On the other hand, "and the Almighty (*veShaddai*) has brought misfortune upon me" refers to Hashem's *middas harachamim,* as in Yaakov's prayer (*Bereishis* 43:14), "May El Shaddai grant you mercy before the man," on which *Rashi* comments that the word "*Shaddai*" implies the One who has mercy and Who has the power to grant mercy.

Thus, we can continue with the explanation, as follows: In the *Mahadura Basra* of the *Maharsha* on *Maseches Chullin* (86a), where the *gemara* states, "The whole world is provided with food because of Chanina My son, and Chanina My son subsists on a *kav* of carobs from one *Shabbos* eve to the next," *Maharsha* explains that Hashem created the world using both *din* (strict justice) and *rachamim* (mercy). Thus, if all of the world, or the majority of the world, are sinners and are deserving of being destroyed, *chas veshalom,* due to *middas hadin* (the attribute of strict justice) it is through *middas harachamim* (the attribute of mercy) that Hashem can take pity on them. Thus, while half goes to *middas hadin* and half to *middas harachamim,* a single righteous man can balance out the entire world. As Hashem gave precedence to *middas harachamim* over *middas hadin, middas harachamim* has the right to choose which part it wants, and it chooses all the rest of the world, leaving the righteous man to *middas hadin.* Thus we see that "The whole world is provided with food because of Chanina," in that *middas harachamim* takes the rest of the world for itself, and it is thus that the world is provided with food, while *middas hadin* is given R' Chanina.[1] Thus Naomi said, "Hashem did not act with me as He had when He created the world with half to *middas hadin* and half to *middas harachamim,* for 'I was full when I went away, but Hashem has brought me back empty,' where *middas harachamim* took nothing. Rather, 'Hashem has testified against me, and the Almighty has brought misfortune upon me.' " The reason for this was that Elimelech's sin was that he did not pity the poor and he left Eretz Yisrael because of his miserliness in that he wouldn't carry the burden of those who suffered because of the famine. His punishment was that *middas harachamim* did not take pity on him, and "Hashem has brought me back empty."

22. וַתָּשָׁב נָעֳמִי וְרוּת הַמּוֹאֲבִיָּה כַלָּתָהּ עִמָּהּ הַשָּׁבָה מִשְּׂדֵי מוֹאָב — And so Naomi returned, and Ruth the Moabite, her daughter-in-law, with her — who returned from the fields of Moab.

This entire verse seems to be superfluous, because we know all its information from previous verses, and it would be sufficient just to write the last few words of the verse, "They came to Bethlehem at the beginning of the barley harvest."

It appears, though, that the aim of this verse is to tell us that in Heaven Naomi's repentance and her confession had been accepted, and she returned to her previous spiritual state as she had been before she left Bethlehem. And similarly with Ruth, who, even though she had come from the fields of Moab, also had her repentance for all the sins she had done in Moab accepted, in accordance with the promise of Hashem to Avraham, "Yours is the dew of your youth," that all the years before he came to a realization of the existence of Hashem would be forgiven (*Bereishis Rabbah* 39:9). The same is true here, that Ruth's repentance was

1. It is worth checking out this source, for it contains fundamental concepts.

[22] *And so Naomi returned, and Ruth the Moabite, her daughter-in-law, with her — who returned from the fields*

---

accepted, and all of her sins in the fields of Moab were forgiven.

Now we can understand the seeming redundancy of "Naomi returned . . . who returned from the fields of Moab," in that Naomi's return was to her prior spiritual state, and Ruth the Moabite returned from the fields of Moab, in that her repentance was accepted even though she had not yet converted entirely, and, as we will explain below (3:9), her repentance was nevertheless enough to forgive all her sins. Thus, the author of *Lev Eliyahu* (in *Parshas Acharei Mos,* p. 35) quotes R' Yitzchak Blaser, that the repentance of those of the other nations absolves them from any punishment for their sins, but the sins themselves are not forgiven even if they repented greatly. In the case of Ruth, we have a new concept however, for by saying "your people are my people," etc., she was able to achieve complete repentance, as we explained.[1] The idea of repentance is hinted at in the present verse, when they returned to Eretz Yisrael, as *Eitz Yosef* writes on the Midrash there that the promise to Avraham, that "Yours is the dew of your youth" was said to him when he succeeded in Hashem's test in going to Eretz Yisrael, as stated by *Eitz Yosef* (in "your sins will fly away"): "He was sanctified through the sanctity of the land whose inhabitants are forgiven of sins." Similarly, when Naomi and Ruth returned to Eretz Yisrael, they were forgiven for their sins.

❧ ❧ ❧

It appears that we can also explain from another apparent redundancy in the verse that Naomi received a hint from Heaven that when the Torah says (*Devarim* 23:4), "An Ammonite or Moabite shall not enter the congregation of Hashem," it applies only to a male Moabite and not to a female Moabite.

We can learn this from the fact that while Naomi indeed returned to Eretz Yisrael from Moab, that was not true for Ruth, and the verse should have stated in regard to Ruth, "who came from the fields of Moab" rather than "who returned from the fields of Moab." From this we can learn that Ruth felt as if she had always belonged in Eretz Yisrael, and she was returning from Moab rather than coming from it. The verse wished to emphasize that Ruth herself felt she was returning from the fields of Moab and was not just coming from them. Indeed, we find in the Holy Books that the souls of true converts are indeed souls of the Jewish people, except

---

1. Also see above, what I wrote on the verse, "Where you die, I will die."

that at the time of the sin of Adam they somehow went into the bodies of members of the other nations.

❦ ❦ ❦

This also explains the end of the verse, "They came to Bethlehem at the beginning of the barley harvest." *Rashi* states that this was the harvesting of the *omer,* and the verses comes to hint at the fact that the *mitzvah* of the *omer* was one whose merit Ruth also enjoyed. This we see in *Midrash Rabbah* (*Vayikra* 28:6), where R' Yochanan said: "Never let the *mitzvah* of the *omer* be regarded by you lightly, for it was through the *mitzvah* of the *omer* that Avraham was granted the inheritance of the land of Canaan." Similarly, as a result of the merit of the *mitzvah* of the *omer* Ruth was granted an inheritance in Eretz Yisrael, because the prohibition is only against a male Moabite and not a female Moabite to become part of Hashem's Congregation.

It would appear that this is also an allusion to the return of Lot to Eretz Yisrael, for Ruth came from Moab, i.e., from Lot, and since Lot went together with Avraham in the test of "*Lech lecha,*" he was granted some sort of link to Eretz Yisrael. Thus it is proper to write about Ruth, his descendant, that she returned from the fields of Moab, for the verse here hints that nine generations after the separation of Avraham and Lot a descendant of Lot returned to join with a descendant of Avraham [Avraham, Yitzchak, Yaakov, Yehudah, Peretz, Chetzron, Ram, Amindavav, Nachson, Tov), and that is why there are nine Hebrew words in the first part of the verse, "And so Naomi returned, and Ruth the Moabite, her daughter-in-law, with her — who returned from the fields of Moab" (1:22). Thus, from the time that Avraham and Lot left Egypt together and began to go toward the land of Yehudah, as it states (*Bereishis* 13:1), "So Abram went up from Egypt . . . and Lot with him, to the south," nine generations passed. *Rashi* writes that on this trip they were on their way to the south of Eretz Yisrael, that being the portion of Yehudah.

Lot had a complaint against Avraham, as hinted at and deduced by *Chazal* on the verse where it states (ibid. v. 11), "Lot traveled to the south (*mikedem*)," from which *Chazal* deduced that Lot traveled away from the Ancient One (*mikadmono*) of the World, and said, "I do not want either Avraham or his God" (and see *Rashi* there). After Lot had done kindness to Avraham and had not revealed Avraham's secret to Pharaoh and therefore Avraham was saved by him, and yet Avraham had rejected him, he felt hurt and rejected, which led him to say, "I do not want either Avraham or his God." He was therefore punished in that the separation between *of Moab. They came to Bethlehem at the beginning of the barley harvest.*

Lot and Avraham lasted for nine generations, and this is hinted at in the verse, "And so Naomi returned, and Ruth the Moabite, her daughter-in-law, with her — who returned from the fields of Moab" (1:22). And in the ninth generation there was a fulfillment of their coming to Bethlehem in Yehudah.

וְהֵמָּה בָּאוּ בֵּית לֶחֶם בִּתְחִלַּת קְצִיר שְׂעֹרִים — They came to Bethlehem at the beginning of the barley harvest.

We need to explain what difference it made as to what season it was when they returned. *Rashi* on the verse (*Bereishis* 40:1), "And it happened after these things that the cupbearer of the king of Egypt and the baker transgressed," states that "Because that cursed woman (i.e., Potiphar's wife) got everyone accustomed to speak about [Yosef], Hashem brought the offenses of the two [i.e., that of the cupbearer and that of the baker] to light, so that people would pay attention to them and not to him, and He also caused relief to come through them." Along the same line, one can say that since "the entire city was tumultuous over them and the women said, 'Could this be Naomi?' " with everyone talking disparagingly about Naomi, Hashem arranged that they should return at the beginning of the barley harvest, so that the women would not have any time to engage in idle talk. Furthermore, Naomi's and Ruth's deliverance came through the barley harvest, for the story of Ruth takes place in the fields of Boaz when she comes to gather up the dropped and forgotten grain stalks.

Indeed deliverance came to Naomi and Ruth through the harvesting of the barley, to teach, instruct and strengthen us about the importance of *tzedakah.* Thus we find in *Kesubos* 66b: "*Chazal* learned: Once R' Yochanan ben Zakkai was riding on a donkey and left Yerushalayim and his students were walking behind him. He saw a certain young woman collecting barley among the dung heaps of the animals of Arabs. When she saw him, she wrapped herself with her hair and stood up before him. She said to him, 'Rebbi, feed me.' He said to her, 'My daughter, who are you?' She told him, 'I am the daughter of Nakdimon ben Gurion.' He said to her, 'My daughter, where did the money of your father's house go?' She told him, 'Rebbi, isn't there a proverb in Jerusalem that the salt (i.e., the preservation) of money is by diminution (by giving money away to charity)?' (and evidently they had lost their money because they had not given money to charity) . . . R' Yochanan ben Zakkai cried and said, 'How happy are Israel. When they do the will of Hashem there is no nation or tongue which can rule over them, and when they do not do the will of

א וּלְנָעֳמִ֞י °מידע [°מוֹדַ֣ע ק׳] לְאִישָׁ֗הּ אִ֣ישׁ גִּבּ֣וֹר חַ֔יִל
ב מִמִּשְׁפַּ֖חַת אֱלִימֶ֑לֶךְ וּשְׁמ֖וֹ בֹּֽעַז׃ וַתֹּ֨אמֶר

Hashem they are handed over to a low people, and not only a low people, but even the animals of a low people.' "

In the case of Naomi and Ruth, Hashem's attribute of strict justice helped them and they were able to gather the barley honorably, and were not given the punishment of the daughter of Nakdimon ben Gurion who had to glean stalks of barley among the dung heaps of the animals of Arabs. From this one can learn that a person who can help the Jewish poor and does not do so is punished measure for measure by having to live off the food of animals. The difference between the human and the animal is that the human's purpose is to help other people, as we see in the words of R' Chaim of Volozhin to his son (in his introduction to *Nefesh HaChaim*): "Man was not created for himself, but to help others wherever he has the power to do so." Animals, on the other hand, eat and work only for themselves. Thus anyone who can aid the Jewish poor and does not do so is acting like an animal and is punished by having to eat the food of animals.

Ruth and Naomi were able, through their repentance (as we explained above) to become a symbol of those who are involved in *tzedakah* and lovingkindness with the unfortunate poor and to show how great is their reward.

II

1. וּלְנָעֳמִי מוֹדַע לְאִישָׁהּ אִישׁ גִּבּוֹר חַיִל מִמִּשְׁפַּחַת אֱלִימֶלֶךְ וּשְׁמוֹ בֹּעַז — Naomi had a relative through her husband, a man of substance, from the family of Elimelech, whose name was Boaz.

The commentators ask how it was that Boaz, her husband's relative, did not come to Naomi's aid immediately. After all, he was a wealthy man and the judge of Israel. There is no doubt that he had heard of her return, as we see in (1:19), "The entire city was tumultuous over them." Why, then, did he not immediately take pity on them and help them?[1]

It would appear that he definitely brought Naomi provisions but she refused to accept the gifts, for she knew that she had been punished by the deaths of her husband and sons for having left Eretz Yisrael and living in Moab. Now, when she returned, her goal was to rectify that wrong and to do *teshuvah* — to repent. That was why she refused to accept anything from Boaz. Had she accepted his aid, everyone would have said that the reason she returned from Moab was because she wanted Boaz to support

---

1. Another response to this question is offered below.

1 Naomi had a relative through her husband, a man
of substance, from the family of Elimelech, whose
name was Boaz.

---

her, while her return was totally in order to repent. She was also afraid that if she took his assistance she herself might come to feel that she had returned to Eretz Yisrael in order to receive help from Boaz, and the thinking of such thoughts decreases the perfection of one's *teshuvah*, in that one has to rectify the wrong which one did.

וּלְנָעֳמִי מוֹדַע לְאִישָׁהּ אִישׁ גִּבּוֹר חַיִל מִמִּשְׁפַּחַת אֱלִימֶלֶךְ וּשְׁמוֹ בֹּעַז — Naomi had a relative through her husband, a man of substance, from the family of Elimelech, whose name was Boaz.

Even though Naomi could have relied on Boaz to aid and support her, as he was a man of substance and a judge, she did not want to rely on mortals for her sustenance. Rather, she acted in accordance with (*Tehillim* 55:23), "Cast upon Hashem your burden and He will sustain you," and thus Ruth went like all the other poor women to glean in the fields.

That, indeed, is the way that Hashem deals with man: If a person places his full trust in Hashem, Hashem ensures that he will be provided for, even in a "miraculous" way if necessary, while if a person feels that he needs to take care of his own needs, Hashem allows him to be subjected to all the vagaries of the world.

Now, a person can place his faith in Hashem when he sees he is being treated with mercy, but Naomi saw that Hashem was treating her with the full measure of strict justice, "for the Almighty has dealt very bitterly with me" (1:20). In spite of this, she placed her trust in Hashem. Along these same lines, we find that R' Moshe Feinstein, in addressing people who had survived the horrors of the Nazis, told them that in the Torah we find that the *tochechah* (the "rebuke") is followed by the *parshah* of *arachin*, which deals with the different valuations of people whose value was pledged to charity. From this juxtaposition, he learned that one who survived the *tochechah* of the *Sho'ah* and nevertheless remained strong in his faith is a person of great value.

We can also ask on our verse why there is a seeming repetition, in that it mentions both that Boaz was "a relative" and tells us that he was "from the family of Elimelech."

The answer is that it is possible to find a relative who does not feel close to oneself, while in other relationships one finds a relative to whom one feels close. Here, then, the verse tells us that not only was Boaz a relative, but he felt himself to be a member of the family. Further, the verse also adds that he was "a man of substance" (*ish gibor chayil*), namely a true

Torah scholar, in whom ("*bo*") there was the might ("*oz*") of Torah — Boaz. Yet, in spite of all of that, Naomi did not want to receive any support from Boaz but wanted to rely on Hashem alone, like the dove in the case of Noach (*Bereishis* 8:11) which said that it preferred to have its food come from Hashem even if it was as bitter as an olive, rather than receiving it from a mortal, even it was as sweet as honey.

וּלְנָעֳמִי מוֹדַע לְאִישָׁהּ אִישׁ גִּבּוֹר חַיִל מִמִּשְׁפַּחַת אֱלִימֶלֶךְ וּשְׁמוֹ בֹּעַז — Naomi had a relative through her husband, a man of substance, from the family of Elimelech, whose name was Boaz.

There are a number of points in this verse which need clarification. First, we know that Boaz was the judge of Israel, as noted by *Rashi* on verse 1:1 above; second, that the generations were supported by the judges; and third, that this occurred in the days of Ivtzan, and *Chazal* say that Ivtzan was Boaz. Why, then, doesn't the verse mention the major attribute of Boaz, in that he was a judge? Also, since he was the judge of Israel, why does the verse list him as a relative of Elimelech? As one generally links a lesser person to a greater person, shouldn't the verse have stated that Elimelech was a relative of Boaz, and not as we have it here?

The author of *Geza Yishai* notes that since Naomi and Boaz were relatives, both through Elimelech and in their own right (for *Chazal* tell us that Naomi's father, Elimelech, and Salmon — the father of Boaz — were all children of Nachshon ben Aminadav), how can it be that when Naomi and Ruth came to Bethlehem and "the entire city was tumultuous over them" (1:19), Boaz did not immediately send for them and offer to support them? After all, he was a wealthy man and the provider of the generation. Even though there were certainly good reasons why Boaz did not do so, as *Geza Yishai* points out, he nevertheless did not act as the judges of those days did. After all, it was the duty of the judge to be the provider of the generation, as *Rashi* notes. Thus, in answer to our question above as to why Boaz was not identified as a judge, we can say that this is because he did not act toward Naomi as the judges of his times did. Furthermore, the Hebrew word for relative used here, *moda*, is not written here with the customary letter *vav* between the *mem* and the *daled*, but with a *yud* instead, to show us that Boaz did not act like a close relative but as someone who was distant. Furthermore, as we saw earlier how Elimelech was so miserly that he left Eretz Yisrael because of all the beggars who were beseeching him, the verse here tells us that Elimelech's relative, Boaz, acted in the same way, and did not hasten to offer aid to Naomi and Ruth.

One can explain that Boaz's intentions in not hurrying to aid them was in accordance with *Bava Basra* 10, regarding a question that Turnus Rufus the Wicked asked R' Akiva: "If your God loves the poor, why doesn't He support them?" R' Akiva answered: "So that through them we will be saved from the decree of *Gehinnom*." Turnus Rufus replied: "On the contrary, this will make you deserving of *Gehinnom*. Let me give you an analogy. What is this like? It is like a king of flesh and blood who became angry at his servant and imprisoned him, and then ordered the jailers not to give him food or drink. One man then went and fed him and gave him food and drink. When the king heard this would he not become angry at him? Yet you (the Jewish people) are called servants, as it states (*Vayikra* 25:55), 'For the Children of Israel are servants to Me' " (in other words, by helping the poor one is contradicting Hashem's desires). R' Akiva said to him, "Let me give you an analogy. What is this like? It is like a king of flesh and blood who became angry at his son and imprisoned him, and then ordered the jailers not to give him food or drink. One man then went and fed him and gave him to drink. When the king heard this, wouldn't he send him a gift? And we are called sons, as it states (*Devarim* 14:1), 'You are children to Hashem, your God.' " [Turnus Rufus] went on and said to R' Akiva: 'You are called sons and you are called servants. When you do the will of Hashem you are called sons and when you do not do the will of Hashem you are called servants."

Now that Boaz saw what had happened to Naomi, who had been afflicted through *middas hadin* (the attribute of Hashem's strict justice), he saw that Hashem had treated her like a servant rather than a child, and he therefore did not want to come to her aid. The *navi* who wrote *Megillas Ruth* nevertheless has complaints against him, because a person should not delve into Hashem's concealed matters and into those areas that belong to Him. Each person must treat the other like a child of Hashem and help people whenever they are in distress. It is just for this that Shlomo wrote (*Mishlei* 17:17), "a brother is born for [times of] affliction," and as R' Akiva said to Turnus Rufus, the Scriptures teach that Hashem desires us to give charity even when we have earned condemnation because of our transgressions.

וּלְנָעֳמִי מוֹדַע לְאִישָׁהּ אִישׁ גִּבּוֹר חַיִל מִמִּשְׁפַּחַת אֱלִימֶלֶךְ וּשְׁמוֹ בֹּעַז — Naomi had a relative through her husband, a man of substance, from the family of Elimelech, whose name was Boaz.

Ramo, in his *Meishiv Nefesh*, asks whether this verse is not superfluous, because we see below (v. 3) that, "Her fate made her happen upon a parcel of land belonging to Boaz, who was of the family of Elimelech." Furthermore, what is the intention of this introductory verse and how does the next verse follow, when we are told, "Ruth the Moabite said to Naomi, 'Let me go out to the field and glean among the ears of grain . . .' 'Go ahead, my daughter,' she said to her"?

Beis HaLevi writes (at the end of *Parshas Vayeishev*) that the obligation for a person to attempt to support himself, about which it states (*Devarim* 15;18), "Hashem, your God, will bless you in everything you do," is dependent upon the degree of *bitachon* (trust in Hashem) the person has, and the greater a person's *bitachon* the less he has to work at supporting himself. Thus, for example, Yosef the *Tzaddik,* due to the degree of his *bitachon*, did not need to have Pharaoh's wine bearer intercede for him. One who lacks *bitachon*, to the extent that he lacks it, will need to try that much harder to support himself, and only through working at it will he see blessing.

These verses, then, come to teach us about Ruth's level of *bitachon*. Naomi's level of *bitachon* was undoubtedly very great, and all that she had to do in attempting to support herself was to have a relative such as Boaz — a valiant man who would obviously arrange for her support — maintain her properly, as eventually occurred. Ruth, though, according to her level of *bitachon*, needed to actually take action, and that meant to search for the dropped and forgotten grain stalks. That is what this sequence of verses tells us. Naomi did not say to her, "Go, my daughter, to collect stalks in the field," because based on her own level of *bitachon* she would not need to resort to such work. Ruth, on the other hand, told Naomi (2:2), "Let me go out to the field, and glean among the ears of grain."

Now we can understand why the text stresses that (2:2) "Ruth the Moabite said." What this verse tells us is that there still remained within Ruth a certain underlying foundation from Moab, and she had not yet attained Naomi's level of *bitachon*. Similarly, when the verse ends with, "Go ahead, my daughter," we may ask: Was Ruth, then, her daughter? The point, though, is that she had attained the level of a daughter.

Meshech Chochmah (*Parshas Va'eschanan*) discusses the three terms by which the Jewish people have been called: my daughter, my sister, my mother. "My daughter" was the level of the Jewish people when they left Egypt, where only through Hashem's great mercy were they taken out, in spite of the fact that they did not deserve to be taken out. It was in that sense that Naomi referred to Ruth as "my daughter," as one who was not yet fit to be supported due to her own merits in *bitachon* and was supported only through Hashem's kindness, like a father who supports his daughter.

וּלְנָעֳמִי מוֹדַע לְאִישָׁהּ — Naomi had a relative through her husband.

See what *Rashi* writes (and this is from *Bava Basra* 91): " 'A relative' — he was the son of Elimelech's brother." *Chazal* said that Elimelech; Salmon, the father of Boaz; Ploni Almoni, the redeemer; and Naomi's father were all sons of Nachshon ben Aminadav, and nevertheless the merits of their fathers were to no avail to those who left Eretz Yisrael. Indeed, we have seen it asked why *Chazal* stated that when they left Eretz Yisrael the merits of their forefathers ended, which would imply that the one is dependent on the other.

Rabbeinu Bachya, in *Parshas Beshalach*, asks why when Moshe prayed to Hashem after the sin of the spies, he did not mention the merits of our forefathers, as he did in regard to the sin of the Golden Calf. He answers that even though the merits of our forefathers can help us even in the worst of sins, when the spies rejected the precious land of our forefathers and spoke negatively about the land which our forefathers inherited, they were not worthy of the forefather's merits. Thus, *Chazal* said the same thing here: When they left Eretz Yisrael, they were no longer worthy of the merits of the forefathers.

And to go into it more deeply, we can study the verse in *Parshas Chukas* (*Bamidbar* 20:14): "Moshe sent emissaries from Kadesh to the king of Edom: 'So said your brother Israel.' " *Rashi* asks why Moshe decided to mention brotherliness here. He answers that what Moshe wanted to point out was that we are both descendants of Avraham, of whom it was said (*Bereishis* 15:13), "Your offspring will be aliens in a land not their own." Now, in reality, both of us — Yisrael and Edom — were obligated to pay that debt, yet it was the children of Yaakov who paid it.

I have also heard a question asked about the latter statement — i.e., that both sides were obligated to pay the debt — because even though the verse states, "Your offspring will be aliens in a land not their own," *Chazal* stated clearly on the verse (ibid. 21:12), "through Yitzchak will offspring be considered yours" that "through Yitzchak" means "not all of Yitzchak," i.e., that only through Yaakov and not through Eisav was this debt to be repaid.

One can answer this by saying that the very fact that Hashem chose Yaakov to pay Avraham's debt made Yaakov the chosen offspring of Avraham. Furthermore, since Eisav chose Mount Seir for himself and left Eretz Yisrael, saying, "I shall leave because I have no portion in this land, neither in the gift which You gave to him nor in repaying the debt" [see *Rashi* in *Parshas Vayishlach*, on the verse (*Bereishis* 36:7), "For their wealth was too abundant for them to dwell together"], he removed himself from being considered the offspring of Avraham.

Now, when Elimelech left Eretz Yisrael that act brought an end for him to the merits of the forefathers, because by his actions he was no longer considered one of their descendants. As a result he could no longer benefit from their merits, for the merits of the forefathers are dependent on one being an "offspring of the forefathers," and being an "offspring of the forefathers" depends on one's choosing Eretz Yisrael, the gift of the forefathers.

אִישׁ גִּבּוֹר חַיִל — A man of substance.

The *Targum* translates this as a man who is knowledgeable in the Torah. We can explain this by what *Ben Yehoyada* wrote on *Pesachim* (50a), to

רוּת הַמּוֹאֲבִיָּה אֶל־נָעֳמִי אֵלְכָה־נָּא הַשָּׂדֶה
וַאֲלַקֳטָה בַשִּׁבֳּלִים אַחַר אֲשֶׁר אֶמְצָא־חֵן

---

explain the meaning of *Chazal* that "Fortunate is the one who comes here with his learning in his hand." On this, *Ben Yehoyada* notes, "There is Torah learning . . . which can raise people to the heights which were set aside for them . . . without the assistance or support of other *tzaddikim*. Other people are very weak and cannot be raised to those heights except through combining their learning with the learning of other *tzaddikim*." It is in reference to this that we learned that "Fortunate is the one who comes here with his learning in his hand," i.e., fortunate is the person who does not need the power of other *tzaddikim* to support him, and whose learning is based totally on his own efforts and abilities. That is the praise that we have here for Boaz, "a man of substance," one who was knowledgeable in the Torah, and who had reached his goals based only on his own abilities.

איש גבור חיל ממשפחת אֱלִימֶלֶךְ — A man of substance, from the family of Elimelech.

We know that Boaz was a judge, for our Sages tell us (*Bava Basra* 91a), Boaz was Ivtzan, and we are told in *Shoftim* 12:8 that "Ivtzan of Bethlehem judged Israel." Now, since Boaz was an important person, wouldn't it have been more appropriate for the verse to have stated that Elimelech was a member of the family of Boaz, in that one generally attributes membership in a family in terms of the more important person?

It is possible that the reason this verse was written in this manner is to tell us that Elimelech was worthy of being a judge. In fact, our Sages tell us that the name "Elimelech" implies "*eilai melech* — to me belongs the kingship," in that the monarchy would come from him. It also appears that he would have been worthy of being the judge, but since he left Eretz Yisrael and did not put up with the suffering of the poor there, he lost his chance to be the founder of the Jewish monarchy and of being a judge in Israel. Boaz, then, received these in his place. Thus, as Elimelech had originally been the one who should have received these honors, and only as a result of his actions were they transferred to Boaz, the verse attributed Boaz's family to that of Elimelech.

2. וַתֹּאמֶר רוּת הַמּוֹאֲבִיָּה אֶל נָעֳמִי אֵלְכָה נָּא הַשָּׂדֶה וַאֲלַקֳטָה בַשִּׁבֳּלִים אַחַר אֲשֶׁר אֶמְצָא חֵן בְּעֵינָיו וַתֹּאמֶר לָהּ לְכִי בִתִּי — Ruth the Moabite said to Naomi, "Let me go out to the field, and glean among the ears of grain behind someone in whose eyes I shall find favor." "Go ahead, my daughter," she said.

In verse 3:1 she is referred to as "Naomi, her mother-in-law." Why did the

[2] *Ruth the Moabite said to Naomi, "Let me go out to the field and glean among the ears of grain behind someone in whose eyes I shall find favor."*

---

verse here leave out "her mother-in-law," and simply refer to her as "Naomi"?

It would appear that Naomi was both Ruth's mother-in-law and her teacher, the one who taught her Jewish law and ritual. Indeed, when Ruth asked for permission to go out to the field, she was really asking Naomi to teach her the laws covering gleaning in the fields — what was permitted and what was forbidden. Thus, the question was one to Naomi as Ruth's teacher, and that is why the term "her mother-in-law" was omitted in this verse.

Ruth was worthy of that which we learn in *Avos* 6:1, that whoever studies Torah for its own sake becomes like a steadily strengthening fountain and like an unceasing river. For men, who are obligated to learn Torah, the progression is: "Great is the study of Torah, which brings one to do deeds." In the case of women, who are exempt from studying the Torah, and in fact (*Sotah* 21b), "Whoever teaches his daughter Torah teaches her frivolity," the case is different, and it is through performing *mitzvos* for their own sake that they can become like a steadily strengthening fountain and like an unceasing river.

It would appear that by performing one specific *mitzvah* women can become worthy of what is promised by the Torah in *Avos,* and that is the *mitzvah* of *gemilas chasadim* — helping others. Women who perform *gemilas chasadim* for its own sake achieve that which men achieve through learning for its own sake, namely that they become like a steadily strengthening fountain and like an unceasing river. Now, as Ruth was involved constantly in *gemilas chasadim* for its own sake with her mother-in-law — and, as we are told in *Yalkut Shimoni* (601): "R' Zeira said: This *Megillah* (i.e., the Book of *Ruth*) has nothing about ritual purity or ritual impurity, nothing about what is permitted and what is forbidden, and why was it written? To teach us the reward for those who help others" — she merited learning the laws related to gleaning in the fields, modesty, etc.

There is also a hint here at the receiving of the Torah; we are told that, in preparation for receiving the Torah (*Shemos* 19:2), "Israel encamped there, opposite the mountain." On this *Mechilta* comments, "like one person, with one heart." *Or HaChaim* comments that by joining together with one heart they became like a single person, and were thus worthy of receiving the Torah. Similarly, women who band together to perform *gemilas chasadim* fulfill thereby "Israel encamped there, opposite the mountain," and are worthy of becoming like an unceasing river to understand thereby everything in the Torah in regard to fulfilling their *mitzvos*.

Using the above foundation, it occurred to me to explain what we learn in *Sanhedrin* 99b: "The students of R' Elazar asked him: 'What can a person do to save himself from the pangs of the coming of *Mashiach*?' He answered them, 'Let him engage in learning Torah and in *gemilas chasadim*.' " It appears from this that one must do both — study Torah and perform *gemilas chasadim*. Why would it not be enough just to study Torah, as we see in *Tanna d'Vei Eliyahu Rabbah* (Ch. 7), "If you see that you are suffering agony, run to Torah study, and the agony will immediately leave you, as it states (*Yeshayahu* 26:2), 'Go, my people, enter your rooms.' Regarding this it states (*Shir HaShirim* 1:4), 'The King brought me into His cloud-pillared chamber.' "

The answer is that while for Torah scholars the main thing is Torah study, for the others — those who support the Torah and the women — they need to engage in *gemilas chasadim*, and through this they can be worthy of the promises which were given to those who study Torah.

וַתֹּאמֶר רוּת הַמּוֹאֲבִיָּה אֶל נָעֳמִי אֵלְכָה נָּא הַשָּׂדֶה וַאֲלַקֳטָה בַשִּׁבֳּלִים אַחַר אֲשֶׁר אֶמְצָא חֵן בְּעֵינָיו וַתֹּאמֶר לָהּ לְכִי בִתִּי — Ruth the Moabite said to Naomi, "Let me go out to the field, and glean among the ears of grain behind someone in whose eyes I shall find favor." "Go ahead, my daughter," she said.

This verse teaches us a great deal about *derech eretz* — proper behavior.

(A) Why does the verse state, "Ruth the Moabite," when we already know she was from Moab? This teaches us that even though she was from Moab, and the Moabites were very much despised by the Jewish people — for regarding Moab it says (*Devarim* 23:5), "because of the fact that they did not greet you with bread and water on the road when you were leaving Egypt" — Ruth nevertheless did not ask Naomi to accompany her. Of course, had Naomi gone with her to glean, the owner of the field would have greeted them graciously and would have given them whatever they sought. Ruth nevertheless went all by herself in order to prevent her mother-in-law from being humiliated, and went to look for "someone in whose eyes I shall find favor."

(B) Ruth declared, "I will glean among the ears of grain behind someone in whose eyes I shall find favor." Even though the owner of a field is required by *halachah* to leave over the dropped and forgotten stalks and the corner of the field for the poor and the stranger, Ruth did not take it for granted that these would be anything left over for her, as required by *halachah*, but regarded any such gleanings as being a favor done to the poor by the owner of the field. I heard from my grandfather (author of *Or Yechezkel*) regarding Rivkah, that whoever is grateful to someone else is in reality grateful to Hashem, by Whose word the world was created. So too was Ruth grateful to the owner of the field even though the *halachah* required him to leave over for the poor the dropped and forgotten stalks.

(C) It further appears that the verse shows *derech eretz*, in that even though such gleanings are ownerless and may be taken by the poor — with the owner not permitted to stop the taker — it is nevertheless *derech eretz* not to do so without the approval the owner of the field. Just as it is not *derech eretz* to eat food at the home of a person who does not have sufficient food even if it is offered, so too is it not *derech eretz* to take the gifts of the poor against the owner's wishes — even though that is permissible — as we see in the verse (*Mishlei* 23:6), "Do not eat the bread of the miserly."

With this, we can also explain the meaning of the verse (2:8), "Boaz said to Ruth, 'You have heard, my daughter. Do not go to glean in another field, and do not leave here.' " It would seem that the words, "Hear me well, my daughter," are superfluous, for it would have been enough to write simply, "Boaz said to Ruth, 'Do not go to glean in another field.' " Rather, what Boaz was telling Ruth was to pay attention to what he was saying, and that what he had said about not going to another field was not just out of politeness but because he really wanted her to know that he meant it from the bottom of his heart. It was only because he put it this way that Ruth decided to come only to his field to glean.

וַתֹּאמֶר רוּת הַמּוֹאֲבִיָּה אֶל נָעֳמִי אֵלְכָה נָּא הַשָּׂדֶה וַאֲלַקֳטָה בַשִּׁבֳּלִים — Ruth the Moabite said to Naomi, "Let me go out to the field, and glean among the ears of grain."

Why should Ruth have needed to ask Naomi for permission? After all, if she did not glean in the fields, they would die of hunger! Rather, this is to teach us proper behavior, that since Ruth came back with Naomi in order for them to live together, it was not seemly behavior on her part to leave Naomi throughout the entire day while she went to glean grain, without receiving Naomi's permission to do so. That was why Ruth asked Naomi for permission.

Yet, even though Ruth asked Naomi for permission, the verse refers to her as "Ruth the Moabite" even though we already know that fact, because by her behavior here she showed some traits of her Moabite ancestors. Instead of asking whether or not she should go to the fields to glean grain, she merely asked permission to do so. Thus the term "Ruth the Moabite" in this verse expresses criticism of her actions.

ב/ג וַתֵּלֶךְ וַתָּבוֹא וַתְּלַקֵּט בַּשָּׂדֶה אַחֲרֵי הַקֹּצְרִים וַיִּקֶר מִקְרֶהָ
חֶלְקַת הַשָּׂדֶה לְבֹעַז אֲשֶׁר מִמִּשְׁפַּחַת אֱלִימֶלֶךְ׃

---

3. וַתֵּלֶךְ וַתָּבוֹא וַתְּלַקֵּט בַּשָּׂדֶה אַחֲרֵי הַקֹּצְרִים וַיִּקֶר מִקְרֶהָ חֶלְקַת הַשָּׂדֶה לְבֹעַז אֲשֶׁר מִמִּשְׁפַּחַת אֱלִימֶלֶךְ — So off she went. She came and gleaned in the field behind the harvesters. Her fate made her happen upon a parcel of land belonging to Boaz, who was of the family of Elimelech.

Rashi wonders about the seeming repetition in the verse of "she went" followed by "she came." On this he comments that she marked out her path before she went into the fields, so that she would be able to find her way out.

There is still another problem with the wording of this verse, because wouldn't the logical order be that she first chanced upon the fields of Boaz and then began gleaning, while the sequence here is reversed?

In reality, though, what happened was that she first gleaned in other fields before chancing upon the fields of Boaz, but in each of the other fields she did not feel comfortable and left them soon after entering, until she chanced upon the fields of Boaz, of the family of Elimelech. Now, even though we were already told earlier that Boaz was of the family of Elimelech, here it is repeated to stress that the fields were of the family of Elimelech and that is why she felt comfortable in this field.

וַתֵּלֶךְ וַתָּבוֹא וַתְּלַקֵּט בַּשָּׂדֶה אַחֲרֵי הַקֹּצְרִים וַיִּקֶר מִקְרֶהָ חֶלְקַת הַשָּׂדֶה לְבֹעַז אֲשֶׁר מִמִּשְׁפַּחַת אֱלִימֶלֶךְ — So off she went. She came and gleaned in the field behind the harvesters. Her fate made her happen upon a parcel of land belonging to Boaz, who was of the family of Elimelech.

There is a problem with the wording of this verse, because wouldn't the logical order be that she first chanced upon the fields of Boaz and then began gleaning, while the sequence here is reversed? Further, why does the verse again tell us that Boaz was of the family of Elimelech?

It appears that this verse is to tell us about Hashem's Divine Providence, that even though Boaz owned a number of fields of his own, the events which took place did so specifically in the one field which Boaz had redeemed from Elimelech, so that Boaz would realize that it was not just coincidence that Ruth was in a field of a relative of Elimelech, but that it was the very field which Boaz had redeemed from Elimelech.

Boaz saw clearly that Hashem's Divine Providence had led Ruth there, because she had entered another field first and gleaned after the harvesters, but had found that she had been greeted with hostility. Seeing

2/3 *She came and gleaned in the field behind the harvesters. Her fate made her happen upon a parcel of land belonging to Boaz, who was of the family of Elimelech.*

---

this, she had left the field, even though by Torah law she could have remained there and gleaned. However, because of her extreme modesty and good manners she had not remained in that field. Thus she left the first field and by fate came to the field of Boaz, which he had redeemed from Elimelech.

Since she had been so considerate and left the field where she felt she was not wanted and looked for a field where she would be welcomed, she merited having fate bring her to the field of Boaz.

וַתֵּלֶךְ וַתָּבוֹא וַתְּלַקֵּט בַּשָּׂדֶה — So off she went. She came and gleaned in the field.

Rashi quotes a Midrash which states that before Ruth entered a field, she would make signs along the way, so that she would not get lost in the different paths and would know how to return. We must ask: Is the only purpose of this verse to tell us about a common-sense method which Ruth used to find her way? Surely there must be more behind this verse than that. Maybe what this is teaching us is that once Ruth decided that she would make an effort to support herself rather than relying on *bitachon* alone to see her through, she decided that her efforts would need to be done in the best possible manner.

It is told that the Vilna Gaon once entered the home of his brother, R' Avraham (author of *Ma'alos HaTorah*), and saw that a doctor was visiting his brother, who was sick. The Gaon cried out, "What is a doctor doing in Hashem's house?" The Gaon's spiritual level was so great that he did not use doctors, because — as explained by the *Ramban* and *Ibn Ezra* — those with full *bitachon* do not use doctors. Nevertheless, based on the spiritual level of the present generation, one must go to the best possible doctor and make the greatest possible effort to find a cure. *Shoresh Yishai* explains the verse differently. What Ruth did was out of *tznius* (modesty) in that she wanted to be sure that she would not get lost on her way back and would not need to ask for directions, for when asking she might be humiliated.

It occurred to me that Ruth came from Moab, whose women were promiscuous, as we know from the episode where they caused the Jewish people to sin, as suggested by Balaam. Regarding this event, *Chazal* tell us that they were as promiscuous as their ancestors, the daughters of Lot. How, then, did Ruth know how to act with *tznius*, along with all that it entails, as the different commentators state? Furthermore, how did she know all the laws governing the gift to the poor (*pe'ah, shich'chah, leket* — leaving the corner of the field unharvested, not coming back for grain forgotten in the field, and not picking up one or two stalks that fell to the ground while harvesting) in the short time since she had arrived in Eretz Yisrael?

From this we can bring proof to what the *Alter* of Kelm in his *Chochmah U'Mussar* (Part 2, p. 44) wrote on the verse in *Tehillim* (139:14), "My soul knows it well": Man's soul knows a great deal, and it is only because it must associate with man's body that its spiritual knowledge is dulled. It is just because of this that all the *mitzvos* were given — so that the soul should not become sullied from the vulgarity of the body. This is because man's soul is part of Hashem above, and Hashem gave us His Torah — that being His will. Therefore, if a person purifies himself from his body, his soul knows by itself what Hashem wants. This is what *Chazal* said (quoted in *Tosfos* on *Kesubos* 104 — "*lo neheneisi*") that rather than having a person pray to have Torah enter his body, he should rather pray first that fine tidbits should not enter his body. The point is that if the body is purified, his soul will know by itself the wishes of Hashem and His Torah. Thus, when Ruth was able to purify her body she already knew the laws of the gifts to the poor and the laws of *tznius* and the lofty values these include.

I also saw in *Pri Tzaddik* (*Rosh Chodesh Sivan*, p. 22) regarding what the *gemara* in *Nedarim* 22b means, where it states, "Had Israel not sinned, they would only have received the Five Books of the Torah and the Book of *Yehoshua*, as it states (*Koheles* 1:8), 'For much wisdom proceeds from much anger' " — in that it was because of Hashem's anger that He gave us additional works. In other words, had they not sinned there would have been no need to give them any other of Hashem's works, because their souls would have been so pure that there would not be any need for any others. However, as they did indeed sin with the Golden Calf and their souls were tainted by their bodies, the second set of the Ten Commandments was given to them, along with the Oral Torah. In the World to Come, though, the souls will once again be purified, as we see in *Yirmiyahu* (31:33), "They will no longer teach — each man his fellow, each man his brother . . . for all of them will know Me."

וַיִּקֶר מִקְרֶהָ חֶלְקַת הַשָּׂדֶה לְבֹעַז אֲשֶׁר מִמִּשְׁפַּחַת אֱלִימֶלֶךְ — Her fate made her happen upon a parcel of land belonging to Boaz, who was of the family of Elimelech.

We read (*Mishlei* 19:21), "Many designs are in a man's heart, but the counsel of Hashem, only it will prevail." Hashem prepared matters so that the words of both would be fulfilled — both the *bitachon* of Naomi that deliverance and support would come from Boaz, and the plan of Ruth to find sustenance through her fulfillment of the *mitzvah* of *tzedakah*. Indeed, as it states in the Torah (*Devarim* 15:11), "For destitute people will not cease to exist within the land," it is the function of the poor people to make themselves available to the rich, so that the rich will perform the *mitzvah* of *tzedakah* and thereby earn the World to Come. This is stated in *Bava Basra* 10. Ruth therefore went, with this intention, to make herself available to the rich so that they would thereby earn the World to Come. It was through the merits of both of them — the *bitachon* of Naomi and the proper intentions of Ruth (as Ruth states later on [v. 19], "The name of the man for whom I worked today is Boaz" — from which *Chazal* deduced that as much as the rich man does for the poor man, the poor man does more for the rich man, in that he enables the rich man to merit the World to Come), that she merited "Her fate made her happen upon a parcel of land belonging to Boaz," for there was no man in that generation who was more fitting to fulfill this *mitzvah* than Boaz.

וַיִּקֶר מִקְרֶהָ חֶלְקַת הַשָּׂדֶה לְבֹעַז אֲשֶׁר מִמִּשְׁפַּחַת אֱלִימֶלֶךְ — Her fate made her happen upon a parcel of land belonging to Boaz, who was of the family of Elimelech.

Why does this verse mention that Boaz was of the family of Elimelech, when we are already told that in the first verse of the chapter? Furthermore, why does the verse say, "a parcel of land belonging to Boaz," when it could simply have said, "the land parcel of Boaz"? It is possible that this verse is coming to tell us that this field had originally belonged to Elimelech before he left Eretz Yisrael, and fate made it happen that the land now belonged to Boaz, as he was of the family of Elimelech.

Now we can understand somewhat why the young lad in charge of the harvesting permitted Ruth to gather the gleanings there, for we see from how he first answered with disparaging words against Ruth that she did not find favor in his eyes, and he really could have prevented her from entering. Even though the *halachah* is that one supports the poor who are non-Jewish along with the Jewish poor, that applies to the poor of other nations, but would not apply to a Moabite woman, because at that time they had not yet determined that the *halachah* barring Moabite converts applies only to Moabite men but not to Moabite women. Thus he could have prevented her from entering and could claim that he was fulfilling the verse (*Devarim* 23:7), "You shall not seek their peace or welfare." The verse here explains why he did not prevent her from doing so, because the field had original been Elimelech's, and Naomi could still redeem it from Boaz. The young lad who was overseeing the harvesters felt obligated to let Ruth glean as the field had once belonged to Naomi and she still had the right to redeem the field.

ד וְהִנֵּה־בֹעַז בָּא מִבֵּית לֶחֶם וַיֹּאמֶר לַקּוֹצְרִים
ה יהוה עִמָּכֶם וַיֹּאמְרוּ לוֹ יְבָרֶכְךָ יהוה: וַיֹּאמֶר בֹּעַז

---

4. וְהִנֵּה בֹעַז בָּא מִבֵּית לֶחֶם וַיֹּאמֶר לַקּוֹצְרִים יהוה עִמָּכֶם וַיֹּאמְרוּ לוֹ יְבָרֶכְךָ יהוה — Behold, Boaz arrived from Bethlehem. He greeted the harvesters, "Hashem be with you." And they answered him, "May Hashem bless you."

In terms of respect for their employer and especially as Boaz was a great Torah scholar and the judge of the generation, shouldn't the harvesters have greeted Boaz before he greeted them?

This, however, is proof to what we are told in *Kiddushin* 33 that a workman is not permitted to stand up (as a sign of respect) for a Torah scholar while the workman is busy working (because he would be depriving his employer of his labor during that time). Here, they were workers hired for the day, and were not permitted to interrupt their work to greet Boaz. Boaz, on his part, showed his great humility and his love of his fellow Jews by greeting them first. As they were his workers, he had the right to interrupt their work and greet them.

Even then, he did not spend any extra time speaking to them, but merely spoke to his servant who was supervising the others, who was his own employee, and asked him about the young woman who was gleaning in the fields. On the other hand, he did not talk to any of the others — the daily employees — in order not to have them learn erroneously that one is permitted to interrupt one's work to answer, as a sign of respect. They would not realize that this was different from other cases in that Boaz was the one employing them and could thus forgo their work while they answered him. On the other hand, if they were engaged for daily work at any other employer, they would not be permitted to interrupt their work and answer any other person. When he spoke to his servant, who was a regular employee of his, Boaz was not afraid that the others would learn from this that they might interrupt their work, for the servant was employed by him on a regular basis, while the others might find themselves in different persons' fields every day. Thus, he only spoke to his servant at length, but not to the harvesters.

וְהִנֵּה בֹעַז בָּא מִבֵּית לֶחֶם — Behold (*vehinei*), Boaz arrived from Bethlehem.

Alshich asks why the verse is phrased as it is, rather than simply saying, "Boaz arrived from Bethlehem."

Devash HaSadeh quotes R' Menachem Mendel of Rimanov, who explains the *akeidah* — Avraham's offering of Yitzchak — in the following

[4] *Behold, Boaz arrived from Bethlehem. He greeted the harvesters, "HASHEM be with you." And they answered him, "May HASHEM bless you."* [5] *Boaz then said*

---

way. Avraham, by observing the entire Torah even before it was given, purified all his body organs. Thus, for every *mitzvah* which he was to perform, all his bodily organs would hasten happily and eagerly to perform it, and whenever something was against Hashem's will, his bodily organs became heavy and there was no way he could perform such an action. Now, when Hashem told him to take Yitzchak, his legs became light and he ran eagerly, early in the morning, and the whole time he was happy. This feeling of eagerness and happiness lasted until he wanted to take the slaughtering knife and sacrifice his son, when his hand suddenly felt very heavy and he could not grip the knife. That is why the verse says (*Bereishis* 22:10), "Avraham stretched out his hand, and took the knife to slaughter his son." In truth, Hashem's command was to bring Yitzchak up, and not to slaughter him [quoted in *Melitzei Eish*, Part I, p. 271].

This also explains the words of David HaMelech (as quoted in *Midrash Rabbah* to *Vayikra* 35:1), on the verse (*Tehillim* 119:59), "I considered my ways, and returned my feet to Your testimonies." David said, "Lord of the Universe, each day I would consider and say, 'I am going to this particular place and this particular home, but my feet brought me to the *batei knesses* (shuls) and *batei midrash* (study halls).' " This is also what David said (*Tehillim* 119:105), "Your word is a lamp for my feet and a light for my path," for just as light shows a person the way in the dark, David's feet showed him the way and taught him the proper path, because if his feet felt light he knew that he was going to a *mitzvah*, and if they became heavy he realized that what he wanted to do was not Hashem's will.

It appears that Boaz, too, attained that level, and Boaz saw that his legs were leading him to a field, specifically the field in which Ruth was, even though he had a number of other fields. That is what is meant by, "Behold, Boaz arrived."

וְהִנֵּה בֹעַז בָּא מִבֵּית לֶחֶם — Behold (*vehinei*), Boaz arrived from Bethlehem.

See *Meishiv Nefesh*, who notes that the verse does not say, "Boaz came from Bethlehem," but rather, "Behold (ve*hinei*), Boaz arrived from Bethlehem," for Hashem arranged it specially for Boaz to come, unlike his usual habit, and to make a special trip to the field from Bethlehem in order to set in motion what would eventually happen. This is in accordance with the Midrash below (Ch. 4), on the verse (4:1), "Boaz, meanwhile, had gone up to the gate, and sat down there. Just then ("*vehinei*") the redeemer of whom Boaz had spoken passed by." On this R' Shmuel bar Nachmani said, "Even if he had been at the end of the world, the Holy One, Blessed is He, would have caused him to fly and would have brought him there so that that righteous man would not sit and grieve there." Similarly, here too, Hashem brought Boaz from Bethlehem so that that righteous woman would not feel like a poor woman who was gleaning among the sheaves, but as a resident, as Boaz arranged for her.

This behavior which Hashem showed is at the foundation of what *Mesillas Yesharim* (Ch. 1) wrote: "If you delve more deeply into the matter you will see that the world was created for man's use . . . and if he controls himself and cleaves to his Creator and utilizes the world to help him in his service of his Creator, he will be raised up and the world will be raised up with him, for this is a great ascent for all of Creation, as the servants of the perfect man, who is sanctified with His sanctity, may He be blessed."

This might also be a hint to what David said in *Tehillim* 40:8, "Then I said, 'Behold ("*hinei*") I have come, with the Scroll of the Book that is written for me.' " This "Scroll" is a reference to *Megillas Ruth*, "that is written for me," because the primary purpose of the Book is to show the genealogy of David, where the miracle that ultimately led to the birth of David began with "Behold ("*hinei*") I have come." And that *hinei* is a reference to "Behold (ve*hinei*), Boaz arrived from Bethlehem," for just as an angel led Ruth to that particular field [as we see in *Midrash Rabbah* on the verse (2:3), "and her fate made her happen" ("*vayiker mikreh*") — this teaches us that an angel led her, as in *Bamidbar* 23:4, "Hashem ("*vayiker*") happened upon Balaam"], Boaz's legs brought him from Bethlehem to the field to see Ruth, as we have explained.

וְהִנֵּה בֹעַז בָּא מִבֵּית לֶחֶם וַיֹּאמֶר לַקּוֹצְרִים יהוה עִמָּכֶם — Behold, Boaz arrived from Bethlehem. He greeted the harvesters, "Hashem be with you."

We need to understand why we are told that Boaz came from Bethlehem. Couldn't the verse simply say that Boaz arrived and greeted the harvesters? What difference did it make from where he was coming?

On the verse (2:11), "Boaz replied and said to her: 'I have been fully informed ("*hageid hugad*" in Hebrew) of all that you have done for your mother-in-law . . .,' " the *Targum* states, "Boaz said, 'I have been fully informed about the statement of our Sages that when the law was stated (i.e., about Ammonites and Moabites not being allowed to join the community of Israel) it did not include women but only men, and I was told by prophecy that from you will come kings and prophets, because of the kind way you treated your mother-in-law in that you supported her after your husband died.' "

What the *Targum* wishes to do is to explain the double use of the verb *hageid hugad*. It explains that the first refers to the fact that it had become clear to Boaz that the prohibition "Ammonite and Moabite" only applied to the males, whereas the second refers to the prophecy which Boaz had received that Ruth would be the mother of prophets and kings. The rule (see *Temurah* 15) is that a prophet may not come up with any new *halachah* based on prophecy, and that was why the verse here — as stated by the *Targum* — dealt with two separate ideas: "Moabite male and not Moabite female," which is a *halachah* Boaz had deduced, and the fact that Ruth would be the mother of prophets and kings, which was not a *halachah* but rather something which Boaz had received by prophecy.

It would appear that the teaching that "Moabite" only applied to males was something that Boaz had only arrived at that day in Bethlehem, and that is why the verse mentions that he came from Bethlehem, happy with the Torah teaching he had just learned. He then asked the young man there about the young woman who was so modestly gleaning in the field. To this, the young man replied (2:6), "She is a Moabite girl . . . the one who returned with Naomi from the fields of Moab." Boaz thus saw how Hashem had arranged matters that on the same day he had come to the conclusion that the prohibition only applied to Moabite males, he could apply that rule right there and then in terms of Ruth. We are also told that (2:11), "Boaz replied and said to her," where the verb, "he replied" is given in Hebrew as "*va'ya'an*." Now, we know from our Sages in *Sotah* 32b that the use of that verb in regard to the First Fruits means that the declaration must be made in a loud voice. Here, too, Boaz made his statement in a loud voice so that all the harvesters would hear and learn that the prohibition of "Moabite" only applied to Moabite males but not to Moabite females, and that Ruth could join the community of Israel.

וְהִנֵּה בֹעַז בָּא מִבֵּית לֶחֶם וַיֹּאמֶר לַקּוֹצְרִים יהוה עִמָּכֶם — Behold, Boaz arrived from Bethlehem. He greeted the harvesters, "Hashem be with you."

We can ask: What difference does it made where Boaz had come from? Rather, this teaches us the remarkable qualities of Boaz, for even though he came from Bethlehem, namely from his *beis din*, and of course was treated there with the respect due a judge and the leader of his generation, he nevertheless went down to his field as a sign of respect to his harvesters, simple people who worked for him, and never thought for a second that to do so was unbecoming behavior for him. After all, he was afraid that his laborers might violate the *halachos* of gifts to the poor, and where there is a potential violation of *halachah* the question of respect for an honored person does not enter into the picture.

וְהִנֵּה בֹעַז בָּא מִבֵּית לֶחֶם וַיֹּאמֶר לַקּוֹצְרִים יהוה עִמָּכֶם — Behold, Boaz arrived from Bethlehem. He greeted the harvesters, "Hashem be with you."

Boaz saw that the harvest was blessed, and attributed it to the harvesters. "And they answered him, 'May Hashem bless you,' " namely that the harvest had been blessed because of the merits of Boaz and help from Hashem, in that Hashem had blessed Boaz.

Boaz was not satisfied with their answer and sought to find out through whose merit this field had indeed been blessed. He looked around in the field and saw that there was a young woman who was acting with great modesty and wisdom, and thought that the blessing of the field might have come about through her merit, similar to the words of Lavan (*Bereishis* 30:27), "Hashem has blessed me on your account." "Boaz then said to his young man who was overseeing the harvesters, 'To whom does that young woman belong?' " (2:5), as he thought that the blessing might have come about through her.

" 'She is a Moabite girl,' the young man who was overseeing the harvesters replied, saying [raising his voice to insult her] — 'the one who returned with Naomi from the fields of Moab' " (2:6). There are a number of points that can be deduced from this verse. First, it states, *ha'na'ar* ("the young man") rather than *na'ar Bo'az* ("the young man belonging to Boaz"), because Boaz saw what the young man didn't see. Boaz saw the great virtues in Ruth while the young man was foolish and saw none of these virtues but, on the contrary, saw only defects. The verse goes on to mention "who was overseeing the harvesters" to explain why the young man said what he said. It was because he had an inflated sense of pride since he was in charge of other people, even though the people he oversaw were simply farm laborers. Nevertheless, the fact that he had been appointed to this position blinded him and he was unable to see Ruth's good qualities and to realize that the blessing had come on account of her.

וַיֹּאמֶר לַקּוֹצְרִים יהוה עִמָּכֶם — He greeted the harvesters, "Hashem be with you."

The Mishnah at the end of *Berachos* states that it was Boaz who initiated the practice that one should greet one's fellow with Hashem's Name. It would appear that *Megillas Ruth*, while revealing some aspects, conceals much about the greatness of Boaz, who would always be the first one to greet his fellow. Similarly, in *Berachos* 17 R' Yochanan ben Zakkai says, "Never did any person greet me first." I also heard from the author of *Pachad Yitzchak* that the reason Boaz began this custom was because his heart was filled with love for all his fellow Jews, so that when he met a fellow Jew he received such enjoyment that he felt like reciting a blessing — just as when one eats something he must recite a *berachah*. He was thus permitted to use Hashem's Name because of the enjoyment which he *to his young man who was overseeing the harvesters, "To whom does that young woman belong?"*

---

received. What Boaz innovated was that just as one is forbidden to enjoy any food in this world without a *berachah,* so too is one forbidden to enjoy meeting one's friend without a *berachah*. And it was from the heart of such a lover of the Jewish people that David was descended, for David's heart was the heart of all of Israel (*Rambam, Hilchos Melachim* 3). This fact explains the *yichus* of David HaMelech, and is for that reason that this episode is mentioned in *Megillas Ruth*.

וַיֹּאמֶר לַקּוֹצְרִים יהוה עִמָּכֶם וַיֹּאמְרוּ לוֹ יְבָרֶכְךָ יהוה — He greeted the harvesters, "Hashem be with you." And they answered him, "May Hashem bless you."

The prayer of the community is greater than the prayer of an individual. Thus, we are told in *Rosh Hashanah* 18 that if the community prays together, even if its verdict had already been sealed, the verdict is torn up, as it states (*Devarim* 4:7), "whenever *we* call Him" — i.e., that the community is answered whenever it collectively calls Hashem. For the individual, on the other hand, we read (*Yeshayahu* 55:6), "Seek Hashem when He can be found," and certain times are more propitious than others.

Similarly, a blessing given to the community is of greater effect, and that was why Boaz used the plural in saying, "Hashem be with you," where he used the plural form *"imachem"* rather than the singular form *"imecha*." They, too, answered him collectively, "May Hashem bless you."

5. וַיֹּאמֶר בֹּעַז לְנַעֲרוֹ הַנִּצָּב עַל הַקּוֹצְרִים לְמִי הַנַּעֲרָה הַזֹּאת — Boaz then said to his young man who was overseeing the harvesters, "To whom does that young woman belong?"

Boaz did not say "Who ("*mi*" in Hebrew) is that young woman?" but instead said, "To whom ("*le'mi*") does that young woman belong?" The reason for this is that it is respectful to have a woman known in relation to her father or her husband. Thus he asked, "To whom does that young woman belong?"

Rashi asks: "Was it then Boaz's way to ask about women? [The reason he did so was] that he saw in her *tznius* and wisdom; she would glean two stalks but not three; she would glean standing stalks while standing and lying stalks while seated, in order not to uncover herself."

The question nevertheless remains: Was it then Boaz's way to speak to modest and wise women? It appears that Boaz wanted to understand the ways of Hashem, and when he saw a modest and wise woman, he found it hard to understand why a woman such as that should be so poor as to need to glean in the fields, following the harvesters. After all, if a woman was so modest, shouldn't Hashem have helped so that she could have remained at home, in terms of (*Tehillim* 45:14), "the honorable princess dwells within"? Also, there is a general rule that one who comes to purify himself is assisted in his efforts (*Shabbos* 94). Why, then, was Ruth subjected to the temptation of having to glean in others' fields? Thus, when Boaz asked, "To whom does that young woman belong?" he wanted to try to understand Hashem's ways.

I heard a comment from *Kelalos Yechezkel* on *Yalkut* (*Yirmiyahu* 326): When they took Yirmiyahu out of the pit where he had been in extreme danger until they lowered a rope to him to enable him to escape, *Yalkut* states that Yirmiyahu said, "I wish I had a ladder." The Holy One, Blessed is He, said to him, "Is it a ladder you want? Just as your ancestor (Rachav) lowered [the spies in Jericho] with ropes, the same will be with you." Then (*Yirmiyahu* 38:13), "they pulled Yirmiyahu with the ropes and raised him out of the pit."

Now, Yirmiyahu was in great danger there, and how great was his joy when they pulled him out of the pit. How, then, could he have complained at such a time and exclaimed, "I wish I had a ladder?" Further, what had he done that warranted having Hashem answer him and tell him, "Just as your ancestor lowered [the spies in Jericho] with ropes, the same will be with you"?

Rather, Yirmiyahu wanted to know the reasons for Hashem's treatment of him, for he knew that everything that occurs is by Divine Providence and that Hashem acts according to the rule of "measure for measure." That was why he wanted to understand why he had to be taken out with ropes rather than with a ladder. Now, one who seeks to understand why Hashem acts in a specific way is answered, and Hashem explained to him that it was "measure for measure," and that just as Rachav his ancestor had lowered the spies with ropes, so too was he to be raised with ropes rather than with a ladder.

וַיֹּאמֶר בֹּעַז לְנַעֲרוֹ הַנִּצָּב עַל הַקּוֹצְרִים לְמִי הַנַּעֲרָה הַזֹּאת — Boaz then said to his young man who was overseeing the harvesters, "To whom does that young woman belong?"

Rashi asks: "Was it then Boaz's way to ask about women? [The reason he did so was] that he saw in her *tznius* and wisdom; she would glean two stalks but not three; she would glean standing stalks while standing and lying stalks while seated, in order not to uncover herself."

We still need to ask: Was it then the way of Boaz to look at women? Further, why did the commentators ask only about whether it was Boaz's way to ask about women, and not ask whether it was his way to look at women? The answer to this is that that generation was rife with theft, as we see later (3:2), where *Rashi* notes that the generation had a great deal of theft, and Boaz would sleep in his threshing floor to guard it. It would appear that he did not sleep there to protect his wealth, for he was the leader of the nation, and the well-being of the nation was his concern. Therefore it is more plausible to say that he wanted to protect his generation from violating the laws of theft, for we see in *Succah* 29b: "Rav said: For four causes people's possessions are lost to them: for not paying the wages of their hired help on time, for withholding the wages of laborers . . ." Thus we see that as a result of theft — and not paying one's workers is theft — people's possessions are lost to them. Now the country had just undergone a great famine, and Boaz attributed that to the sin of theft. He therefore ordained that people should be very careful not to violate the prohibition against theft and made a point of sleeping in his threshing floor so as to prevent people from violating that prohibition. By the same token, he looked after his fields during the time that the poor came to glean, so that the poor would not violate the prohibition against theft, for if a poor person took a group of three or more stalks that had fallen together that would be stealing. He therefore permitted himself to look around, and that was how he observed the actions of Ruth. *Rashi*, as we saw, first mentions *tznius* and only then mentions wisdom, but when relating the actions of Ruth her wisdom is mentioned before her *tznius*. The reason for this is in accordance with the statement of the *tanna* in *Maseches Avos* (3:13): "Whoever's fear of sin takes precedence over his wisdom, his wisdom will remain; and whoever's wisdom takes precedence over fear of sin, his wisdom will not remain." Now, *tznius* is fear of sin, and that is why *Rashi* mentioned *tznius* before wisdom. However, since an ignoramus cannot be truly pious, *Rashi* mentions the wisdom that he saw in her — that she gleaned two stalks and not three — before mentioning her fear of sin — that she would glean the standing grain while standing and the grain on the ground while sitting, in order not to uncover herself.

וַיֹּאמֶר בֹּעַז לְנַעֲרוֹ הַנִּצָּב עַל הַקּוֹצְרִים לְמִי הַנַּעֲרָה הַזֹּאת — Boaz then said to his young man who was overseeing the harvesters, "To whom does that young woman belong?"

" 'She is a Moabite girl,' the young man who was overseeing the harvesters replied, saying — 'the one who returned with Naomi from the fields of Moab; and she had said, "Please let me glean, and gather among the sheaves behind the harvesters." So she came, and has stood since the morning until now; [except for] her resting a little in the hut' " (2:5-7).

There are many deductions to be made from these verses, and I will attempt to explain them. (a) The words, "who was overseeing the harvesters" in v. 6 seem superfluous, because we already know this about him from v. 5. (b) Why does v. 6 mention "saying" ("*vayomer*") when it already states that he replied ("*vaya'an*")? (c) All that Boaz asked was, "To

ב/ו ו וַיַּעַן הַנַּעַר הַנִּצָּב עַל־הַקּוֹצְרִים וַיֹּאמַר נַעֲרָה מוֹאֲבִיָּה הִיא הַשָּׁבָה עִם־נָעֳמִי מִשְּׂדֵה מוֹאָב:

---

whom does that young woman belong?" The young man should merely have replied, "She is a Moabite girl who returned with Naomi." Why does the young man go on to mention, "She had said, 'Please let me glean . . .' So she came, and has stood etc."?

I was able to explain these verses in the same way that I saw Rav Yosef Dov Soloveitchik do so, namely, that this whole episode was a *halachic* discussion back and forth. Here, "the young man who was overseeing the harvesters" was the *mashgiach* (supervisor) whose job it was to make *halachic* decisions about *pe'ah, shich'chah,* and *leket*, and when Boaz asked him, his answer was based on Boaz's question.

We find in *Maseches Pe'ah* (4:5) that there are three times during the day when the poor are allowed in to glean *pe'ah*, and outside these times they are not allowed into the fields for this purpose. That is how *Rambam* rules (*Hilchos Matnos Aniyim* 2:17). The reason for these restrictions is that if there were no fixed times, if the owner of the field had a relative who was poor he would tell him at what time he was leaving over the *pe'ah* and none of the other poor people would know about it. The poor relative would then take everything and leave nothing for any other poor person. This is what *Rambam* meant when he wrote that this is so that there should be a fixed time for the poor to gather together and to take *pe'ah.* [The reason why these specific three times for gathering *pe'ah* were chosen and not others is explained by *Rambam* in accordance with the *Yerushalmi*, for the young children and the old people, but the reason there are fixed times for *pe'ah* in the first place is as we mentioned earlier.]

Now Boaz came to the field and saw a young woman gleaning at a different time than these three times, and he thought this must be because one of the young men had let her in as she was a poor relative of his [which is exactly what the rule of the three specific times was meant to avoid], and he therefore asked, "To whom does that young woman belong?" i.e., to whom is she related? The young man who was the *mashgiach* answered that she had no relatives. As to why she was gathering at this non-standard time, it was because she said, "Please let me glean" — i.e., the dropped stalks (*leket*), "and gather among the sheaves behind the harvesters," namely the forgotten stalks (*shich'chah*). She did not mention *pe'ah* because she knew it had fixed times, unlike the other two, as proven by the fact that *Rambam* only brings this law of the fixed times in regard to *pe'ah*, but not in regard to *leket* and *shich'chah*.

The *mashgiach* continued: If you would wish to differ and say that there

6 *"She is a Moabite girl," the young man who was overseeing the harvesters replied, saying — "the one who returned with Naomi from the fields of Moab;*

---

should be a *gezeirah* (rabbinic ordinance), that these three specific restricted times should apply to *leket* and *shich'chah* as well, the fact is that the young woman "came, and has stood since the morning until now." Now, one only allows the poor in at these specific times, but if they entered at one of these permitted times one is forbidden to chase them out after that time. The times only regulate when they may come in, but once they come in they have the right to stay as long as they want. That is what the young man told Boaz: She had indeed come in at the appointed time in the morning, but had stayed ever since. Thus, the fact that she was in the field at this time was not because some relative had let her in, but because she had come in at the appropriate time and had stayed ever since.

וַיֹּאמֶר בֹּעַז לְנַעֲרוֹ הַנִּצָּב עַל הַקּוֹצְרִים לְמִי הַנַּעֲרָה הַזֹּאת — Boaz then said to his young man who was overseeing the harvesters, "To whom does that young woman belong?"

Rashi asks: "Was it then Boaz's way to ask about women? [The reason he did so was] that he saw in her *tznius* and wisdom," etc. I heard from R' Eliyahu Lopian that a person with *ruach hakodesh* (Divine inspiration) is able to tell from looking at a person what that person's spiritual level is.[1]

The question can then be asked: Since Boaz had *ruach hakodesh* and should have been able to tell simply by looking at Ruth that she was a worthy woman, why did he only learn this from her modest actions? The answer may be that Ruth's modesty was so great that she was able to even hide the nobleness of her character, as is said about R' Shalom Sharabi and about R' Aryeh, the son of the *Pnei Yehoshua* (*Yalkut Yosef, Bamidbar*).

6. וַיַּעַן הַנַּעַר הַנִּצָּב עַל הַקּוֹצְרִים וַיֹּאמַר נַעֲרָה מוֹאֲבִיָּה הִיא הַשָּׁבָה עִם נָעֳמִי מִשְּׂדֵי מוֹאָב — "She is a Moabite girl," the young man who was overseeing the harvesters replied — "the one who returned with Naomi from the fields of Moab."

From the fact that the verse uses the word "*va'ya'an*" in regard to the young man's speech, it implies that he spoke in a loud voice. The young

---

1. A story is told about R' Aharon the Great, that he sent a person who wanted to be a *ba'al teshuvah* (a person who wants to repent) to his *Rebbe,* the Maggid of Mezrich, in that he himself felt unable to help the person, for the person was totally immersed in sin. When the man came to the Maggid, the Maggid said that the man was not so terrible, and that all the effort and discomfort involved in coming to the Maggid had removed most of the blemishes of his character.

ב/ז־ח ז וַתֹּאמֶר אֲלַקֳטָה־נָּא וְאָסַפְתִּי בָעֳמָרִים אַחֲרֵי הַקּוֹצְרִים
וַתָּבוֹא וַתַּעֲמוֹד מֵאָז הַבֹּקֶר וְעַד־עַתָּה זֶה שִׁבְתָּהּ הַבַּיִת
ח מְעָט׃ וַיֹּאמֶר בֹּעַז אֶל־רוּת הֲלֹא שָׁמַעַתְּ בִּתִּי

---

man was intent on not having Boaz do anything special for Ruth, and as a result he raised his voice to humiliate her and referred to her aloud as a Moabite girl. Furthermore, he mentioned that she was the one who had returned with Naomi from Moab, to remind Boaz of the terrible sin which Naomi had committed in leaving Eretz Yisrael, and of the fact that Naomi had returned only when she had faced troubles in Moab. This was similar to the complaint of Yiftach to the elders of Gilad (*Shoftim* 11:7), "Why have you come to me now when you are in distress?"

Therefore, when Boaz wanted to praise Ruth, it states (2:11), "Boaz replied and said to her, 'I have been fully informed of all that you have done for your mother-in-law after the death of your husband — how you left your father and mother and the land of your birth and went to a people you had never known before' " (2:11). There, too, the verb used is *"va'ya'an,"* for Boaz said what he had to say in a loud voice, so that the young man in charge of the harvesters would hear about Ruth's good qualities and about what a great person she was, and would treat her with respect.

וַיַּעַן הַנַּעַר הַנִּצָּב עַל הַקּוֹצְרִים וַיֹּאמַר נַעֲרָה מוֹאֲבִיָּה הִיא הַשָּׁבָה עִם נָעֳמִי מִשְּׂדֵי מוֹאָב — "She is a Moabite girl," the young man who was overseeing the harvesters replied, saying — "the one who returned with Naomi from the fields of Moab."

What the young man was saying to Boaz was that what was happening was "measure for measure": Since Ruth was with Naomi, who had returned from the fields of Moab, and as Naomi had left Eretz Yisrael because of the hard times suffered by the Jewish people, the punishment was that Ruth — who was extremely modest — had to glean grain and suffer all the humiliation involved in following the harvesters and picking up that which they had dropped or forgotten. When the young man mentioned "the one who returned with Naomi from the fields of Moab," what he meant to convey was that because of the sin of having left Eretz Yisrael because of want, Naomi was being punished in having to send the modest Ruth from their home to glean in the fields.

וַיַּעַן הַנַּעַר הַנִּצָּב עַל הַקּוֹצְרִים וַיֹּאמַר — The young man who was overseeing the harvesters replied.

As the previous verse already mentioned that Boaz addressed his question to "the young man who was overseeing the harvesters," why was it necessary in this verse as well to describe him as being the one

[7] *and she had said, 'Please let me glean and gather among the sheaves behind the harvesters.' So she came, and has stood since the morning until now; [except for] her resting a little in the hut."*

[8] *Then Boaz said to Ruth, "You have heard, my daughter.*

---

overseeing the harvesters? Rather, what this repetition teaches us is that this "power" the young man had went to his head and he had become conceited. As a result, he answered Boaz insolently and in a loud voice (as we saw before, the word "*va'ya'an*" implies speaking with a loud voice), and it is certainly not polite to address another person — especially a person of the stature of Boaz — in a loud voice.

The verse continues, "And she had said: 'Please let me glean and gather among the sheaves behind the harvesters.' So she came, and has stood since the morning until now; [except for] her resting a little in the hut" (2:7). Everything that the young man said was meant to disparage Ruth, for he believed that Boaz was thinking of marrying her, and he thought it was improper for an important person such as Boaz — a judge and a great Torah scholar — to marry a Moabite woman. That was why he spoke so negatively.

Boaz did not answer him in any way, because of his great modesty, but just stood and listened silently.[1]

8. וַיֹּאמֶר בֹּעַז אֶל רוּת הֲלֹא שָׁמַעַתְּ בִּתִּי אַל תֵּלְכִי לִלְקֹט בְּשָׂדֶה אַחֵר וְגַם לֹא תַעֲבוּרִי מִזֶּה וְכֹה תִדְבָּקִין עִם נַעֲרֹתָי — Then Boaz said to Ruth, "You have heard, my daughter. Do not go to glean in another field, and do not leave here, but stay close to my maidens."

Yalkut states that Boaz warned her against two prohibitions: (a) "Do not go to glean in another field" — that she should have no other gods; and

---

1. A story is told about the *Sefas Emes,* who was once studying Torah with a *chavrusa* (study companion) at night, and because they were so engrossed they did not realize that dawn had broken. They then prayed *vasikin* (at the earliest preferable time for the *Shacharis* prayer) and went to sleep. That morning, the grandfather of the *Sefas Emes*, the *Chiddushei Harim*, noticed that his grandson was not there for the *Shacharis* prayer, and he thought that the *Sefas Emes* was not present because he had overslept. Later that morning, the *Chiddushei Harim* called over his grandson and rebuked him for missing the prayers. The *Sefas Emes* didn't say a word in his defense, and simply listened to his grandfather's criticism.

After the *Chiddushei Harim* had finished criticizing the *Sefas Emes*, the *Sefas Emes* went back to learn with his *chavrusa.* His *chavrusa* asked him why he had not told his grandfather what had actually happened, and that he had spent the whole night learning and had prayed *vasikin* and had not missed the prayer time after all. The *Sefas Emes* answered him, "Why should I stop my grandfather from rebuking me? It is worth the humiliation in order to be rebuked by him."

אַל־תֵּלְכִי לִלְקֹט בְּשָׂדֶה אַחֵר וְגַם לֹא תַעֲבוּרִי
ט מִזֶּה וְכֹה תִדְבָּקִין עִם־נַעֲרֹתָי: עֵינַיִךְ בַּשָּׂדֶה

(b) "do not leave here" ("*mizeh*" in Hebrew) — do not forget (*Shemos* 15:2) "this ("*zeh*") is my God and I will glorify Him." And he reminded her of two positive commandments: "but stay close" ("*tidbakin*") as in (*Devarim* 4:4), "But you who cling ("*hadeveikim*") to Hashem"; "to my maidens" — that refers to cleaving to the righteous.

It would appear that in this commentary *Yalkut's* reference to "This ("*zeh*") is my God and I will glorify Him" relates to what we learn in *Menachos* 53b, namely that the word "*zeh*" refers to Hashem, as we see in the verse, "This ("*zeh*") is my God and I will glorify Him." So too do we find in the *Zohar*, *Parshas Vayechi* (221) that Hashem's Holy Spirit is referred to as "*zeh.*" The meaning of "do not leave here," then, is that when a person causes his mind to be bound to Hashem, there is aroused within him a tremendous desire to praise, adulate and glorify Hashem. So too do we see that on the above verse (*Shemos* 15:2), "This ("*zeh*") is my God and I will glorify Him," *Rashi* interprets it to mean, "I will recount His splendor and praise to all the creatures of the world, as [was done when Israel proclaimed to the whole world] (*Shir HaShirim* 5:9), "With what does your exalted God excel all others?" By cleaving to Hashem, one sees the beauty and splendor, and then one has a tremendous desire to praise Hashem for the splendor which one sees and feels.

We still need to explain why the verse, "This is my God and I will glorify him" has to do with prohibitions, as stated above by *Yalkut*, rather than being a positive commandment. Shouldn't it refer to a positive commandment, that a person should praise Hashem, that just as the Jewish people did at the Sea of Reeds, we should always praise Hashem?

What one can say is that the degree to which a person must praise Hashem is not a uniform one for every person, but is dependent on how much the person feels and recognizes the good which he has received from Hashem, the Source of all good. One who doesn't praise Hashem commensurate with the good that was done to him is considered an ingrate. Thus, when Boaz told Ruth, "Do not leave here," he was telling her not to be remiss in praising Hashem for all the good He had done for her, because the amount of praise must equal the amount of good done to the person.

It is told that the Chafetz Chaim would go up into the attic in his home and would sit there and enumerate all the good Hashem had done for him from when he was first conscious of his actions until that day, and would thank Hashem for everything. This task would take him a number of hours. The greater the person the more he recognizes the good and mercy which Hashem has done for him. One who does not praise and extol

Do not go to glean in another field, and do not leave here, but stay close to my maidens. [9] *Keep your eyes on the*

Hashem in accordance with the good which he has received from Him is considered to have violated the prohibition of "do not leave here."

וַיֹּאמֶר בֹּעַז אֶל רוּת הֲלֹא שָׁמַעַתְּ בִּתִּי אַל תֵּלְכִי לִלְקֹט בְּשָׂדֶה אַחֵר וְגַם לֹא תַעֲבוּרִי מִזֶּה וְכֹה תִדְבָּקִין עִם נַעֲרֹתָי — Then Boaz said to Ruth, "You have heard, my daughter. Do not go to glean in another field, and do not leave here, but stay close to my maidens."

We must examine what it was that Ruth had heard. It would appear that what she had heard is what we explained earlier. At first, the young man had treated Ruth with disdain, as she was a Moabite, and it is written that the Moabites should not enter the congregation, and the young man did not yet know that the law regarding Moabites only applied to Moabite men and not to Moabite women. Furthermore, Ruth had come back with Naomi from the fields of Moab, after Naomi had left Eretz Yisrael because of all the troubles, not caring for those she left behind.

We are told in *Berachos* 31b, "R' Elazar said: One who suspected his fellow without grounds for doing so must appease him. Not only that, but he must bless him." Boaz now fulfilled that *halachah*, because the young man overseeing the harvesters had suspected Ruth without reason. Therefore, in order to appease her, Boaz told her, "Stay close to my maidens . . . Should you become thirsty, go to the jugs and drink . . ." (2:8-9) Then he blessed her with the words, "May Hashem reward your actions, and may your payment be full from Hashem" (2:12).

However, as it was the young man who had suspected her and not Boaz himself, why should Boaz have been the one to appease her? Regarding this, Boaz said, "You have heard, my daughter," that I heard the disdain with which you were treated, and it is known that if one heard words of disdain said about another, that is a sign that the person who heard it is also connected to these words in some way, in terms of (*Makkot* 10b), "A person is led along the path which he wishes to pursue," and in accordance with (*Mishlei* 3:34), "If [one is drawn] to the scoffers, he will scoff." Thus, Boaz said to Ruth, "You have heard, my daughter," how you were humiliated, and since I was present at the time, I, too, am somewhat responsible, and I must appease you."

וַיֹּאמֶר בֹּעַז אֶל רוּת הֲלֹא שָׁמַעַתְּ בִּתִּי אַל תֵּלְכִי לִלְקֹט בְּשָׂדֶה אַחֵר וְגַם לֹא תַעֲבוּרִי מִזֶּה וְכֹה תִדְבָּקִין עִם נַעֲרֹתָי — Then Boaz said to Ruth, "You have heard, my daughter. Do not go to glean in another field, and do not leave here, but stay close to my maidens."

We can give another explanation of what Boaz meant when he said to

Ruth, "You have heard, my daughter," without specifying what she had heard. We also have to clarify the meaning of *Chazal* (*Yalkut* II:601) about "Do not go to glean in another field" and how it is linked to (*Shemos* 20:2), "You shall not recognize the gods of others." "Do not leave here" is linked to (*Shemos* 15:2), "I shall sing to Hashem, for He is exalted"; and "but stay close to my maidens" refers to the righteous, who are called maidens, as we see in (*Iyov* 40:29), "Could you sport with him as a bird, or tether him for your maidens?"

When Ruth heard the way the young lad was humiliating her, Boaz was afraid that she might turn away and go back to her old ways, and if a convert turns away that is a very bad thing, and it is easy for one of them to turn back. He therefore said, "You have heard, my daughter," as we see in *Avos* 6:2: "R' Yehoshua ben Levi said: Each day a *bas kol* (a Divine Voice) goes out from Mount Chorev and proclaims, saying: 'Woe to those creatures who have contempt for the Torah.' " The commentators ask: Why is it necessary to have a *bas kol* go out daily if no one can hear it? I heard quoted from the Satmar Rebbe, R' Yoel Teitelbaum, that whoever is moved to do *teshuvah,* to abandon his evil ways and go to the good path, is moved by that *bas kol*, which causes him to draw closer. Thus, what Boaz said to Ruth was: "You have heard, my daughter," the *bas kol*, and therefore "do not go to glean in another field," namely among the other nations of the world. Also, "do not leave here," because a day will come when you will sing together with our nation the words, "I shall sing to Hashem, for He is exalted," as the Jewish people did when the Sea of Reeds was split, for it was the children — of whom it was said (*Devarim* 32:13), "He would suckle him with honey from a stone, and oil from a flinty rock" — who first recognized Hashem. "But stay close" means to stay close to the Torah, of which it is said (*Devarim* 4:4), "You who cling to Hashem your God — you are all alive today," while "to my maidens" refers to the righteous, who are those who learn the Torah.

וַיֹּאמֶר בֹּעַז אֶל רוּת הֲלֹא שָׁמַעַתְּ בִּתִּי אַל תֵּלְכִי לִלְקֹט בְּשָׂדֶה אַחֵר וְגַם לֹא תַעֲבוּרִי מִזֶּה וְכֹה תִדְבָּקִין עִם נַעֲרֹתָי — Then Boaz said to Ruth, "You have heard, my daughter. Do not go to glean in another field, and do not leave here, but ("*ko*") stay close to my maidens."

It appears that when he used the word "*ko,*" Boaz was hinting at the blessing of Avraham (*Bereishis* 15:5), "So ("*ko*") shall your offspring be," and saying that if Ruth stayed close to Boaz's maidens, she would merit the blessing of Avraham, which rested upon Israel, for, just as we are told in *Makkos* 5b that one who accompanies someone performing a *mitzvah* is considered as if he himself had performed it, so too does one who joins the Jewish people receives the blessings of the Jewish people.

It appears that that was also Yaakov's intention when he told the angels to say to Eisav (*Bereishis* 32:5), "Thus ("*ko*") shall you say to my lord, to Eisav, 'So said your servant Yaakov,' " for Eisav had come to destroy Yaakov, while Hashem had promised Avraham, "So ("*ko*") shall your offspring be." This blessing was then transferred to Yitzchak and to Yaakov, as it states (*Bereishis* 21:12), "Through Yitzchak will offspring be considered yours," and not through *all* of Yitzchak, i.e., only through Yaakov. This blessing of Hashem to Avraham about the eternity of his offspring was transferred to Yitzchak and then to Yaakov, and therefore no war against them can succeed.

וְכֹה תִדְבָּקִין עִם נַעֲרֹתָי — "But stay close ("*ve'cho sidbakin*") to my maidens."

By using the word "*ko,*" it appears that he was hinting to her about the first word mentioned in the Torah regarding *birkas kohanim*, which begins with the words *ko sevarechu* (*Bamidbar* 6:23), because in order to merit blessing and peace, which encompass within themselves all the other blessings, one needs to cleave to Hashem, Who is the source of all blessings, and to *tzaddikim*, as we see in *Berachos* 32b: "R' China bar Abba said: All the prophecies of the prophets [both the good tidings and the consolations] were only on behalf of one who marries off his daughter to a *talmid chacham* or conducts business on behalf of a *talmid chacham*, for that is considered cleaving to a *talmid chacham*."

Ba'al HaTurim there notes that the word *berachah* appears 25 times in the *Chumash* (and 25 in Hebrew is *chaf heh* — "*ko*"), and thus *birkas kohanim* begins with a *berachah* and ends with "*shalom*" (that being the last word of *birkas kohanim*). Boaz thus promised Ruth that if she would stay close to his maidens she would merit all the blessings encompassed in the word *ko*.

9. עֵינַיִךְ בַּשָּׂדֶה אֲשֶׁר יִקְצֹרוּן — "Keep your eyes on the field which they are harvesting."

Boaz asked Ruth to look at the field because just as an *ayin hara* (Evil Eye) can cause damage to a field and one is therefore forbidden to stand next to the field of one's fellow when the stalks of grain are standing (*Bava Basra* 2b) because of potential *hezik re'iyah* (damage caused by looking), so too does an *ayin tov* (the opposite of *ayin hara*) cause a blessing upon the field. This we see in *Rashi* on the verse (*Bereishis* 1:31), "Hashem saw all that He had made, and behold it was very good," for Hashem's "seeing" was what made the world exist. So too do we find in *Ramban* in *Parshas Bamidbar* (1:45) regarding the counting of *Bnei Yisrael*: The purpose of the counting was to have everyone pass Moshe and Aharon, who would look at everyone, and their looking at *Bnei Yisrael* would ensure that the Jewish people would survive. Similarly, Boaz wanted Ruth's looking at the field to bring a blessing upon it.

ב/י אֲשֶׁר־יִקְצֹרוּן וְהָלַכְתְּ אַחֲרֵיהֶן הֲלוֹא צִוִּיתִי אֶת־
הַנְּעָרִים לְבִלְתִּי נָגְעֵךְ וְצָמִת וְהָלַכְתְּ אֶל־
י הַכֵּלִים וְשָׁתִית מֵאֲשֶׁר יִשְׁאֲבוּן הַנְּעָרִים׃ וַתִּפֹּל

It is known that even the non-Jews in Radin believes that if the Chafetz Chaim would pass by their fields, their fields would be blessed. I also saw in *Zichron Yaakov* of R' Yaakov Lipschitz, that there was a certain *gadol* whose farm animals were taken by non-Jews to their fields, so that when he came to retrieve them he would look at the fields and thus the fields would be blessed.

עֵינַיִךְ בַּשָּׂדֶה אֲשֶׁר יִקְצֹרוּן וְהָלַכְתְּ אַחֲרֵיהֶן הֲלוֹא צִוִּיתִי אֶת הַנְּעָרִים לְבִלְתִּי נָגְעֵךְ — "Keep your eyes on the field which they are harvesting and follow after them. I have ordered the young men not to touch you."

I have seen it asked: Why did Boaz have to order the young men not to touch her? After all, Ruth was coming to glean grain that belongs to the poor, and why would they interfere with her and not allow her to glean?

I saw in *Shai HaTorah* by R' Yosef Dov Soloveitchik that Ruth was still a non-Jew at the time, because only afterwards does it say, "Therefore, bathe and anoint yourself," (3:3) which *Rashi* says was her acceptance of the *mitzvos*. Therefore, as far as the actual *halachah* was concerned there is no obligation to allow a non-Jew to glean, but this is permitted because of *darkei shalom* — to live at peace with the non-Jews by not differentiating between Jews and non-Jews. *Kesef Mishneh* (*Hilchos Matnos Aniyim*) quotes *Ran* that the *halachah* that one supports non-Jewish poor along with Jewish poor only applies if there are Jewish poor there as well, but there is no such obligation when there are no Jewish poor, as then *darkei shalom* does not apply. Thus Boaz ordered his young men not to interfere with Ruth even when she was all alone in the field, and that they should not prevent her from gleaning.

I find this somewhat difficult, because even though Ruth had not converted, she still had the status of a *ger toshav* — a person who has accepted the seven Noahide laws, as quoted in *Shai HaTorah*. *Pesachim* 21b brings the verse (*Devarim* 14:12), "To the stranger who is in your cities you shall give it that he may eat it," from which we learn that we are required to support a *ger toshav*. So too does it state (*Vayikra* 25:35), "If your brother becomes impoverished and his means falter in your proximity, you shall strengthen him — proselyte or resident ("*ger vetoshav*") — so that he can live with you." On the word *toshav*, *Rashi* states that this refers to anyone who has undertaken to refrain from idol

2/9 *field which they are harvesting and follow after them. I have ordered the young men not to touch you. Should you become thirsty, go to the jugs and drink from that which the servants have drawn."*

---

worship but who eats meat that was not slaughtered *halachically*. Thus we see that we are required to support a *ger toshav* and to give him *tzedakah* (*Rambam, Hilchos Matnos Aniyim* 7:1), and only in the case of idol worshipers is the requirement to support them only because of *darkei shalom.*

— עֵינַיִךְ בַּשָּׂדֶה אֲשֶׁר יִקְצֹרוּן וְהָלַכְתְּ אַחֲרֵיהֶן הֲלוֹא צִוִּיתִי אֶת הַנְּעָרִים לְבִלְתִּי נָגְעֵךְ "Keep your eyes on the field which they are harvesting and follow after them. I have ordered the young men not to touch you."

As the young men worked for Boaz and Boaz was a *tzaddik* (a righteous man) he chose servants who were *tzaddikim*. Why, then, was Boaz concerned enough to warn his young men not to disturb Ruth? If, on the other hand, these young men were not *tzaddikim*, what difference would such a warning make?

It would appear that since Boaz asked Ruth to remain only in his field, it is part of the *mitzvah* of *hachnasas orchim* (welcoming guests) to ensure that no harm befalls one's guests, and it is the duty of the host to take care of all their needs, even to the extent of being willing to give his life to ensure their protection. Indeed, this is what we saw with Lot, when he said to the people of S'dom (*Bereishis* 19:8), "To these men do nothing, inasmuch as they have come under the shelter of my roof." On this *Ramban* states that he tried exceedingly hard to protect them, as they had come under his roof. Thus Boaz tried with all his might to ensure that all of Ruth's needs were met fully.

Along these lines, I would like to explain the punishment that Noach received for being late in supplying the lion with food, about which it is said (*Mishlei* 11:31), "A righteous person is punished on earth." (And see *Rashi* on the verse (*Bereishis* 7:23), "Only Noach survived.") *Chochmah U'Mussar Ma'amar* 134 asks: Why is it that when Noach had to take care of so many different animals, and he was only late one time in the feeding of one particular animal, that he should have been punished immediately by having the lion bite him. The answer might be that as Noach was the owner of the Ark and all the animals on it were his guests — having come within his confines — and his responsibility to take care of them extended even to the extent of endangering his life, he was punished immediately after having fed the lion late.

ב/יא עַל־פָּנֶיהָ וַתִּשְׁתַּחוּ אָרְצָה וַתֹּאמֶר אֵלָיו מַדּוּעַ מָצָאתִי
יא חֵן בְּעֵינֶיךָ לְהַכִּירֵנִי וְאָנֹכִי נָכְרִיָּה׃ וַיַּעַן בֹּעַז
וַיֹּאמֶר לָהּ הֻגֵּד הֻגַּד לִי כֹּל אֲשֶׁר־עָשִׂית אֶת־חֲמוֹתֵךְ
אַחֲרֵי מוֹת אִישֵׁךְ וַתַּעַזְבִי אָבִיךְ וְאִמֵּךְ וְאֶרֶץ מוֹלַדְתֵּךְ
וַתֵּלְכִי אֶל־עַם אֲשֶׁר לֹא־יָדַעַתְּ תְּמוֹל שִׁלְשׁוֹם׃

---

10. וַתִּפֹּל עַל פָּנֶיהָ — Then she fell on her face.

Meishiv Nefesh states that Ruth did so because she was deeply ashamed, as we see with Moshe in *Parshas Korach* (*Bamidbar* 16:4), "Moshe heard and fell on his face," for Moshe was deeply ashamed when he heard that he was suspected of adultery, as stated in *Sanhedrin* 100b. We see from this the truth in the words of R' Yitzchak Blaser, that being humble in the complete sense means that both praise and disgrace bring a person to shame. Ruth was ashamed when Boaz praised her for something she thought she was undeserving of, just as Moshe was ashamed when he was suspected of adultery, for there is no greater disgrace than adultery. In both Moshe's and Ruth's cases it states that they fell on their face.

מַדּוּעַ מָצָאתִי חֵן בְּעֵינֶיךָ לְהַכִּירֵנִי — "Why have I found favor in your eyes that you should recognize me."

What does it mean when she said that Boaz was just now going to "recognize" her? After all, he had already promised to do her a number of favors. Rather, she was referring back to the very first favor Boaz had done to her in recognizing her, for every great *mitzvah* that a person does comes about from a lesser *mitzvah*, in that (*Avos* 4:1) "one *mitzvah* begets another." Here, Boaz merited receiving all the good because of the minor action he had taken in "recognizing" Ruth, for it was from that action that everything else began. We see from this that there is nothing small in the world. Rather each *mitzvah* is a major act, and only in our limited perception do we consider it to be small. In reality, then, every action of obeying the will of Hashem is of infinite greatness.

וְאָנֹכִי נָכְרִיָּה — "Though I am a foreigner."

Even though she had already converted,[1] this was still at a time when the prohibition against Moabites was considered to include Moabite

---

1. In reality, there are two opinions on this matter. One view is that she had converted fully while the other is that she only had the status of *ger toshav*.

[10] *Then she fell on her face, bowing down to the ground, and said to him, "Why have I found favor in your eyes that you should recognize me though I am a foreigner?"*

[11] *Boaz replied and said to her, "I have been fully informed of all that you have done for your mother-in-law after the death of your husband — how you left your father and mother and the land of your birth and went to a people you had never known before.*

---

women as well, so she was still considered to be a person who could not cleave to the Jewish people [for in regard to marriage it states, "he will cleave to his wife"], as she was considered a foreigner.[1]

It appears further that in regard to marriage there is no such thing as conversion by an Ammonite or a Moabite male, and they are unable to leave the status of being non-Jewish. I also saw in the name of the Novominsker Rebbe [R' Yaakov Perlow] who deduces this from the language of *Rambam* (*Hilchos Issurei Bi'ah* 12:17), who writes, "except . . . for Ammon and Moab . . . and if one of them converts he is like a Jew in every way, except for becoming part of the community": Not only is there a prohibition against converting them, but in terms of marriage they are not considered to have converted, and for that reason they cannot become part of the community.

11. וַיַּעַן בֹּעַז וַיֹּאמֶר לָהּ הֻגֵּד הֻגַּד לִי כֹּל אֲשֶׁר עָשִׂית אֶת חֲמוֹתֵךְ אַחֲרֵי מוֹת אִישֵׁךְ וַתַּעַזְבִי אָבִיךְ וְאִמֵּךְ וְאֶרֶץ מוֹלַדְתֵּךְ וַתֵּלְכִי אֶל עַם אֲשֶׁר לֹא יָדַעַתְּ תְּמוֹל שִׁלְשׁוֹם — Boaz replied and said to her, "I have been fully informed of all that you have done for your mother-in-law after the death of your husband — how you left your father and mother and the land of your birth and went to a people you had never known before."

See the *Targum,* which states: "I was told about the statement of our Sages that when Hashem made the decree, it was not against women but only against men." It appears that Boaz realized this when he saw Ruth and her actions, because the reason why (*Devarim* 23:4), "An Ammonite or Moabite shall not enter the congregation of Hashem" is because "they did not greet you with bread and water on the road when you were leaving Egypt." *Ramban* on *Devarim* 23:5 explains that since the Jewish people are merciful and help others, and Moab is far removed from these qualities, it is impossible for the two to mix together and for Moab to

---

1. See the *Targum,* which states this specifically.

ב/יב יב יְשַׁלֵּם יהוה פָּעֳלֵךְ וּתְהִי מַשְׂכֻּרְתֵּךְ שְׁלֵמָה מֵעִם
יהוה אֱלֹהֵי יִשְׂרָאֵל אֲשֶׁר־בָּאת לַחֲסוֹת תַּחַת־

become part of the Jewish people, for two opposites cannot mix together to form a unified whole. However, when Boaz saw "all that you have done for your mother-in-law after the death of your husband . . .," it was clear that the female Moabites are different than the males, in that only the males had this corrupt nature and not the females [we find an example of this in the children of Nachor and in the children of Haran, where the females were righteous women — Sarah, Rivkah, Rachel, Leah — but the men were not righteous], and that is why the prohibition applied only to the men and not to the women.

Do not be surprised that we bring proof from Ruth, even though she was a lone individual who might have been different from the other Moabite women. On the contrary, we learn from this that if a single person was created with these powers, every other person has the ability and power to reach the level of Ruth, because each was born in the image of Hashem, and it is through that image that one can attain such a level. The source of our words is in *Yoma* 35b, where we learn, "When the poor, the rich, and the evil come up for judgment, the poor man is asked, 'Why did you not study Torah . . . were you poorer than Hillel?' " Thus we see that Hillel was not an exception, but everyone could do what Hillel did.

When Eliezer went to find a wife for Yitzchak, he tested Rivkah in terms of her willingness to help others, by seeing if she would offer to bring water for his camels as well. A well-known question that is asked is how that test was a sufficient one. After all, Rivkah might *chas veshalom* have been an idol worshiper who did not believe in Hashem. How, then, was this test sufficient? The answer given is that for a person to do such kindness for other people, one needs superhuman powers, and only one who cleaves to Hashem and to His attributes ["just as He is merciful, you are to be merciful; just as He is compassionate, you are to be compassionate"] is able to do what she did. Therefore, this test — bringing water to the camels — was sufficient to establish her belief in Hashem.

Along these lines, I would like to answer this section in Ruth as well, for the lovingkindness which Ruth showed in leaving her parents and her homeland, and in going to a country which was not even willing to accept her, and who did this only because she wanted to remain with Naomi, was an act of supernatural lovingkindness, and came about because she cleaved to Hashem and to His attributes. Therefore, when Boaz saw that Ruth had cleaved to Hashem, in that she had performed an act of lovingkindness that can come only through cleaving to Hashem, he

12 *May* HASHEM *reward your actions, and may your payment be full from* HASHEM, *the God of Israel, under Whose wings you have come to seek refuge."*

---

understood that (*Devarim* 23:4), "An Ammonite or Moabite shall not enter the congregation of Hashem" applied only to the men and not to the women, for such an act of lovingkindness can only come through cleaving to Hashem. Thus she would be permitted to become part of the Jewish people. That was what Boaz answered when Ruth asked him why he was being so kind when she was but a foreigner.

וַיַּעַן בֹּעַז וַיֹּאמֶר לָהּ הֻגֵּד הֻגַּד לִי כֹּל אֲשֶׁר עָשִׂית אֶת חֲמוֹתֵךְ אַחֲרֵי מוֹת אִישֵׁךְ — "I have been fully informed of all that you have done for your mother-in-law after the death of your husband."

Chazal say that if a person keeps a single Jew alive, it is as if he kept the entire world alive. This explains why the reward that Ruth received was equivalent to that of Miriam. As the *Targum* puts it, "I was told in a prophecy that in the future there will come out from you kings and prophets because of the kindness you did with your mother-in-law, in that you supported her after your husband died." And that, too, was the reward which Miriam received, as we see in *Parshas Shemos* regarding the midwives. Thus *Rashi* explains the verse (*Shemos* 1:20), "Hashem benefited the midwives" as meaning that he made for them houses — houses of *Kohanim* and *Leviim* and kings — as meaning that these would be their descendants.

The midwives, of course, helped all the Jewish people and kept the male children alive, whereas Ruth only helped Naomi. From this we see that if a person keeps a single Jewish person alive — namely Naomi in this case — it is as if he kept the entire world alive, namely all the male children kept alive by Yocheved and Miriam.

12. יְשַׁלֵּם יהוה פָּעֳלֵךְ וּתְהִי מַשְׂכֻּרְתֵּךְ שְׁלֵמָה מֵעִם יהוה אֱלֹהֵי יִשְׂרָאֵל אֲשֶׁר בָּאת לַחֲסוֹת תַּחַת כְּנָפָיו — "May Hashem reward your actions, and may your payment be full from Hashem, the God of Israel, under Whose wings you have come to seek refuge."

We need to explain why the verse seems to repeat itself. There is no doubt that Hashem pays a reward to anyone who does something good even if there is no specific command to do that particular action. Thus, we see in *Kiddushin* 31 that Hashem paid a non-Jew for the respect he showed for his father and paid Nebuchadnezzar for the three steps that he ran in honor of Hashem, as stated in *Sanhedrin* 96, for Hashem pays people who do good. However, once the Torah was given the reward is a complete one, as the person has followed that which he was commanded in the

Torah. Thus, "May Hashem reward your actions" meant that Ruth would be rewarded even without the Torah and even if she did not convert, for she had done a good deed in helping Naomi. Now, though, that she had converted and accepted upon herself the *mitzvos*, " may your payment be full from Hashem, the God of Israel," because the *mitzvos* were performed for Hashem, "under Whose wings you have come to seek refuge." This is in accordance with the words of R' Chanina (*Kiddushin* 31), that one who is commanded to perform a *mitzvah* and performs it is greater than one who performs it without having been commanded to do so. That is why Ruth's reward for aiding Naomi was doubled and redoubled.

On the other hand, the opposite of this is also true: Hashem punishes the wicked even if their wicked actions were not specifically prohibited, because Hashem set up the world so that evil is repaid by evil. This was what Hillel meant when he said when he saw a skull floating on the water (*Avos* 2:6): "Because you drowned others, they have drowned you."[1] The case with Hillel was one of measure for measure. Even though in theory a skull should sink to the bottom because it is heavier than water, here it floated in order to teach the world why it was in the water.

יְשַׁלֵּם יהוה פָּעֳלֵךְ וּתְהִי מַשְׂכֻּרְתֵּךְ שְׁלֵמָה מֵעִם יהוה אֱלֹהֵי יִשְׂרָאֵל אֲשֶׁר בָּאת לַחֲסוֹת תַּחַת כְּנָפָיו — "May Hashem reward your actions, and may your payment be full from Hashem, the God of Israel, under Whose wings you have come to seek refuge."

The *Targum* writes, "May Hashem reward you in this world for your good deeds, and may your reward be complete before Hashem, the God of Israel, in that you came to convert . . ." In other words, even though the righteous of the other nations have a part in the World to Come, as stated in *Rambam Hilchos Teshuvah* (3:35), their reward is not complete. *Ramchal* writes in *Derech Hashem* 2:4, "In the World to Come one will not find any other nations except for Yisrael, and the souls of the righteous of the nations will be given a different form which will be attached to Yisrael, and they will be to them as a garment to a person, and it is in that form that they will benefit from the good, and there is nothing in their law which will have them attain more than this."

The *Targum* there concludes, "And with that merit you will be saved from *Gehinnom* and your portion will be with Sarah, Rivkah, Rachel and Leah." We need to explain why one needs merits to escape from *Gehinnom*. It appears that this must be a reference to *Yevamos* 48b, where we learned, "Rav Chanania the son of Rabban Gamaliel says: Why is it that in these times converts are oppressed and afflicted? It is because they

1. See *Melitzei Eish* of 3 *Sivan* on R' Yoel Chassid, who discusses this at length.

delayed entering under the wings of the *Shechinah*. R' Avahu — and some say Rav Chanina — said: Where is there a verse [to support this]? 'May Hashem reward your actions, and may your payment be full from Hashem, the God of Israel, under Whose wings you have come to seek refuge' (2:12)." Upon this, *Rashi* comments that "You hastened and did not delay."

Tosfos there asks on the statement by *Rashi* that "You hastened and did not delay." According to our accounting, Ruth was already an old woman, the granddaughter of Eglon, the king of Moab. How, then, can we say that she hastened and did not delay? However, the *Targum* writes on verse 11, "Boaz replied and said to her," that only then had he learned that the prohibition only applies to Moabite males but not Moabite females. Thus only at that time was Ruth able to convert. Boaz was therefore correct when he told her, "You will be saved from *Gehinnom* because you hastened and did not delay."

יְשַׁלֵּם יהוה פָּעֳלֵךְ וּתְהִי מַשְׂכֻּרְתֵּךְ שְׁלֵמָה מֵעִם יהוה אֱלֹהֵי יִשְׂרָאֵל — "May Hashem reward your actions, and may your payment be full from Hashem, the God of Israel."

We must explain why Boaz referred to "the God of Israel" rather than to "the God of Avraham" or "the God of Yitzchak." By doing so, though, Boaz was hinting at the words of David in *Tehillim* (121:1-2), "A song of ascents. I raise my eyes upon the mountains, whence will come my help? My help is from Hashem, Maker of heaven and earth." *Midrash Rabbah*, at the beginning of *Parshas Vayeitzei* (68:2), states that that was what Yaakov said when he went to Lavan. The Midrash says: "R' Shmuel bar Nachmani began: 'A song of ascents. I raise my eyes upon the mountains' ("*heharim*") — I will raise my eyes to my instructors ("*hehorim*") [i.e., my teachers who taught me the Torah] and to my teachers [i.e., those who taught me how to serve Hashem and observe His *mitzvos*]. 'Whence will come my help?' [This refers to a wife, who is referred to as a helpmate — *ezer*]. When Eliezer went to bring Rivkah, what does it say? 'The servant took ten camels' etc., while I (i.e., Yaakov) do not have a single ring or bracelet. He then said differently: Shall I lose confidence in my Creator? *Chas veshalom*! I will not lose confidence in my Creator, for My help is from Hashem, Maker of heaven and earth."

I heard from R' Eliyah Lopian who explained the verse "whence will my help come?" in the name of the Gaon: When I have no person who can help me, my help *must* then come "from Hashem, Maker of heaven and earth," just as He can make substance out of nothing. That is what Boaz told Ruth, in order to strengthen her spiritually, for she, too, feared "whence will my help come?" After all, she was a convert, from Moab, and poor. What she needed was to be able to have substance created from nothing. That was why "My help is from Hashem, Maker of heaven and earth." Just as Yaakov's deliverance came from Hashem, so too would Hashem's deliverance come and save her from her distress.

In that same chapter in *Tehillim*, it states (v. 5), "Hashem is your guardian, Hashem is your protective Shade at your right hand." *Shelah* (I:22) quotes the Midrash that Hashem told Moshe to tell the Jews that: My name is *Eheyeh asher Eheyeh*. What does *Eheyeh asher Eheyeh* mean? Just as you are with Me, I am with you. So, too, did David say, "Hashem is your guardian, Hashem is your protective Shade at your right hand." What is meant by "Hashem is your protective Shade"? Hashem is like your shadow; just as if you play with your shadow your shadows plays back with you and if you cry it cries and if you are angry it appears to be angry, Hashem, too, is your shadow. Just as you act with Him, he acts with you. *Ramban* in *Parshas Shemos* (3:14) bring a similar Midrash, which says, "What does *Eheyeh asher Eheyeh* mean? Just as you are with Me, I am with you. If people open their hands and give *tzedakah*, I, too, will open My hand, as it states (*Devarim* 28:12), 'Hashem shall open for you His storehouse of goodness,' and if they do not open their hands . . ."

It now follows that this is a continuation of the verses where Boaz had said (2:11-12), "I have been fully informed of all that you have done for your mother-in-law after the death of your husband . . . May Hashem reward your actions, and may your payment be full from Hashem, the God of Israel." Since you opened your hands to do *tzedakah* and *chessed*, Hashem will open His full and broad hand to do *tzedakah* and *chessed*, for that is His way — "Hashem is your protective Shade at your right hand."

יְשַׁלֵּם יהוה פָּעֳלֵךְ וּתְהִי מַשְׂכֻּרְתֵּךְ שְׁלֵמָה מֵעִם יהוה אֱלֹהֵי יִשְׂרָאֵל — "May Hashem reward your actions, and may your payment be full from Hashem, the God of Israel."

Midrash Rabbah (5:4) as well as *Yalkut Shimoni*, states that "may your payment be full" ("*sheleimah*") is a hint at Shlomo HaMelech. This Midrash needs explanation. *Eim HaMelech* explains the Midrash to mean that Ruth would live to see Shlomo the son of David, her great-grandson, as it states (I *Melachim* 2:19), "He placed a chair for the king's mother," namely for Ruth, who was the Mother of Royalty.

It appears that one can explain this hint at Shlomo in a different way. The *Targum* on this verse states, "May Hashem reward you in this world for your good deeds, and may your reward be complete before Hashem, the God of Israel, in that you came before Hashem, the God of Israel, to convert and to be taken under the shadow of the *Shechinah*, and with that merit you will be saved from *Gehinnom* and your portion will be with

Sarah, Rivkah, Rachel and Leah." As Boaz had already promised Ruth, "May your payment be full from Hashem, the God of Israel," what did he add when he said, "and with that merit you will be saved from *Gehinnom*"? After all, if she was to receive so great a reward, she certainly would not be punished in *Gehinnom*. This requires clarification.

It appears that the *Targum*[1] is referring to *Yevamos* 48b, where "Rav Chanania the son of Rabban Gamliel says: Why is it that in these times converts are oppressed and afflicted? . . . Others say: It is because they delayed entering under the wings of the *Shechinah*. R' Avahu — and some say Rav Chanina — said: Where is there a verse [to support this]? 'May Hashem reward your actions, and may your payment be full from Hashem, the God of Israel, under Whose wings you have come to seek refuge' (2:12)." Upon this, *Rashi* comments that "You hastened and did not delay." In other words, converts are oppressed and afflicted in this world in order to have them atone for having delayed and not having converted earlier, and is through this affliction that they find atonement. Then, when they die, they immediately enter *Gan Eden* and the World to Come. Boaz told Ruth that she had hurried and had not delayed, and it was because of that merit that she would not go to *Gehinnom* and her portion would be with Sarah, Rivkah, Rachel and Leah and she would not need any atonement.

Now we can understand why there was a hint in "may your payment be full" ("*sheleimah*") to Shlomo HaMelech. We are told in *Sanhedrin* 104b that *Chazal* wanted to list Shlomo with the four kings who have no place in the World to Come, but a *bas kol* came forth and said to them (*Mishlei* 22:29), "Have you seen a man with alacrity in his work? He will stand before kings. He will not stand before [men of] darkness. He who gave precedence to My House over his, and built My House in seven years, but his own in thirteen, he shall stand before kings, he shall not stand before men of darkness." Thus we see that Shlomo merited the World to Come because of his alacrity in building Hashem's House. Thus Boaz hinted to Ruth that it was because of the merit of her alacrity and her not delaying her conversion that she was saved from *Gehinnom* and granted a portion with Sarah, Rivkah, Rachel and Leah. By the same reasoning, Shlomo was also saved from *Gehinnom*.

אֲשֶׁר בָּאת לַחֲסוֹת תַּחַת כְּנָפָיו — "Under Whose wings you have come to seek refuge."

The word "*lechasos*" (to seek or take refuge) appears three times in *Tanach:* "It is better to take refuge in Hashem than to rely on man" (*Tehillim* 118:8); It is better to take refuge in Hashem than to rely on

1. See the *Targum* quoted in our discussion of 2:5, above.

יג כְּנָפָיו: וַתֹּאמֶר אֶמְצָא־חֵן בְּעֵינֶיךָ אֲדֹנִי כִּי
נִחַמְתָּנִי וְכִי דִבַּרְתָּ עַל־לֵב שִׁפְחָתֶךָ וְאָנֹכִי לֹא
יד אֶהְיֶה כְּאַחַת שִׁפְחֹתֶיךָ: וַיֹּאמֶר לָה בֹעַז לְעֵת
הָאֹכֶל גֹּשִׁי הֲלֹם וְאָכַלְתְּ מִן־הַלֶּחֶם וְטָבַלְתְּ פִּתֵּךְ
בַּחֹמֶץ וַתֵּשֶׁב מִצַּד הַקֹּצְרִים וַיִּצְבָּט־לָהּ קָלִי

---

benefactors (ibid. v. 9); "Under whose wings you have come to seek refuge" (*Ruth* 2:12).

It appears that by saying this Boaz hinted to her that even though he had helped her and he had become a person she could rely on, where she could gather in his fields as much as she needed, she should nevertheless not place all her trust in him. "Do not rely on nobles, nor on a human being, for he holds no salvation" (*Tehillim* 146:3), "Just as you first did not place your trust in man, even though you knew that Naomi had a relative who is a man of means, you nevertheless went to the field which Hashem's Providence led you to, and so too, did you say to your mother-in-law, 'Let me go out to the field and glean among the ears of grain behind someone in whose eyes I shall find favor.' " Thus Boaz hinted that she should remain with her trust in Hashem and not place her trust in human beings.

To explain the words of David HaMelech, we should mention a story of R' Meir Shapiro who was asked by a gentile judge, how it is that *Chazal* said that (*Bava Metzia* 114b), "Only you [i.e., the Jewish people] are designated as man ("*adam*")." "Does that mean that the non-Jews are but animals?" asked the judge. R' Meir told him that "man" has four different names in Hebrew: *adam, ish, gever, enosh*. The latter three have plural forms, while there is no plural form for *adam*. When the *gemara* refers to only the Jewish people as "*adam,*" that is because the Jews all unite as a single person with a single heart, and such unity cannot be found among non-Jews.

This is what David HaMelech said when he exclaimed, "It is better to take refuge in Hashem than to rely on man" (*Tehillim* 118:8). Even if a person deserves the title of *adam* because he has a heart that feels for others just as for himself, one should trust better in Hashem. The same is true for a person who is a *nadiv* — a person with a reputation as a generous individual. Even then, one must put one's trust in Hashem rather than in a *nadiv*.

13. וְאָנֹכִי לֹא אֶהְיֶה כְּאַחַת שִׁפְחֹתֶיךָ — "Though I am not even [as worthy] as one of your maidservants."

Shoresh Yishai explained that after Boaz had promised Ruth the World

[13] *Then she said, "May I continue to find favor in your eyes, my lord, because you have comforted me, and because you have spoken to the heart of your maidservant, though I am not even [as worthy] as one of your maidservants."*

[14] *At mealtime, Boaz said to her, "Come over here and partake of the bread, and dip your morsel in the vinegar." So she sat beside the harvesters. He handed her parched grain,*

---

to Come, as we brought above[1] from the *Targum*, she exclaimed that she had never dreamed of having the merit of entering the World to Come like one of Boaz's maidservants. We see this in *Kesubos* 111, where R' Avahu said that even a Canaanite maidservant [*Maharsha* says that this refers to a woman who immerses herself in a *mikveh* in order to become a maidservant] is guaranteed a place in the World to Come, for it states (*Yeshayahu* 42:5), "Who gave a soul to the people upon it."

The explanation of this is as follows: Ruth thought that since the Torah stated (*Devarim* 23:7), "You shall not seek their peace or welfare, all your days, forever," that she certainly had no merit for the World to Come, for that is what is hinted at in "all your days, forever," i.e., the World to Come. As she nevertheless came to shelter under the wings of the *Shechinah*, that was a clear acceptance of conversion without any reward, and that is the acceptance of conversion due to love, as we explained earlier, "I am not even worthy of being your maidservant."

14. וַיִּצְבָּט לָהּ קָלִי — He handed her parched grain.

Rashi writes he offered it to her. The Midrash notes that if Boaz had known that Hashem would write, "He handed her parched grain, and she ate," he would have offered her fattened heifers. It appears what the Midrash means to tell us is that Boaz himself offered her the parched grain, even though he was the judge and was wealthy, with many young men to assist him. He nevertheless took care of this by himself because when it comes to performing a *mitzvah*, the *mitzvah* is greater when the person performs it himself rather than through a messenger (see *Kiddushin* 41).

The Midrash concludes that even though Boaz went out of his way to perform the *mitzvah* himself, he would have made an even greater effort had he but known the full value of the performance of every *mitzvah,* to the extent that he would have fed her fattened heifers.

---

1. See our discussion of 2:5, above.

טו וַתֹּאכַל וַתִּשְׂבַּע וַתֹּתַר׃ וַתָּקָם לְלַקֵּט וַיְצַו בֹּעַז אֶת־
נְעָרָיו לֵאמֹר גַּם בֵּין הָעֳמָרִים תְּלַקֵּט וְלֹא תַכְלִימוּהָ׃
טז וְגַם שֹׁל־תָּשֹׁלּוּ לָהּ מִן־הַצְּבָתִים וַעֲזַבְתֶּם וְלִקְּטָה
יז וְלֹא תִגְעֲרוּ־בָהּ׃ וַתְּלַקֵּט בַּשָּׂדֶה עַד־הָעָרֶב
וַתַּחְבֹּט אֵת אֲשֶׁר־לִקֵּטָה וַיְהִי כְּאֵיפָה שְׂעֹרִים׃
יח וַתִּשָּׂא וַתָּבוֹא הָעִיר וַתֵּרֶא חֲמוֹתָהּ אֵת אֲשֶׁר־לִקֵּטָה

וַיִּצְבָּט לָהּ קָלִי וַתֹּאכַל וַתִּשְׂבַּע וַתֹּתַר — He handed her parched grain, and she ate and was satisfied, and had some left over.

See *Rashi*, that he proffered it to her, and the Midrash (5:6) states that he gave her just a pinch between his two fingers. How then do we reconcile this with "she ate and was satisfied"? R' Yitzchak said that a blessing resided in the stomach of that righteous woman. *Michtav MeEliyahu* notes that even for that small gesture Boaz merited having the monarchy of David and of the *Mashiach* descend from him (*Ruth Rabbah*). How is it, he asks, that for such a small deed Boaz received such a merit?

The answer to this is that by his deed Boaz showed that when it comes to doing *chessed* (deeds of lovingkindness) for another person there is no such thing as a small *chessed*, and every such deed is great. That is why he merited to have the House of David descend from him. This idea we see in *Shemos Rabbah* (2:3): "The Holy One, Blessed is He, does not make a person great until he tests him in some small matter. Only afterwards does He raise him to greatness. Thus there were two great leaders whom the Holy One, Blessed is He, tested in a small matter, and when they were found to be trustworthy He raised them to greatness. He tested David with his flock . . . So too with Moshe, it states (*Shemos* 3:1), 'He guided the sheep far into the wilderness.' " As Boaz was so careful in doing *chessed* with both small and large matters, David his descendant merited doing *chessed* with his flock in a way which made him deserve to be entrusted with the children of Hashem, the Children of Israel.

15-16. וַתָּקָם לְלַקֵּט וַיְצַו בֹּעַז אֶת נְעָרָיו לֵאמֹר גַּם בֵּין הָעֳמָרִים תְּלַקֵּט וְלֹא תַכְלִימוּהָ . . . — Then she got up to glean, and Boaz ordered his young men, saying, "Let her glean even among the sheaves; do not embarrass her. And even deliberately pull out some for her from the heaps and leave them for her to glean; don't rebuke her."

If Boaz ordered his young men not to embarrass her, wouldn't that already include not to rebuke her? Why, then, do the verses mention both?

It appears from verses 9 and 15 that some of the young men were in charge of the field and all its needs, while others were harvesters (verses 3

and she ate and was satisfied, and had some left over.
15 Then she got up to glean, and Boaz ordered his
young men, saying, "Let her glean even among the
sheaves; do not embarrass her. 16 And even deliber-
ately pull out some for her from the heaps and leave
them for her to glean; don't rebuke her."
17 So she gleaned in the field until evening, and
she beat out what she had gleaned; it was about an
ephah of barley. 18 She carried it and came to the
city. Her mother-in-law saw what she had gleaned,

---

and 14) who were simply country workers who worked in the fields. Boaz thus ordered his young men to tell the harvesters not to embarrass her when she gathered stalks from among the sheaves, namely that they should not use any type of language of scorn or mockery. However, in regard to those in charge of the field, he ordered them not to rebuke her if they saw what she was doing went beyond the *halachos* regarding what may and may not be gleaned, by taking wheat which she thought was *leket* or *shich'chah* even though it wasn't. Instead, they were to tell her gently what was included and what was not.

We still have to explain why (in verse 9), when Boaz told Ruth, "I have ordered the young men not to touch you," he did not at that time tell the young men not to embarrass or rebuke her, and only after they had eaten did he order this, as it states, "Then she got up to glean, and Boaz ordered his young men saying: 'Let her glean even among the sheaves; do not embarrass her.' "

The Midrash (5:6), in the name of R' Yochanan, states on verse 14, "At mealtime, Boaz said to her, 'Come over here and partake of the bread, and dip your morsel in the vinegar,' " that this refers to David HaMelech, where "Come over here" refers to the monarchy. Boaz saw through *ruach hakodesh* (Divine inspiration) that Ruth was destined for the monarchy. He therefore made a point of telling the young men to honor her as if she were a queen, because it is understood that the honor one gives a king is different than the honor one gives an ordinary person.

18. וַתִּשָּׂא וַתָּבוֹא הָעִיר וַתֵּרֶא חֲמוֹתָהּ אֵת אֲשֶׁר לִקֵּטָה — She carried it and came to the city. Her mother-in-law saw what she had gleaned.

Meshech Chochmah explains that in *Sotah* 43b we are told that a poor person who gathers *leket* or *shich'chah* and makes a pile of his gleaning is required to give *ma'aser* (a tithe) because of *mar'is ayin* (an outward appearance of wrongdoing — because otherwise it would look as if he had

יט וַתּוֹצֵא וַתִּתֶּן־לָהּ אֵת אֲשֶׁר־הוֹתִרָה מִשָּׂבְעָהּ: וַתֹּאמֶר
לָהּ חֲמוֹתָהּ אֵיפֹה לִקַּטְתְּ הַיּוֹם וְאָנָה עָשִׂית יְהִי

---

harvested without giving *ma'aser* — *Rashi*). Thus, when we are told, "Her mother-in-law saw what she had gleaned," it means that it was clearly apparent that it was the gleaning, and that is why Ruth took what she had left over and gave it to Naomi.

It appears that the way *Meshech Chochmah* understood this was that Ruth was already a full convert at the time, who was therefore obligated to give *ma'asros*, because if we say as we did before (on verses 2 and 9) that Ruth was still in the category of *ger toshav,* she would be exempted from *ma'asros* on the gleanings she had gathered because she was not Jewish. Nor can we say that Ruth had gathered on behalf of Naomi, because one person is forbidden to gather for another. This is because the person who does so is seizing grain on behalf of one "creditor" (a poor person, who has the right to the gleanings) at a time when there are other "creditors," as stated in *Bava Metzia* 9b. Therefore Ruth gathered on her own behalf, and she was therefore exempt from *ma'asros*, unless we say that *Meshech Chochmah* believes that Naomi acted above the letter of the law and acted as if Ruth were a true convert, even though *halachically* her status was that of a *ger toshav*, and nevertheless took *ma'asros* from the gleanings.

וַתּוֹצֵא וַתִּתֶּן לָהּ אֵת אֲשֶׁר הוֹתִרָה מִשָּׂבְעָהּ — She took out and gave her what she had left over after her fill.

The words "after her fill" seem superfluous. After all, "what she had left over" refers to the bread and parched corn. We should examine why these extra words were mentioned.

Shulchan Aruch, Orach Chaim 170:19, rules that guests who are invited to someone's home for a meal are forbidden to take of the food offered them and to give it to the host's child or servant unless given permission to do so by the host. *Taz* on *Even HaEzer* 28:34 states that this is all the more true about giving the food to others without the host's permission. Thus, Ruth was forbidden to give of her portion to Naomi without the permission of Boaz.

That was why *Megillas Ruth* added "what she had left over." What is forbidden is to give food away to another in the host's presence, but if the guest took a normal portion for himself and left over some of the food which he had taken for himself, the host certainly expects to give the guest whatever was left over of the guest's portion, and the guest can then give that food away to anyone he wishes. Thus, what happened here was that Boaz gave Ruth a normal portion of food, and Ruth was so righteous that there was a blessing in her stomach and she needed very little food to fill it.

and she took out and gave her what she had left over after her fill.

19 *"Where did you glean today?" her mother-in-law asked her. "Where did you work? May the one*

She was thus able to leave over the rest of her food for Naomi, and this was totally permissible. This is a fulfillment of the verse (*Vayikra* 26:5), "You will eat your bread to satiety," upon which *Rashi* comments, "The person will eat very little but there will be a blessing in his stomach."

We can bring proof to this differentiation between giving a host's food away and taking of one's own portion and giving it away from *Rama* in *Even HaEzer* 28:17, who rules that if a person is a guest at another person's house and takes the portion given to him and uses it to perform *kiddushin* with a woman, the woman is considered to be married. *Taz* (34) finds this ruling surprising, because we are told in *Chullin* 94b that guests are not allowed to take of the food before them and to give it to the host's son or daughter, and all the more so not to others without the host's permission. Why, then, can a person use it to perform *kiddushin*? It would appear that in the case mentioned in *Chullin*, the host put a communal food plate on the table, from which each person takes what he wants. In such a case, the guest is forbidden to take from the communal plate and give it to the host's children. However, if the host gave each person his own individual portion — and *Rama* specifies that the person takes the portion *given to him* — and the guest then takes whatever is left over of what was given to him, he has the right to give it to the host's children, for it belongs to him. The host has certainly renounced his ownership over that food, because the host expects a normal person to eat all the food given to him.[1]

וַתִּתֶּן לָהּ אֵת אֲשֶׁר הוֹתִרָה מִשָּׂבְעָהּ — She gave her what she had left over after her fill.

It appears that Ruth gave Naomi only whatever she had left after eating her fill, and not from the rest of her gleanings, to fulfill what we read in the verse (*Mishlei* 22:9), "One with a good eye will be blessed, for he has given of his bread to the poor." When Ruth gave of her own personal bread to the poor, that was a clear example of a "good eye."

19. וַתֹּאמֶר לָהּ חֲמוֹתָהּ אֵיפֹה לִקַּטְתְּ הַיּוֹם וְאָנָה עָשִׂית — " 'Where did you glean today?" her mother-in-law asked her. "Where did you work?"

It appears that she added, "Where did you work?" because what Ruth had

1. Also see *Tosfos* on *Pesachim* 29, beginning *"Be'din hu,"* who explain that the food belongs to the guest in terms of who would violate the *halachah* if it is *chametz* and the time for owning *chametz* has passed. Also see there what *Sefas Emes* writes about this.

ב/יט מַכִּירֵךְ בָּרוּךְ וַתַּגֵּד לַחֲמוֹתָהּ אֵת אֲשֶׁר־עָשְׂתָה עִמּוֹ וַתֹּאמֶר שֵׁם הָאִישׁ אֲשֶׁר עָשִׂיתִי עִמּוֹ הַיּוֹם

---

brought her was wheat that had already been ground, as stated earlier: "And she beat out what she had gleaned" (2:17). Indeed Boaz had instructed his young men, "And even deliberately pull out some for her from the heaps and leave them for her to glean" (2:16), which *Rashi* explains to mean that he instructed his young men to deliberately "forget" some of the grain for her. The reason that Boaz winnowed the grain for her was that this way the grain was exempt from *ma'aser* because of *lakuach* (grain acquired from another person) since grain acquired from another person is exempt from *ma'aser* by Torah law. *Meshech Chochmah* asks, though, that according to *Rambam* if one took it before the winnowing one is obligated to give *ma'aser* by Torah law, so why would this grain be exempt? That is why it states, "And even deliberately pull out some for her from the heaps and leave them for her to glean," but not to let it belong to her, meaning that as long as there was still winnowing to be done it would be the property of Boaz. Only after the winnowing would it belong to Ruth, and would therefore be exempt because of *lakuach*. Therefore it states, "So she gleaned in the field — and she beat out what she had gleaned" (2:17). This means that she winnowed in the field and not at home, because the grain was not hers until after the winnowing, in order to be exempt from *ma'aser.*[1] This explains why Naomi added the words, "May the one that took [such generous] notice of you be blessed." *Rashi* explains that this is referring to the owner of the field who favored her in having her glean in his field. One might ask what type of favor this was, because the owner of a field is required to allow the poor to glean in his fields. However Naomi saw two things in Boaz's behavior: first, that he acted toward Ruth graciously, and second, that he gave her more than the *halachah* required — and that was why she said, "May [he] be blessed."

וַתֹּאמֶר לָהּ חֲמוֹתָהּ אֵיפֹה לִקַּטְתְּ הַיּוֹם וְאָנָה עָשִׂית יְהִי מַכִּירֵךְ בָּרוּךְ וַתַּגֵּד לַחֲמוֹתָהּ אֵת אֲשֶׁר עָשְׂתָה עִמּוֹ וַתֹּאמֶר שֵׁם הָאִישׁ אֲשֶׁר עָשִׂיתִי עִמּוֹ הַיּוֹם בֹּעַז — "Where did you glean today?" her mother-in-law asked her. "Where did you work? May the one that took [such generous] notice of you be blessed." So she told her mother-in-law for whom she had worked, and said, "The name of the man for whom I worked today is Boaz."

The Midrash (5:9) states in the name of R' Yehoshua that more than the *ba'al habayis* (the owner of the property) does for the poor person, the poor person does for the *ba'al habayis*, because Ruth said to Naomi, "*for* whom

---

1. See *Meshech Chochmah* on this.

2/19 *that took [such generous] notice of you be blessed." So she told her mother-in-law for whom she had worked, and said, "The name of the man for whom I worked today is Boaz."*

I worked" (i.e., the one who benefited from my work) and not "*by* whom I worked."

Chasam Sofer (*Derashos* 79c) asked what this verse is doing here, and why Ruth hinted at this at this point. Also, why did Naomi ask her where she had gleaned? After all, Ruth had gone to glean in any field which she might find.

As we explained earlier (on verse 2:1), Naomi's degree of *bitachon* in Hashem was not to go out of her way to accomplish anything, but to wait for Hashem's deliverance to come, and not through any gift from a human being. That was why Naomi did not send out Ruth to glean, and Ruth went out on her own. Ruth, at that time, was not on a high enough level, and she had to take action to be able to support herself. When Naomi asked her, "Where did you glean today and where did you work?" she was really asking Ruth how much effort she had needed to make in order to obtain her wheat. By this, Naomi would be able to gauge how close Ruth had drawn to Hashem, and how close she was to having fulfilled (*Shemos* 23:25), "He shall bless your bread and water," as we see in *Berachos* 35b, that when the Jews do Hashem's will, their work is performed by others, as it states (*Yeshayahu* 61:5), "Foreigners will stand and tend your flocks," etc.

Thus Ruth answered, "the man for whom I worked" and not "by whom I worked," because the implication is that whatever Ruth did was not for herself but for Boaz, for by his helping her he would merit the World to Come. This we see in *Bava Basra* 10, where Turnus Rufus the Wicked asked R' Akiva: "If your God loves the poor, why doesn't He support them?" R' Akiva answered: "So that through them we will be saved from the decree of *Gehinnom*." Thus, whatever Ruth was doing was not for herself but for Boaz, so that he should gain all the merit.

This now explains why at first it states, "her mother-in-law asked her" (2:19), as if in a non-friendly manner, but after Ruth answered her it states, "Naomi said to her daughter-in-law" (2:20), indicating she was happy with the effort Ruth had put in.

וַתַּגֵּד לַחֲמוֹתָהּ אֵת אֲשֶׁר עָשְׂתָה עִמּוֹ וַתֹּאמֶר שֵׁם הָאִישׁ אֲשֶׁר עָשִׂיתִי עִמּוֹ הַיּוֹם בֹּעַז — So she told her mother-in-law for whom she had worked, and said, "The name of the man for whom I worked today is Boaz."

Chelek Bnei Yehudah notes that the Midrash (5:9) states that more than the *ba'al habayis* does for the poor person, the poor person does for the *ba'al habayis*, because Ruth said to Naomi, "The name of the man for whom

ב/כ בֹּעַז׃ כ וַתֹּאמֶר נָעֳמִי לְכַלָּתָהּ בָּרוּךְ הוּא
לַיהוָה אֲשֶׁר לֹא־עָזַב חַסְדּוֹ אֶת־הַחַיִּים וְאֶת־

I worked" (i.e., the one who benefited from my work) and not "by whom I worked." We can ask: Why was this not deduced from the fact that it states, at the beginning of the verse, "She told her mother-in-law for whom she had worked" (2:19) rather than saying "by whom she had worked?" However, both verses are needed, to teach us that more than the *ba'al habayis* does for the poor person, the poor person does for the *ba'al habayis*. I might have thought that what helps the *ba'al habayis* is the fact that he performs the *mitzvah*, regardless of who the poor person is. However, from these verses we learn that it makes a difference who the poor person is, and if the poor person is a *yirei Shamayim* (a God-fearing Jew) the *ba'al habayis* receives a greater reward than if the poor person is not such. Proof of this is from *Chazal* (*Bava Kamma* 1b) on the verse (*Yirmiyahu* 18:23), "May they be caused to stumble before You. At the time of Your anger, act against them!" Yirmiyahu said to Hashem, "Lord of the Universe, even when they perform *tzedakah* cause them to stumble by having them give *tzedakah* to people who are unworthy." Thus we see that Yirmiyahu cursed the people of Anasos that even if they would give *tzedakah* they should give it to unworthy people. We see that it depends on who the poor person is as to how much of a reward the *ba'al habayis* will earn.

One can deduce this from the text in *Bava Basra* which we brought above (on 2:1) regarding R' Akiva and Turnus Rufus as to why, if Hashem loves the poor, He does not support them. R' Akiva answered that this is to rescue those who give *tzedakah* from *Gehinnom*. Turnus Rufus replied: "On the contrary, this will make you deserving of *Gehinnom*. Let me give you an analogy. What is this like? It is like a king of flesh and blood who became angry at his servant and imprisoned him, and then ordered the jailers not to give him food or drink. One man then went and fed him and gave him food and drink. When the king heard this would he not become angry at him? Yet you (the Jewish people) are called servants, as it states (*Vayikra* 25:55), 'For the Children of Israel are servants to Me' " (in other words, by helping the poor one is contradicting Hashem's desires). R' Akiva said to him, "Let me give you an analogy. What is this like? It is like a king of flesh and blood who became angry at his son and imprisoned him, and then ordered the jailers not to give him food or drink. One man then went and fed him and gave him to drink. When the king heard this, wouldn't he send him a gift? And we are called sons, as it states (*Devarim* 14:1), 'You are children to Hashem your God.' " Now, the analogy of R' Akiva was about a person who performed a *chessed* (a deed of lovingkindness) without being commanded to by the

[20] *Naomi said to her daughter-in-law, "Blessed is he to Hashem, for not failing in His kindness to the living or to*

---

king, and here too, it is the poor man himself who saves the rich man from *Gehinnom*, and not only the *mitzvah*, or Hashem's command.

Another proof that the greatness of the *mitzvah* depends on with whom one performs it can be found in what *Chazal* said (*Bava Basra* 11b): "Whoever keep alive a single Jew — i.e., by supporting him and saving him from death — is as if he had saved the entire world." Yet the *mitzvah* of *tzedakah* applies in giving a worthy person what he lacks, even (in the case of a rich person who became poor) up to a horse for him to ride on and a servant to run before him, as stated in *Kesubos* 67b. Thus, on the one hand, we have the story brought there about a certain person who had become poor and who came to Rava and asked for his normal food, consisting of fat chickens and old wine (both of which were luxuries) and was given these. On the other hand, we have the story of Binyamin HaTzaddik (*Bava Basra* 11b) who prevented a woman and her seven children from literally starving to death. In both cases we have the same *mitzvah* of *tzedakah;* nevertheless in the case of Binyamin HaTzaddik the angels came to Hashem and said to Him: "Lord of the Universe, you said that a person who keeps alive a single Jew is as if he had saved the entire world . . ." because the greatness of the *mitzvah* depends on the poor man involved and not only on the fact that the person performed the *mitzvah*.

20. וַתֹּאמֶר נָעֳמִי לְכַלָּתָהּ בָּרוּךְ הוּא לַיהוה אֲשֶׁר לֹא עָזַב חַסְדּוֹ אֶת הַחַיִּים וְאֶת הַמֵּתִים — Naomi said to her daughter-in-law, "Blessed is he to Hashem, for not failing in His kindness to the living or to the dead!"

Rashi, quoting the Midrash, states that He is the One who sustains and supports the living and takes care of the needs of the dead. We can ask why, just at this point, Naomi mentioned Hashem's *chessed* (mercy) with the dead. We can understand her mentioning His providing sustenance to the living when she saw what Ruth had gleaned, but as to Hashem's mercy with the dead, in terms of supplying the shrouds of her husband and sons, that was something that had happened a long time earlier, so why mention it now?

It would appear that this statement of Naomi's was a reaction to what Ruth had said. Evidently, Ruth had felt that her success was due to her own efforts, for she noted that " the man for whom I worked," implying that it was through her efforts that Boaz had benefited. Naomi answered, "Blessed is he to Hashem, for not failing in His kindness to the living or the dead!" (2:20), for just as Hashem had helped with supplying the shrouds of her husband and two sons when she owned absolutely nothing (as explained by *Eitz Yosef*), we can see that Hashem can help when there is no aid whatsoever from any mortal.

ב/כא-כב הַמֵּתִ֑ים וַתֹּ֤אמֶר לָהּ֙ נָֽעֳמִ֔י קָר֥וֹב לָ֙נוּ֙ הָאִ֔ישׁ מִֽגֹּאֲלֵ֖נוּ
כא הֽוּא׃ וַתֹּ֖אמֶר ר֣וּת הַמּוֹאֲבִיָּ֑ה גַּ֣ם ׀ כִּֽי־אָמַ֣ר אֵלַ֗י
עִם־הַנְּעָרִ֤ים אֲשֶׁר־לִי֙ תִּדְבָּקִ֔ין עַ֣ד אִם־כִּלּ֔וּ אֵ֥ת כָּל־
כב הַקָּצִ֖יר אֲשֶׁר־לִֽי׃ וַתֹּ֥אמֶר נָעֳמִ֖י אֶל־ר֣וּת כַּלָּתָ֑הּ ט֣וֹב
בִּתִּ֗י כִּ֤י תֵֽצְאִי֙ עִם־נַ֣עֲרוֹתָ֔יו וְלֹ֥א יִפְגְּעוּ־בָ֖ךְ בְּשָׂדֶ֥ה

וַתֹּאמֶר נָעֳמִי לְכַלָּתָהּ בָּרוּךְ הוּא לַיהוה אֲשֶׁר לֹא עָזַב חַסְדּוֹ אֶת הַחַיִּים וְאֶת הַמֵּתִים וַתֹּאמֶר לָהּ נָעֳמִי קָרוֹב לָנוּ הָאִישׁ מִגֹּאֲלֵנוּ הוּא — Naomi said to her daughter-in-law, "Blessed is he to Hashem, for not failing in His kindness to the living or to the dead! The man is closely related to us," Naomi said to her; "he is one of our redeeming kinsmen."

Note that the blessing of Boaz to Ruth, "May Hashem reward your actions, and may your payment be full from Hashem, the God of Israel, under Whose wings you have come to seek refuge," (2:12) has ten words in the Hebrew, while Naomi's comment about Boaz, "Blessed is he to Hashem," has only three Hebrew words. Why did Naomi give such a short blessing? The commentators also ask why twice in the same verse we are told what Naomi said. It would appear that Naomi had a certain complaint against Boaz (as we noted above on verse 2:1), for once he knew that they had come from the fields of Moab without anything, how did he not immediately send them food and money, even if he did not do so *l'shem Shamayim* — for the best of *halachic* motives? Naomi nevertheless felt offended, and therefore she shortened the blessing when she found out that the owner of the field who favored Ruth and had her glean in his fields was Boaz. Ruth then asked her what complaint she might have against Boaz. Naomi answered her on this, and that is why we find twice in the same verse that Naomi answered Ruth. Thus, when she answered Ruth saying, "The man is closely related to us; he is one of our redeeming kinsmen," she was indicating that he was violating (*Yeshayahu* 58:7), "Do not hide yourself from your kin." Now we can understand the continuation of the verses, "Ruth the Moabite said: 'What's more, he even said to me, "Stay close to my young men, until they have finished all my harvest" ' " (2:21). In saying this, Ruth was seeking merit for Boaz, for when people do *chessed* for others they generally do so once or twice, but to continue to do *chessed* for an extended period of time is something only *tzaddikim* who cling to Hashem's ways do, for just as Hashem's *chessed* is unlimited, so is the *chessed* of true *tzaddikim*.

We can thus understand how the *mesorah* (the traditional summation of text) notes that the word *kalu* ("have finished") appears in two places — once here in *Ruth* and once in *Bereishis* 24:19, when Rivkah told Eliezer *the dead! The man is closely related to us," Naomi said to her; "he is one of our redeeming kinsmen."*

21 Ruth the Moabite said, "What's more, he even said to me, 'Stay close to my young men, until they have finished all my harvest.' "
22 Naomi said to her daughter-in-law Ruth, "It is fine, my daughter, that you go out with his young women, so that you will not be annoyed in another field."

---

that she would draw water for his camels "until they have finished drinking." In regard to Rivkah, in fact, a question is asked as to why Eliezer thought that this test was sufficient. After all, she might have a kind heart but possibly be a total non-believer in Hashem. Now, if Avraham did not allow guests into his home with dust on their feet, lest they be worshipers of the dust (as we see in *Rashi* on *Bereishis* 18:4), there is no doubt that he would under no circumstances allow an idol worshiper to enter his house.

I heard from Harav Shraga Moshe Kalmanovich that Eliezer understood from Rivkah's *chessed* (lovingkindness) — from the fact that she did not become weary and did everything with great alacrity until all the camels had enough to drink — that she must be God-fearing, because such *chessed* is impossible unless one cleaves to Hashem. Only through cleaving to Hashem can a person have the strength and stamina to perform *chessed* in such a way.

And that was what Ruth answered Naomi — that from the way Boaz acted it was possible to see that he was cleaving to Hashem's attribute of *chessed*, and it was therefore proper to praise him and bless him, for he was in no way miserly, *chas veshalom*, as we see in the verse (*Mishlei* 23:6), "Do not eat the bread of the miserly."

Naomi answered her that if indeed what she said was correct, "It is fine, my daughter, that you go out with his young women, so that you will not be annoyed in another field" (2:22).

21-22. וַתֹּאמֶר רוּת הַמּוֹאֲבִיָּה גַּם כִּי אָמַר אֵלַי עִם הַנְּעָרִים אֲשֶׁר לִי תִּדְבָּקִין עַד אִם כִּלּוּ אֵת כָּל הַקָּצִיר אֲשֶׁר לִי. וַתֹּאמֶר נָעֳמִי אֶל־רוּת כַּלָּתָהּ טוֹב בִּתִּי כִּי תֵצְאִי עִם־נַעֲרוֹתָיו וְלֹא יִפְגְּעוּ־בָךְ בְּשָׂדֶה אַחֵר — Ruth the Moabite said, "What's more, he even said to me, 'Stay close to my young men, until they have finished all my harvest.' " Naomi said to her daughter-in-law, Ruth, "It is fine, my daughter, that you go out with his young women, so that you will not be annoyed in another field."

See the Midrash (5:11), which states that R' Chanin bar Levi said, "She was certainly a Moabite, because he (Boaz) said, 'Stay close to my maidens' (2:8), while she (Ruth) said, "close to my young men." The Midrash notes

ב/כג כג אַחַר׃ וַתִּדְבַּק בְּנַעֲרוֹת בֹּעַז לְלַקֵּט עַד־כְּלוֹת
קְצִיר־הַשְּׂעֹרִים וּקְצִיר הַחִטִּים וַתֵּשֶׁב אֶת־חֲמוֹתָהּ׃
ג/א־ב א וַתֹּאמֶר לָהּ נָעֳמִי חֲמוֹתָהּ בִּתִּי הֲלֹא אֲבַקֶּשׁ־לָךְ
ב מָנוֹחַ אֲשֶׁר יִיטַב־לָךְ׃ וְעַתָּה הֲלֹא בֹעַז מֹדַעְתָּנוּ

---

that Ruth changed the word "maidens" said by Boaz to "young men." That is why she is referred to as "Ruth the Moabite" instead of just "Ruth," for she did not repeat Boaz's words correctly.

Naomi rebuked her gently by correcting her with the words, "It is fine, my daughter, that you go out with his young women," letting her know that she must be accurate in what she says, because the Jewish people do not lie, and those who lie do not receive the *Shechinah* and do not enjoy the true good.

This also explains why only now did she refer to Ruth as "my daughter," because as Naomi was fulfilling the *mitzvah* of rebuking a person who does something wrong, she began with a loving term to show her that she had nothing against her personally, but whatever she did was out of love. Thus she said, "It is fine, my daughter, that you go out with his young women," and not as you said — to go out with the young men.

III

1. וַתֹּאמֶר לָהּ נָעֳמִי חֲמוֹתָהּ בִּתִּי הֲלֹא אֲבַקֶּשׁ לָךְ מָנוֹחַ אֲשֶׁר יִיטַב לָךְ — Naomi, her mother-in-law, said to her, "My daughter, I must seek security for you, that it may go well with you."

It would seem that Naomi referred to Ruth, her daughter-in-law, as "my daughter" because of her great love for Ruth. *Meshech Chochmah* on the verse (*Devarim* 5:15), "You shall remember you were a slave," quotes the Midrash on *Shir HaShirim* (at the end of Ch. 3): "R' Shimon bar Yochai asked R' Elazar ben Yose: Did you hear from your father the meaning of (*Shir HaShirim* 3:11), 'The crown with which his mother crowned him'? He answered him 'Yes . . .,' with a parable of a king who had an only daughter, of whom he was extremely fond. At first he called her 'my daughter.' He was not satisfied with that, and he then called her, 'my sister.' He was not even satisfied with that until he called her 'my mother.' Thus, the Holy One, Blessed is He, is exceedingly fond of Israel, and called her 'My daughter,' as in the verse (*Tehillim* 45:11), 'Hear, O daughter.' He was not satisfied with that and then called her 'My sister' . . .. He was not even satisfied with that, until He called her 'My mother.' " Commenting on this, *Meshech Chochmah* states that the title "my daughter" shows greater love for a person than does "my sister" or "my mother," and therefore to call someone "my

2/23 [23] *So she stayed close to Boaz' maidens to glean, until*
the end of the barley harvest and of the wheat harvest.
Then she stayed [at home] with her mother-in-law.

3/1-2 [1] *Naomi, her mother-in-law, said to her, "My*
daughter, I must seek security for you, that it
may go well with you. [2] *Now Boaz, our relative,*

---

daughter" is an indication that one is exceedingly fond of that person. Thus Naomi called Ruth "my daughter" to show how exceedingly fond she was of her, and it was out of that great fondness that she was offering her this advice.

Meshech Chochmah notes that the three titles refer to three time periods. Thus the time right after the Exodus from Egypt, when Israel received all its needs from Hashem in abundance, was one of a daughter relationship. At the time of the giving of the Torah the relationship was that of a sister, because there was a reciprocal relationship between Hashem and Israel, Hashem giving us the Torah and us receiving it with the stating of *na'aseh venishmah.* Then, when the *Mishkan* was built the relationship was one of a mother, because the offerings brought in the *Mishkan* influenced the entire world. Based on this, we can say that Naomi told Ruth that even though from the time they had arrived in Bethlehem Ruth had been the one who supported them and was the influential one, that was not in Ruth's best interest. On the contrary, it would be best for Ruth to be like a daughter and to be influenced by Boaz. That was why Ruth should follow Naomi's advice and should do what Naomi told her to.

וַתֹּאמֶר לָהּ נָעֳמִי חֲמוֹתָהּ בִּתִּי הֲלֹא אֲבַקֶּשׁ לָךְ מָנוֹחַ אֲשֶׁר יִיטַב לָךְ — Naomi, her mother-in-law, said to her, "My daughter, I must seek security for you, that it may go well with you."

The term "mother-in-law" seems superfluous, because there was no more than one Naomi. It would appear that this was written to indicate the fine qualities of Naomi, for even though she was her mother-in-law she treated Ruth as a daughter. Indeed, we are told in *Yevamos* 117a that the law is that a woman's mother-in-law is one of the women who is not able to testify to the death of her daughter-in-law's husband (i.e., the woman's son), because she hates her daughter-in-law and seeks to harm her. Thus we can see the fine qualities of Naomi her mother-in-law, who did not rest until she could find security for Ruth, so that it might go well with her.

It appears further that there was a hint to her through *ruach hakodesh* (Divine inspiration) from the word "*mano'ach*" ("security"), for that word spells out the initial letters of the phrase, "*mimeich nolad velad*

אֲשֶׁר הָיִית אֶת־נַעֲרוֹתָיו הִנֵּה־הוּא זֹרֶה אֶת־
ג גֹּרֶן הַשְּׂעֹרִים הַלָּיְלָה׃ וְרָחַצְתְּ ׀ וָסַכְתְּ וְשַׂמְתְּ

---

chacham — from you will be born a wise child." Indeed, *Chazal* said that Ruth was privileged to live to see her descendant, Shlomo, the wisest of all men, as it states (*I Melachim* 2:19), "He placed a chair for the king's (i.e., Shlomo's) mother." On this *Chazal* in *Bava Basra* 91b say that this is a reference to Ruth, the mother of the monarchy (*Ruth Rabbah* 5:5). Thus, through Ruth's marriage she was privileged to be the mother of the monarchy.

2. וְעַתָּה הֲלֹא בֹעַז מֹדַעְתָּנוּ אֲשֶׁר הָיִית אֶת נַעֲרוֹתָיו — "Now Boaz, our relative, with whose maidens you have been."

It appears that Ruth was afraid that Boaz might consider her to be a thief and would curse her, as we see in *Yalkut* [606] on the verse, "In the middle of the night" (3:8), and on the verse (*Tehillim* 119:62), "At midnight I arise to thank You for Your righteous ordinances": Thus did David say, "I must thank You for the miracles you did with my grandfather and grandmother at midnight, for had he cursed her, where would I have come from?'" Naomi, though, told Ruth that there was no reason for her to fear because Boaz was a relative and would take pity on her.

Ruth also feared that one of the young men or young women who was doing the threshing might catch her there, so Naomi assured her that she had already been with the young women, who were all righteous people and who realized that whatever Ruth did was *l'shem Shamayim* — for the sake of Heaven. Thus there was nothing to fear. Furthermore, as Boaz himself was busy winnowing barley that night and was going to sleep on the threshing floor by himself — because it was a generation rife with theft — she did not need to fear that any of the young women would be there.

It appears that the word "*atah* — now" in this verse was meant to be a hint to Ruth at which point in the night to reveal herself to Boaz. We see in *Megillah* 3 that when the man came to Yehoshua and said to him (*Yehoshua* 5:14), "I am the commander of Hashem's legion, now ("*atah*") I have come," *Tosfos* there, quoting *Rivan,* say that the word "*atah*" is a hint to Torah study, about which it states (*Devarim* 31:19), "So now ("*ve'atah*"), write this song for yourselves." Thus in essence Naomi said to Ruth, "After Boaz has finished eating and learning Torah, and has fulfilled 'So now ("*ve'atah*"), write this song' and is happy because of the song of the Torah, you are to appear before him. At that point you will have nothing to fear in terms of a curse, because he will be in good spirits." And that is what Ruth did, as we see in the verse below (3:7), "Boaz ate and drank and his heart

3/3 *with whose maidens you have been, he will be winnowing barley tonight on the threshing floor.* 3 *Bathe*

---

was merry." It was then that "she came stealthily, uncovered his feet, and lay down."

הִנֵּה הוּא זֹרֶה אֶת גֹּרֶן הַשְּׂעֹרִים הַלָּיְלָה — "He will be winnowing barley tonight on the threshing floor."

Rashi states that it was a generation that was steeped in theft, and he slept there to guard his crops. According to the *gemara* in *Bava Basra* [91b], Boaz was Ivtzan and was the *Nasi* — the head — of Israel. Also, according to *Chazal,* Boaz was very old when he married Ruth, and died immediately afterwards. Was it then the proper respect for the Torah for a person of his stature to personally sleep on the threshing floor in order to guard his grain? Where, then, were his young men at that time?

It would appear that Boaz did not sleep there for personal reasons, such as to guard his grain, but in order to ensure that no person would violate the *halachah* against stealing. Similarly, there is a story about the Chafetz Chaim, which relates that he ran after a thief who had stolen a silver cup from his home and told the man, "I want you to know that I forgive you totally and I also want you to know the worth of the cup, so that you should not sell it for less than its true value." He did this so that the person would not violate the *halachah* against theft. Here, too, Boaz guarded his grain so that no person would violate the *halachah* against theft. From this we learn a great lesson: If a person enables someone else to steal from him easily, as, for example, by negligently leaving something in a place where someone can steal it, he, too, is guilty of the sin. Similarly, we see in *Shevuos* 39b that if a person said, "I will swear," those present say to one another, "Let us depart from the tents of these wicked men" (i.e., both the man who swears and the one who makes him swear are considered to be wicked). The *gemara* asks why both are considered evil. It answers that when it comes to taking an oath, the oath binds both of them: the person taking it and the person who made him take it. On this *Rashi* comments that both are punished because the person who makes the other take an oath did not see to depositing his money with a trustworthy person, and this, in turn, leads to a *chillul Hashem.* Similarly, Boaz was careful not to come to *chillul Hashem* by having people steal grain from the threshing floor of the *Nasi* — the leader of the Jewish people — a person they were required to respect.

Another reason we can give as to why Boaz slept on the threshing floor was to teach the people of his generation not to cause others to sin, for when they saw that the judge himself slept on his threshing floor to guard it, everyone else followed his lead, and thus no one violated the *halachah*

°שמלתך [°שִׂמְלֹתַיִךְ ק] עָלַיִךְ °וירדתי [°וְיָרַדְתְּ ק] הַגֹּרֶן אַל־תִּוָּדְעִי לָאִישׁ עַד כַּלֹּתוֹ לֶאֱכֹל וְלִשְׁתּוֹת:

---

of theft or robbery. Indeed, *Chazal* tell us that (*Succah* 26a) it is the breach in the fence which invites the thief. Thus, it is a *mitzvah* for every person to guard his own possessions in a way that others will not be tempted to stealing them.

3. וְרָחַצְתְּ וָסַכְתְּ — "Bathe and anoint yourself."

Rashi explains "bathing" as referring to Ruth removing the filth of her idol worship and "anointing" as referring to performing the *mitzvos.* It would appear from *Rashi* that only at this time did she become a convert. I found the same in *Shai HaTorah,* quoting by R' Yosef Dov Soloveitchik, son of the Brisker Rav, who uses this to explain what Boaz said to Ruth, "I have ordered the young men not to touch you" (2:9), for Ruth came to glean the grain which must be left for the poor, and why should the young men then have bothered her? *Shai HaTorah* explains that since she had not yet converted and was still considered to be non-Jewish, she had no inherent right to the gleanings of the poor, and would only be entitled to glean because of *darkei shalom* (to maintain the peace) as stated in *Gittin* 61a, that one supports the non-Jewish poor along with the Jewish poor because of *darkei shalom. Kesef Mishneh* (*Hilchos Matnos Aniyim*) quotes *Ran* that the *halachah* that one supports non-Jewish poor along with Jewish poor only applies if there are Jewish poor there as well, but there is no such obligation when there are no Jewish poor, as *darkei shalom* does not apply. Thus Boaz ordered his young men not to interfere with Ruth, even when she was all alone in the field and not entitled to glean.

I find the above difficult, because we see in 1:16 that she had accepted conversion when she said, "Your people are my people, and your God is my God," and in *Yevamos* 47b the *gemara* learns a number of the laws of conversion from here. It is possible that since the *halachah* that the Torah law only forbids a Moabite male and not a Moabite female had not yet been instituted (*Yalkut Ruth* 247), her conversion could not yet take place. Thus, Naomi said to Ruth, "It will be through you that Boaz will be able to overcome the resistance in his *beis din* to the rule that the *halachah* only forbids a Moabite male and not a Moabite female, and therefore please perform a second act of conversion to Judaism."

וְשַׂמְתְּ שִׂמְלֹתַיִךְ עָלַיִךְ וְיָרַדְתְּ הַגֹּרֶן — "Don your finery and go down to the threshing floor."

Rashi comments that this refers to her Shabbos clothes. We should *and anoint yourself, don your finery and go down to the threshing floor, but do not make yourself known to the man until he has finished eating and drinking.*

---

examine why Naomi specified that Ruth should wear her Shabbos clothes. The explanation of this is that *Bach* states that Naomi's advice in this matter was like that of Rivkah to Yaakov. Rivkah told Yaakov to go into his father Yitzchak and receive his blessing, even though this was not with Yitzchak's permission. Just as Rivkah clothed Yaakov in the precious clothes that Adam worn in the Garden of Eden, which had the perfume of the Garden of Eden, so that Yitzchak smelled its scent, so too did Naomi want Ruth, when she entered the threshing floor, to have the scent of Shabbos, because Shabbos is like the Garden of Eden. Similarly, I heard from R' Zalman Rothberg, who once studied under my grandfather (author of *Or Yechezkel*) in Yeshivas Petach Tikvah that one Shabbos my grandfather told him, "You can smell the smell of Shabbos here." Thus, when Naomi asked Ruth to wear her Shabbos clothes when she entered the threshing floor, it was so that the aroma of Shabbos would enter with her.

וְשַׂמְתְּ שִׂמְלֹתַיִךְ עָלַיִךְ וְיָרַדְתְּ הַגֹּרֶן — "Go down ("*veyaradet*") to the threshing floor."

The *kri* (the way the word is read) of the word is *veyaradet,* "you will go down," but the *kesiv* (the way the word is actually written) is *veyaradeti,* "I will go down." On this *Rashi* comments that "my merit will go down with you." *Maharsha* on *Sotah* 45b comments on the *halachah* that if a person is found murdered outside a city, the *chachamim* (the wise men) of the city have to place their hands upon a calf and state, "We did not let the person go without food and did not let him leave without an escort." Based on this, *Maharsha* writes about on the importance of escorting someone on his way within the city. Obviously, the intention is to protect him along the way. Thus, the angels which escort the person performing a *mitzvah* go along with the person being escorted to protect him from injury. This is what Naomi meant when she said, "I will go down," namely that her angels would protect Ruth from injury.

Which injury did Naomi have in mind? First, because Boaz was guarding his threshing floor against thieves, it was important that he should not mistake Ruth for a thief, for a thief who comes secretly at night may be killed. Furthermore, according to the *Midrash Rabbah* (6:1), David praised and thanked Hashem for the kindness which He had done with his ancestors, "that had he (Boaz) uttered a single curse, from where would I have come?"

We can also add that *Bach* wrote (in his *Meishiv Nefesh* 3-4) that everything Naomi did in this regard was with *ruach hakodesh* (Divine

ד וִיהִי בְשָׁכְבוֹ וְיָדַעַתְּ אֶת־הַמָּקוֹם אֲשֶׁר יִשְׁכַּב־שָׁם
וּבָאת וְגִלִּית מַרְגְּלֹתָיו °ושכבתי [°וְשָׁכָבְתְּ ק׳]
ה וְהוּא יַגִּיד לָךְ אֵת אֲשֶׁר תַּעֲשִׂין׃ וַתֹּאמֶר אֵלֶיהָ כֹּל
ו אֲשֶׁר־תֹּאמְרִי [°אֵלַי קרי ולא כתיב] אֶעֱשֶׂה׃ וַתֵּרֶד
ז הַגֹּרֶן וַתַּעַשׂ כְּכֹל אֲשֶׁר־צִוַּתָּה חֲמוֹתָהּ׃ וַיֹּאכַל בֹּעַז

---

inspiration) and in her heart there was total faith that Ruth was the woman whom Hashem had ordained to produce the family of Yishai, which would be a beacon for all the nations. *Chazal* tell us that when they went to anoint Shlomo, David's son, as king, Satan protested this decision. Naomi therefore prayed that her merits should be sufficient to protect Ruth, so that Satan would not impede matters and that things would work out in the best possible way.

It also occurred to me that it states, "go down to the threshing floor" but not "you will come to the threshing floor," which is an allusion to the merits of David and Shlomo who came out of this marriage and who would eventually build the *Beis HaMikdash* on the site of the threshing floor of Aravnah, which David bought. For we are told in *Zevachim* 54b that the *Beis HaMikdash* was not built on the peak of the mountain but rather lower down. That is what is meant by "go *down* to the threshing floor."

5. וַתֹּאמֶר אֵלֶיהָ כֹּל אֲשֶׁר תֹּאמְרִי אֵלַי אֶעֱשֶׂה — She replied, "All that you say to me I will do."

This verse seems difficult, because instead of using the future, "All that you say to me," it should have used the past, "All that you said to me I will do." Rather, what Ruth promised Naomi was that even though Ruth was to leave the domain of Naomi and would enter that of Boaz when she would marry him, she would still remain under the domain of Naomi and would do whatever Naomi told her to.

It also occurred to me that Ruth was prophesying here about what would still happen, in that she still remained in Naomi's domain. Indeed, *Chazal* tell us that the night that Boaz brought Ruth into his home was the last night of his life, and that he died that night and was buried the next morning. In fact, Boaz had already exceeded his allocated days on earth but was kept alive by Hashem so that Ruth would conceive from him and thus lead to the birth of David. Once he had fulfilled this task as appointed by Hashem, he died and Ruth remained once again in Naomi's domain. This we see from the verse (4:16), "Naomi took the child and held it in her bosom, and she became his nurse," for she raised the child herself. Thus

[4] *And when he lies down, note the place where he lies, and go over, uncover his feet, and lie down. He will tell you what you are to do."* [5] *She replied "All that you say to me I will do."*

[6] *So she went down to the threshing floor and did everything as her mother-in-law instructed her.* [7] *Boaz ate*

---

this was a fulfillment of Ruth's prophecy that "All that you say to me I will do," and this referred to the future.

6. וַתֵּרֶד הַגֹּרֶן וַתַּעַשׂ כְּכֹל אֲשֶׁר צִוַּתָּה חֲמוֹתָהּ — So she went down to the threshing floor and did everything as her mother-in-law instructed her.

While Naomi told Ruth to (3:3) "bathe and anoint yourself, don your finery, and go down to the threshing floor," *Rashi* states that Ruth did not do exactly as Naomi had told her and did not dress herself at home in her finery, because she was afraid that if she was all dressed up anyone who saw her might think she was a harlot. Thus she first went down to the threshing floor and only later did she dress up in her finery, as commanded by her mother-in-law.

This, though, seems to contradict the verse, which states that Ruth "did everything as her mother-in-law instructed her." Furthermore, wasn't Naomi aware of such a possibility? The answer to this is that Naomi indeed was aware that this was possible, but she realized that if Ruth came up independently with the idea of donning her finery at a later time rather than earlier, it would be much more appealing to her, for, as *Chazal* tell us, a person prefers a single measure of something which he acquired on his own over nine measures that were just given to him without any effort on his part. Accordingly, Naomi left Ruth room to act in accordance with her own understanding. Thus Ruth "did everything as her mother-in-law instructed her." Indeed, we are told in *Shabbos* 113 that Shlomo HaMelech's statement in *Mishlei* 9:9, "Give the wise man, and he will be wiser," is a reference to Naomi and Ruth.

וַתַּעַשׂ כְּכֹל אֲשֶׁר צִוַּתָּה חֲמוֹתָהּ — She did everything as her mother-in-law instructed her.

The verse does not say, "as her mother-in-law said," because Ruth did exactly as instructed by her mother-in-law without trying to fathom why Naomi had said so. This was because Ruth was extremely modest and accepted unquestioningly whatever Naomi said to her. Indeed, we see Ruth's modesty in the verse (2:5), "Boaz then said to his young man who was overseeing the harvesters, 'To whom does that young woman belong?' " on which *Rashi* asks, "Was it then Boaz's way to ask about women? [The reason he did so was] that he saw in her *tznius* (modesty) and wisdom." *Netziv* writes that the true sign that a person has acquired the attribute of *sheleimus* (perfection) is when that person can, when asked to do so, do the exact opposite of what one might normally expect. For example, Avraham, who was called "*av* — father," was ready, when called upon to so by Hashem, to sacrifice his son, Yitzchak. Here Naomi was asking Ruth to do something which would be a total violation of the laws of modesty — to go to the threshing floor and act as one of the lowliest people. This shows how perfect she had become, in that where necessary she was able to do the exact opposite of what would normally be done.

So too do we find this with Yehudah, where Tamar was a very modest woman but nevertheless covered her face so that Yehudah would not recognize her and would come to her. It would seem from both Tamar and Ruth that the House of David came out of the exact opposite of modesty, for the light of *Mashiach* requires the pure to come forth from the impure, as we see in *Bamidbar Rabbah* (19:1), commenting on the verse (*Iyov* 14:4), " 'Who can produce purity from impurity? Is it not the One?' For example, Avraham (came) from Terach, Chizkiyahu from Achaz . . . the World to Come from this world. Who did this? Who commanded this? Who decreed this? Was it not the Only One of the World?"

7. וַיֹּאכַל בֹּעַז וַיֵּשְׁתְּ וַיִּיטַב לִבּוֹ — Boaz ate and drank and his heart was merry.

Rashi notes that Boaz was studying Torah. The Midrash (5:15) gives a number of explanations of this verse. *Rashi* chose the explanation that he was happy because he was studying Torah, as in the verse (*Tehillim* 119:72), "The Torah of your mouth is better for me than thousands of [pieces of] gold and silver." It appears that what *Rashi* meant to do was to explain what gave Boaz the power to overcome his Evil Inclination. Thus we see in the Midrash (6:4) that R' Yehudah states that that whole night Boaz's Evil Inclination contended with him, saying, "You are unmarried and are looking for a wife and she is unmarried and is looking for a husband. Get up and have conjugal relations with her and make her your wife." He took an oath against his Evil Inclination and said, "I swear by Hashem that I will not touch her." It was only through the power of his Torah learning that night that he had the strength to overcome his Evil Inclination and not to touch her, for the Torah is a

3/7 *and drank and his heart was merry. He went to lie down at the end of the grain pile, and she*

---

shield and protector against the Evil Inclination (*Sotah* 21).

We can also add that *Chazal* tell us that (*Berachos* 5a) "'Good' refers to Torah, as it states (*Mishlei* 4:2), 'For I have given you a good ("*tov*") teaching, do not forsake My Torah.'" Therefore, when the verse here states that his heart was merry ("*vayitav libo*"), we must say that he was studying Torah.

Let us examine this verse (*Mishlei* 4:2), "For I have given you a good teaching, do not forsake My Torah." At first glance, it seems that the second part of the verse contradicts the first part, for if Hashem gave it to us ("I have given you . . ."), how is it still *His* Torah ("do not forsake *My* Torah")? Shouldn't the verse have stated, "Do not forsake *your* Torah?" It would appear that there are two levels of receiving the Torah. There are those who merit having the Torah become their Torah, and there are those who do not merit this, and the Torah remains Hashem's Torah. We see this in *Avodah Zarah* 19a, on the verse (*Tehillim* 1:2), "His desire is in the Torah of Hashem and in his Torah he mediates day and night," where Rava states, "At first it is referred to as Hashem's, as it states, 'His desire is in the Torah of Hashem,' and in the end [after a great deal of effort] it is referred to as the person's, as it states, 'in his Torah he mediates day and night.' " Thus, in *Mishlei* Shlomo HaMelech tells us, "For I have given you a good teaching," and even if the person does not merit having the Torah become his, nevertheless, "do not forsake My Torah."

It would appear that the "*tov*" which is referred to is the hidden light of the Torah and with it one can perceive from one end of the world to the other. Thus *Degel Machaneh Ephraim* (*Parshas Bereishis*) on the verse (1:4), "Hashem saw that the light was good," states that he heard from his grandfather, the Baal Shem Tov, regarding what we are told in *Chagigah* 12 that when Hashem saw that the light was good and set it aside for the *tzaddikim* in the World to Come, He hid it in the Torah. He also set aside the light for the *tzaddikim* of every generation to use when they attain the level of being able to absorb it. This light enables them to see from one end of the world to the other. This was hinted at by *Ba'al HaTurim* on the verse, "Hashem saw that the light," that the *gematria* (numeric value of the letters) of "the light" ("*es ha'or*") is equivalent to 613, the number of *mitzvos* in the Torah. Therefore, those who experience the good of the Torah merit it becoming *their* Torah. That was the level which Boaz attained, and therefore when it states that "his heart was merry," this refers to the fact that he was studying the Torah.

ג/ח ח וַתָּבֹא בַלָּט וַתְּגַל מַרְגְּלֹתָיו וַתִּשְׁכָּב: וַיְהִי בַּחֲצִי הַלַּיְלָה וַיֶּחֱרַד הָאִישׁ וַיִּלָּפֵת וְהִנֵּה

וַתָּבֹא בַלָּט וַתְּגַל מַרְגְּלֹתָיו וַתִּשְׁכָּב — And she came stealthily, uncovered his feet, and lay down.

I saw a remarkable question by *Shoresh Yishai,* who asks that since Boaz was sleeping on the threshing floor to guard his grain from thieves, how is it that neither he nor his young men realized or heard that a young woman had entered the threshing floor, as they would have had there been thieves? Wouldn't the young men be held accountable for not having alerted their master? He brings an answer from R' Yehudah Nasan Provincial, that the word "*balat*" (translated here as "stealthily") is from the same root as (*Shemos* 7:23), "The necromancers of Egypt did the same by means of their incantations" ("*belateihem*"), i.e., the necromancers used a type of magic which enabled them to move about at night without being detected. And the same was true with Ruth, where "*balat*" implies a type of magic. The same was true when Shaul was in the cave (*I Shmuel* 24:5) and "David rose and stealthily ("*balat*") cut off a corner of Shaul's robe." Had it not been for this magic, David would have placed himself in very great danger and he would not have been permitted to do what he did.

I do not understand this answer, for after bringing all the different types of witchcraft practiced by the different nations, *Rambam* (*Hilchos Avodah Zarah* 11:16) writes that "all of these things are lies and deceit, and they used them to deceive the ancient nations into following them. It is not proper for Jews, who are truly wise, to continue with these vanities and to believe that they have any value, for it states (*Bamidbar* 23:23), 'For there is no divination in Jacob and no sorcery in Israel.' Indeed, whoever believes in these things and ones like these and thinks in his heart that they are true and wise except that the Torah forbade using them, is but one of the fools and those who lack knowledge." How, therefore, can one say that Ruth and David used magic to make themselves invisible?

It appears that the meaning of the verse, when it states that Ruth came "*balat*" is that what happened to Ruth looked like the same trickery used by the other nations, but in reality it was something which Hashem did in a miraculous way so that the young men did not see her when she came in. That was also what Hashem did when Shaul did not see David and his men in the cave. This is in accordance with what *Rashi* wrote in *Parshas Shemos,* on the verse (4:11), "Hashem said to [Moshe], 'Who makes a mouth for man, or who makes one dumb or deaf, or sighted or blind? Is it not I, Hashem?' " *Rashi* there explains, "Who made Pharaoh mute . . . and the executioners whose job was to kill — who made them blind so they *came stealthily, uncovered his feet, and lay down.* [8] *In the middle of the night the man was startled, and turned about*

---

would not see when you fled from the execution platform and escaped?" That was what happened to Ruth and to David, where they were able to enter the threshing floor or cave without being seen.

8. וַיְהִי בַּחֲצִי הַלַּיְלָה וַיֶּחֱרַד הָאִישׁ — In the middle of the night the man was startled.

See the Midrash here (6:1) which quotes a verse (*Tehillim* 119:62), "At midnight I arise to thank You for Your righteous ordinances." R' Pinchas said in the name of R' Eliezer ben Yaakov: "A harp and a lyre were suspended over David's head, and when midnight arrived he would get up and play on them," i.e., he would sing praises of Hashem.

What this means is that Boaz woke up at midnight because David would later do so to praise Hashem. This can be best understood if we understand the importance of midnight — "*chatzos.*" I heard an explanation from *Pachad Yitzchak*[1] that its importance lies in the fact that it is linked to the future. Even though the night is the time of Hashem's strict justice and the morning is the time of mercy, from midnight on the time is influenced by the morning, and is considered within the realm of mercy. Thus, the meaning of the Midrash is that due to the merits of King David who would get up at midnight, Boaz arose that midnight to withstand the test of Ruth's presence, and this worked out in the best manner, as it was a time of mercy.

וַיֶּחֱרַד הָאִישׁ וַיִּלָּפֵת — The man was startled, and turned about.

Rashi states that Boaz thought it was a demon and he wanted to cry out but Ruth grabbed him and held him in her arms. The simple meaning is that Boaz was afraid that the demon would harm him, as we see in *Pesachim* 112b, that a *talmid chacham* should not go out alone at night lest a demon harm him. Even though we see in the *gemara* there that in the case of R' Chanina ben Dosa and in the case of Abaye in heaven they announced, "Take heed of Chanina and his Torah," and "Take heed of Nachmani[2] and his Torah," and a demon could not harm either of them — and there is no doubt that Boaz, who was the judge of the generation certainly warranted the same announcement in heaven — nevertheless, Boaz himself, out of his exceeding humility, took pains to be careful. He

---

1. R' Yitzchak Hutner.

2. I.e., Abaye, who was brought up by Rabbah bar Nachman.

was afraid of a demon, and felt that a defect in his Torah learning might render him vulnerable and unprotected.[1]

We are told in *Sotah* 21a that the Torah is compared to light. Just as light protects the world, the Torah protects the world, as it states (*Mishlei* 6:22), "As you go forth, it will guide you." As the *gemara* there states, even if one is not engaged in Torah learning right then, it still protects him. Why, then, wouldn't the Torah have protected Boaz? The answer must be that he was afraid, because of his excessive humility, that there was a defect in his Torah learning, and that was why he felt the Torah might not protect him.

וְהִנֵּה אִשָּׁה שֹׁכֶבֶת מַרְגְּלֹתָיו — And behold! There was a woman lying at his feet!

Chochmah U'Mussar (II:332) states that what happened to Boaz that night on the threshing floor was a test to see whether he was worthy of having the *Mashiach* descend from him. Thus, he underwent a similar test to the one that Yosef underwent in the home of Potiphera, and both of the women who tested them did it *l'shem Shamayim* — for the sake of Heaven. Thus, the wife of Potiphera saw through astrology that she would have descendants through him, but she erred in not realizing that they would come from her daughter rather than from herself. In the end, both men's families were later descended from the woman with whom they had withstood the test. Boaz had Oved from Ruth, while Yosef had Menasheh and Ephraim from the daughter of Potiphera.

To explain why this was so, we must understand that there are two basic elements upon which Hashem leads the world as it revolves: *galus* (exile) and *geulah* (redemption). One is the counterpart of the other. All the exiles of the Jewish people are included within that of Egypt, which came about through the sale of Yosef and his being brought down to Egypt, while the basis for redemption is through *Mashiach* ben David, who is descended from Boaz and Ruth. Thus, just as Yosef, representing *galus,* was tested over conjugal relations, Boaz, who represents *geulah,* was tested in the same way.

The ideas of *galus* and *geulah* are both hinted at in verse 13, where Boaz

1. It is told that at the time when everyone in Eretz Yisrael was afraid that the Iraqis would launch Scud missiles with chemical warheads and all put on gas masks and remained in sealed rooms, R' Chaim Kanievsky remained in his room with the windows open and did not wear a gas mask. He was asked why he acted the way he did. He answered that since Rav Shach lived in Bnei Brak, nothing would happen. He was then asked how it was that Rav Shach himself did wear a gas mask, and he answered that Rav Shach did not know that there was a *gaon* such as Rav Shach to guard the city.

— and behold! there was a woman lying at his feet!
9 *He said, "Who are you?" She answered,*

---

said to Ruth, "Stay the night, then in the morning, if he will redeem you, fine! let him redeem. But if he does not want to redeem you, then I will redeem you. *Chai* Hashem! Lie down until the morning." *Tikkunei Zohar* (*Tikkun* 21, p. 50b) explains that "Stay the night" refers to *galus,* which is called night, whereas "then in the morning" refers to the *geulah* in the future. "If he will redeem you, fine!" refers to the good deeds of the Jewish people, through which they will be redeemed. "But if he does not want to redeem you" means that if redemption is not considered important by the Jewish people, *chas veshalom,* nevertheless Hashem promised that "I will redeem you. *Chai* Hashem! Have patience, and wait until the morning."

We can also see this from the word "*Anochi*" — " 'I' will redeem you" — that through the merit of belief in the "I" ("*Anochi*") of "I am Hashem, your God" there will be the *geulah,* as stated in *Makkos* 24a, "Chabakuk came and reduced it to one principle (*Chabakkuk* 2:4), "The righteous person shall live through his faith."

Chochmah U'Mussar (I:418) notes that immediately after the Jews left Egypt and came to Eretz Yisrael, Hashem tested them with an easy test. At the beginning, when the *shevatim* (the Tribes of Israel) entered Eretz Yisrael, it would have been easy for them to evict the Canaanites from their midst — and this was necessary because, as indeed happened when the Canaanites remained, they caused the Jews to sin. At first, it would have been an easy task, because the Canaanites feared them greatly (*Shemos* 15:14): "People heard — they were agitated; terror gripped the dwellers of Philistia." The Jews, though, were too lazy to drive out the Canaanites who remained in the country. Later, the Jews were no longer able to drive the Canaanites out, and they became mixed with the other nations and learned from their ways. Thus, it is the way of Hashem to test a person with an easy test. If he does not withstand the test, Hashem brings upon him a more difficult test which he can fail, *chas veshalom.* This is the meaning of (*Avos* 4:2), "The reward for a *mitzvah* is a *mitzvah,*" i.e., if a person withstood an easy test he is given an even easier test, and he will surely pass that test and it will be good for him. On the other hand, "the wages of sin are sin," for where a person did not pass an easy test the next test is a harder one, and the person will not be able to pass this test except through a great deal of effort. With this background, we have to explain what sin caused Boaz to have to undergo so great a test as he did that night on the threshing floor.

Sotah 3b brings the verse (*Mishlei* 6:26), "For the sake of a licentious woman [it may be a person will beg] for a loaf of bread." Thus we see from

אָנֹכִי רוּת אֲמָתֶךָ וּפָרַשְׂתָּ כְנָפֶךָ עַל־אֲמָתְךָ כִּי
י גֹּאֵל אָתָּה: וַיֹּאמֶר בְּרוּכָה אַתְּ לַיהוה בִּתִּי
הֵיטַבְתְּ חַסְדֵּךְ הָאַחֲרוֹן מִן־הָרִאשׁוֹן לְבִלְתִּי־
לֶכֶת אַחֲרֵי הַבַּחוּרִים אִם־דַּל וְאִם־עָשִׁיר:
יא וְעַתָּה בִּתִּי אַל־תִּירְאִי כֹּל אֲשֶׁר־תֹּאמְרִי אֶעֱשֶׂה־
לָּךְ כִּי יוֹדֵעַ כָּל־שַׁעַר עַמִּי כִּי אֵשֶׁת חַיִל אָתְּ:

---

the verse that eating bread is related to a licentious woman. We also see in *Bava Basra* 91 that Rabbah bar Rav Huna said in the name of Rav that Boaz made 120 wedding feasts . . . and to none of them did he invite Mano'ach (the father of Shimshon, who at that time had no children, so Mano'ach could not "repay" Boaz by inviting him to any wedding). The *gemara* goes on to mention that all of Boaz's children died in his lifetime. Thus, since Boaz deprived Mano'ach of bread, he was tested with the test of Ruth, "For the sake of a licentious woman [it may be that a person will beg] for a loaf of bread."[1] It appears that the reason why Boaz sent Ruth six measures of barley was in order to rectify the injustice incurred when he did not invite Mano'ach to any of his children's wedding feasts.

9. וַתֹּאמֶר אָנֹכִי רוּת אֲמָתֶךָ וּפָרַשְׂתָּ כְנָפֶךָ עַל אֲמָתְךָ כִּי גֹאֵל אָתָּה — She answered, "I am your maidservant Ruth. Spread your robe over your maidservant, for you are a redeemer."

Rashi comments that "spread your robe" means "spread your robe to cover me with your *tallis,*" and that implies marriage. We need to clarify why spreading a *tallis* should mean marriage. This can be explained by what *Meshech Chochmah* (*Parshas Shelach*) said — that a *tallis* with *tzitzis* is a garment whose end strings have not been completely woven, to show that when a person chooses to follow Hashem's way he needs help from Above to support him. Thus we are told in *Kiddushin* 30b that if not for Hashem's help, the Evil Inclination would overcome all of us. It is with Hashem's help to the one who wants to be purified, and through the *mitzvos* which he performs, that he binds himself to Hashem, and by this he becomes a partner to Hashem in the act of Creation. That is also the foundation of marriage, where the man and woman become partners with Hashem in building and maintaining the world, and join up together as one to further this aim.

---

1. See also *Maharsha,* who explains that Boaz was judged based on his saintliness, because *tzaddikim* are judged by Hashem with the full severity of the *halachah.*

"I am your maidservant Ruth. Spread your robe over
your maidservant, for you are a redeemer."
[10] *And he said, "Be blessed of HASHEM, my daugh-*
ter; you have made your latest act of kindness
greater than the first, in that you have not gone
after the younger men, be they poor or rich. [11] *And*
now, my daughter, do not fear; whatever you say, I
will do for you; for all the men in the gate of
my people know that you are a worthy woman.

וַתֹּאמֶר אָנֹכִי רוּת אֲמָתֶךָ וּפָרַשְׂתָּ כְנָפֶךָ עַל אֲמָתְךָ כִּי גֹאֵל אָתָּה — She answered, "I am your maidservant Ruth. Spread your robe over your maidservant, for you are a redeemer."

The righteous say little and do a lot [see *Avos* 1:15], for Ruth said ten words to Boaz, paralleling the Ten Commandments. That is why her first word — as is the first word of the Ten Commandments — was "*Anochi,*" and by this she meant to ask Boaz to accept upon himself the yoke of marriage, as Boaz had accepted upon himself the yoke of the Kingdom of Heaven at Sinai through the Ten Commandments and in the covenant which he made with Hashem at Sinai.[1] Similarly, Ruth said, "enter with me into the covenant of marriage."

Also, when she said, "Spread your robe (*kanafecha*) over your maidservant," this was an allusion to what Hashem said to the Jewish people at the time of the giving of the Torah (*Shemos* 19:4): "I have borne you on the wings of (*kanfei*) eagles and brought you to Me." Just as Hashem showed His love of the Jewish people in this way, Ruth asked Boaz to show her the love of marriage.

10-11. וַיֹּאמֶר בְּרוּכָה אַתְּ לַיהוה בִּתִּי הֵיטַבְתְּ חַסְדֵּךְ הָאַחֲרוֹן מִן הָרִאשׁוֹן לְבִלְתִּי לֶכֶת אַחֲרֵי הַבַּחוּרִים אִם דַּל וְאִם עָשִׁיר וְעַתָּה בִּתִּי אַל תִּירְאִי כֹּל אֲשֶׁר תֹּאמְרִי אֶעֱשֶׂה לָּךְ כִּי יוֹדֵעַ כָּל שַׁעַר עַמִּי כִּי אֵשֶׁת חַיִל אָתְּ — And he said, "Be blessed of Hashem, my daughter; you have made your latest act of kindness greater than the first, in that you have not gone after the younger men, be they poor or rich. And now, my daughter, do not fear; whatever you say, I will do for you; for all the men in the gate of my people know that you are a worthy woman ("*eishes chayil*")."

Thus we see that through this action of hers Ruth merited being called an "*eishes chayil,*" the term used by Shlomo HaMelech in *Mishlei* to

---

1. This is what Hoshea said when he proclaimed (*Hoshea* 2:21), "I will betroth you to Me forever," referring to the covenant made at Mount Sinai.

יב וְעַתָּה֙ כִּ֣י אָמְנָ֔ם כִּ֥י °אם [°כתיב ולא קרי] גֹאֵ֖ל אָנֹ֑כִי
יג וְגַ֛ם יֵ֥שׁ גֹּאֵ֖ל קָר֥וֹב מִמֶּֽנִּי׃ לִ֣ינִי ׀ הַלַּ֗יְלָה וְהָיָ֤ה

---

describe the great women who had walked the face of the earth, such as our Mother Sarah.

To explain this, R' Moshe David Walli in his work on the Book of *Ruth* states that Ruth's great *chessed* (lovingkindness) was that — contrary to the general rule that a woman prefers a poor young man to a rich old man — she followed what Naomi asked of her, and did great *chessed* for her mother-in-law by being willing to marry Boaz, who was an old man. By this action, the tortured soul of Machlon, Naomi's son, could be redeemed by their kinsman. Thus, when Ruth had a son, the neighbors said that a son had been born to Naomi, because Oved was a *gilgul* (reincarnation) of her son Machlon.

Kesef Tzaruf explains that an *eishes chayil* is a woman whose husband trusts her when he goes out to war, because whenever anyone went to battle on behalf of the House of David he would give his wife a *get* (a divorce) in case he did not come back for any reason. In the case of an *eishes chayil,* when the husband went out to battle he was confident that she would not cheat on him even though she had technically been divorced, and that is the true *eishes chayil.* Now, Ruth showed that she was ready to follow an old man so that her husband's soul could be redeemed, an act which showed her faithfulness to her deceased husband, and that is why she was referred to as an *eishes chayil.*

11. וְעַתָּה בִּתִּי אַל תִּירְאִי כֹּל אֲשֶׁר תֹּאמְרִי אֶעֱשֶׂה לָּךְ — "And now, my daughter, do not fear; whatever you say, I will do for you."

It would seem to appear that the word "*eilai* — to me" is missing, and it should state, "whatever you say *to me.*" Also, how could a *tzaddik* such as Boaz promise her something of which he was unsure, for he immediately told her, "Now, while it is true that I am a redeemer, but there is also another redeemer closer than I. Stay the night, then in the morning, if he will redeem you, fine! let him redeem. But if he does not want to redeem you, then I will redeem you." (3:12-13) How then, did he say to her, "Whatever you say, I will do for you"?

It appears that what Boaz meant was "whatever you say" in your prayers to Hashem "I will do for you," for *Chazal* said on the verse (*Bereishis* 17:29), "Leah's eyes were tender," that she would cry and pray that she should not fall into the hands of Eisav. The Midrash here concludes by saying that prayer is so great that Leah even married Yaakov before her sister did. Similarly, Boaz told Ruth to pray to Hashem and then promised

[12] *Now while it is true that I am a redeemer, but there is also another redeemer closer than I.* [13] *Stay the night, then*

---

her that her prayer would be fulfilled and he would do for her that which she asked.

So too do we see the interpretation of *Chazal* later, on the verse (3:14), "He said, 'Let it not be known that the woman came to the threshing floor,'" where *Chazal* point out that the verse does not say "he said *to her,*" but simply, "he said," for Boaz prostrated himself and said, "Lord of the Universe, it is totally clear to you that I did not touch her. May it be Your will that it should not be known, so that there should not be a public *chillul Hashem.* Thus we see that "He said" connotes praying, and that was Boaz's intention, as we explained.

12. וְעַתָּה כִּי אָמְנָם כִּי אִם גֹאֵל אָנֹכִי וְגַם יֵשׁ גֹּאֵל קָרוֹב מִמֶּנִּי — "Now, while it is true that I am a redeemer, but there is also another redeemer closer than I."

In the Hebrew, the word "*im*" (*alef mem*) is written, but is not read. With that added word, the verse would read, "Now while it is true that I *may* be a redeemer, but there is also another redeemer closer than I." It appears that this is a hint to what *Imrei Yosher* wrote, for it seems strange that since Ruth wanted to marry him and Boaz wanted to marry her, they would have to wait for the other person's approval. After all, there was no requirement by Torah law for the redeemer to marry her.

Imrei Yosher writes that when Ruth said to Boaz, "You are a redeemer," she hinted that she knew from Naomi something which Naomi had found out with *ruach hakodesh* (Divine inspiration) that the Redeemer would come from him. Furthermore, it would only be fitting that Boaz should be the father, because he was from the tribe of Yehudah, of which it states (*Bereishis* 49:10), "The scepter will not depart from Yehudah." Also, Boaz was the head of the Sanhedrin and the most important person of that generation. To this, Boaz answered, "There is also another redeemer closer than I," because the descendants of Amalek would eventually fall to the descendants of Rachel, while Yehudah was a descendant of Leah.

Now we were told that Elimelech and his sons were Ephrathites, and Tov and Elimelech were brothers (as *Rashi* states), and they might also have had the same mother. And in *Tehillim* (132:6) it states, "Behold, we heard of it in Ephrath," on which *Rashi* comments that he came from Ephraim, and *Ibn Ezra* writes the same thing. Here too we can say that on their mother's side they were from the tribe of Ephraim, which is a tribe descended from Rachel, and thus it would be appropriate for Tov to be the forefather of the redeemer. Boaz, though, was only a brother in terms of a

בַבֹּקֶר אִם־יִגְאָלֵךְ טוֹב יִגְאָל וְאִם־לֹא יַחְפֹּץ לְגָאֳלֵךְ וּגְאַלְתִּיךְ אָנֹכִי חַי־יְהוָה שִׁכְבִי עַד־הַבֹּקֶר׃

---

common father, but did not share the same mother. Now we can understand why the word "*im*" is in the verse, for it hints at the reason why Tov was more appropriate than Boaz to be the redeemer — because of his mother's side, even though on their father's side they were both from Yehudah.

13. לִינִי הַלַּיְלָה וְהָיָה בַבֹּקֶר אִם יִגְאָלֵךְ טוֹב יִגְאָל וְאִם לֹא יַחְפֹּץ לְגָאֳלֵךְ וּגְאַלְתִּיךְ אָנֹכִי חַי יהוה שִׁכְבִי עַד הַבֹּקֶר — "Stay the night, then in the morning, if he will redeem you, fine! let him redeem. But if he does not want to redeem you, then I will redeem you. *Chai* Hashem! Lie down until the morning."

It is asked why the *tzaddik* did not send her away immediately, and why he put himself into great spiritual danger, for even if he was saved from sinning, the thoughts of sinning are considered even worse than the sin itself.[1]

It is possible that he acted as he did to show her that he was not rejecting her out of hand, for he had told her that there was a closer redeemer and she might have understood that as a rejection. After all, she herself was exceedingly modest and had totally broken through all barriers of modesty because of the issue at hand and because of Naomi's request. Thus she was worthy of being treated with honor, and he therefore protected her honor and placed himself in danger.

לִינִי הַלַּיְלָה וְהָיָה בַבֹּקֶר אִם יִגְאָלֵךְ טוֹב יִגְאָל — "Stay the night, then in the morning, if he will ("*vehaya*") redeem you, fine! let him redeem."

Chazal tell us that the word "*vehaya*" implies joy.[2] Now, what joy would there be if Tov decided to redeem her, when Ruth wanted to marry Boaz, especially as it was only fitting that the ultimate redeemer should come out of Boaz, the head of the Sanhedrin and the greatest person of his generation, who had performed so much *chessed* for Naomi and Ruth? Why, then does the verse use the word, "*vehaya*" in this context? (see what *Imrei Yosher* writes about this).

The Midrash states that the day after Boaz married Ruth he died, as stated in the Holy Books, for once a person has fulfilled his mission in the world he is taken and returns to his place in *Gan Eden*. Now, the mission

---

1. *Yoma* 29a.

2. *Esther Rabbah* 11.

in the morning, if he will redeem you, fine! let him redeem. But if he does not want to redeem you, then I will redeem you! Chai Hashem! Lie down until the morning."

---

of Boaz was to bring out the soul of David from Ruth, as we see in the writings of Chasam Sofer (brought below in Ch. 4), on the verse (4:4), "That I may know; for there is no one else to redeem it but you, and I am after you," Boaz hinted to Tov that in the end he would marry Ruth regardless, for that was his mission in the world. This, then, explains the joy of "*vehaya,*" because if Tov would redeem Ruth, Boaz would be able to live longer and could serve Hashem in this world until the time eventually came for him to marry Ruth, for a single hour of *teshuvah* and good deeds in this world is greater than all of the World to Come.

וּגְאַלְתִּיךְ אָנֹכִי — "Then I will redeem you."

According to *Sifrei,* Boaz was able to effect *kiddushin* on the threshing floor. Why he did he not do so? After all, he was certainly permitted to marry her, because according to Boaz the prohibition was against "Moabite males but not Moabite females." It is possible to answer this and explain it in two ways. On the one hand, because *Ploni Almoni* was a closer relative than Boaz, according to the laws of *yibum* (levirate marriage) *Ploni Almoni* should have been the first to be offered a chance to marry her. Alternately, one can answer this as follows: *Chazal* tell us that if a student comes and claims he heard a Torah statement from his *rebbi* permitting a certain action, if the student made the statement before taking such an action, he is believed, but if he only says that his *rebbi* permitted it after he had taken the action, he is not believed. Thus, if Boaz would first marry Ruth and only afterwards say that he had heard the *halachah* of "Moabite males but not Moabite females," he would not be believed, for he said it at the time of his action. However, since he did not marry her when he made the statement and, on the contrary, wanted *Ploni Almoni* to marry her, he was believed when he stated, "Moabite males but not Moabite females," because at the time he said this it did not affect him personally.

חַי יהוה שִׁכְבִי עַד הַבֹּקֶר — "*Chai* Hashem! Lie down until the morning."

Rashi says that there are those who interpret his oath as relating to Boaz's Evil Inclination, for his Evil Inclination enticed him, telling him, "She is single and you are single. Why not have relations with her?" He thus swore that he would not have relations with her until they were married. The Midrash (6:4) states that three people were assaulted by their

יד וַתִּשְׁכַּב °מרגלותו [°מַרְגְּלוֹתָיו ק] עַד־הַבֹּקֶר
וַתָּקָם °בטרום [°בְּטֶרֶם ק] יַכִּיר אִישׁ אֶת־רֵעֵהוּ

Evil Inclination and hastened to swear to prevent it from getting the better of them, and they are: Yosef, Boaz and David. The Midrash ends by saying that Boaz was a wise man in that he hastened to take an oath, in keeping with (*Mishlei* 24:5), "The man of knowledge grows stronger."

We need to understand why Boaz took an oath. After all, all Jews are already under oath from Sinai to keep the Torah, and an unmarried male who has intercourse with an unmarried female transgresses, according to *Rambam* the prohibition of (*Devarim* 23:18), "There shall not be a promiscuous woman among the daughters of Israel." What, then, did his oath accomplish in terms of his Evil Inclination? This, actually, is the question in *Nedarim* 8a, where the *gemara* asks, "How do I know that a person may take an oath to fulfill a *mitzvah*? We learn it from (*Tehillim* 119:106), 'I have sworn, and I will fulfill to keep Your righteous ordinances.' But isn't he already under oath from Mount Sinai? Rather, this comes to teach us that a person may (take an oath to) spur himself on."

So too do we see in *Niddah* 30a, that the fetus is not born until it is made to take an oath, as it states (*Yeshayahu* 45:23): " 'To Me shall every knee kneel and every tongue swear.' 'To Me shall every knee kneel' refers to the day of death . . . 'and every tongue swear' — that is the day of birth." Thus even though every person already swore at Mount Sinai (because all the souls were at Mount Sinai), nevertheless the person is made to take another oath, and this requires clarification.

It states in *Bava Basra* 16a that when Hashem allowed Satan to test Iyov, He told him (*Iyov* 2:6), "But preserve his soul [from death]." The *gemara* says that this was a worse torment for Satan than for Iyov, because it is like telling a servant, "Break the cask but do not spill any of its wine." From this we see that Satan only has power over the soul while the person is alive, but not after the person's death. We are also told in *Shevuos* 39a that when Hashem said (*Shemos* 20:7), "You shall not take the Name of Hashem, your God, in vain," the entire world trembled, because the sin of dealing with oaths causes a blot on the person's soul and upon the soul of the entire world. Thus, by making every fetus swear, the sin of breaking an oath becomes one that affects the soul, and Satan has no control over one's soul, in accordance with "But preserve his soul."

Another understanding as to what the oath accomplishes is in accordance with what I saw brought in the name of *Kehillos Yaakov,* in that we know that most sins committed by people are committed after they somehow or other rationalize that it is permitted, for as each person is

[14] *So she lay at his feet until the morning and she arose before one man could recognize another,*

---

concerned for his own well-being, he is able to convince himself that what is bad is really good. Because of his own self-interests, a person will find all types of reasons why in a particular case the law is different, etc. Given this, his oath will indeed help him: If he rationalizes to himself that something is permitted, then the oath he takes now will prevent him from doing it in spite of his rationalization. Also, the oath will help him not to rationalize his behavior in the first place, and that, indeed, is a real incentive.

✿ ✿ ✿

In all three of the cases mentioned above — Yosef, Boaz, and David — they could have found a way to rationalize a violation of the *halachah,* and that was why they needed a separate oath to keep them from any violation. On the verse (*Bereishis* 39:1), "Yosef had been brought down to Egypt," *Rashi* notes that just as Tamar's actions were *l'shem Shamayim* (for the sake of Heaven) the wife of Potiphera's actions were also *l'shem Shamayim,* for she saw by astrology that she would have descendants from him, but did not know whether it was to be through her or through her daughter. Regarding David, it states in *Berachos* 62b that David told Shaul that according to the Torah Shaul deserved to die because he was pursuing David and had the law of a *rodef,* and, as we are told, "If someone wishes to kill you, take the initiative and kill him first." Regarding Boaz, we are told in the Midrash (5:14), on the verse (3:6), "She went down to the threshing floor," that the conception of Moab was through debauchery, but its end was *l'shem Shamayim,* as it states, "She went down to the threshing floor and did everything as her mother-in-law instructed her." Thus, in all three cases the men involved used an oath to fortify themselves against their Evil Inclination, so that it would not enable them to rationalize why their actions should be permitted.

14. וַתָּקָם בְּטֶרֶם יַכִּיר אִישׁ אֶת רֵעֵהוּ — She arose before one man could recognize another.

There is an extra letter *vav* in this verse, in the word "*beterem,*" which, instead of being written *bais, tes, reish, mem,* is written here *bais, tes, reish, vav, mem.* The Midrash (7:1) states that this extra letter *vav* comes to hint to us that Ruth tarried with Boaz for six hours, equivalent to the numerical value of the letter *vav. Bach* adds in his *Meishiv Nefesh* that possibly the reason for this was to teach us that because of those six hours Boaz

טו וַיֹּאמֶר אַל־יִוָּדַע כִּי־בָאָה הָאִשָּׁה הַגֹּרֶן: וַיֹּאמֶר הָבִי
הַמִּטְפַּחַת אֲשֶׁר־עָלַיִךְ וְאֶחֳזִי־בָהּ וַתֹּאחֶז בָּהּ וַיָּמָד
טז שֵׁשׁ־שְׂעֹרִים וַיָּשֶׁת עָלֶיהָ וַיָּבֹא הָעִיר: וַתָּבוֹא

---

merited having six *tzaddikim* come from him, and each of them had six positive attributes: David, Chizkiyahu, etc.

We can say that there are two reasons why Boaz merited this — first, because Ruth tarried with him for six hours, and second, because he was so concerned with Ruth's honor. Thus we see that he had such sterling qualities that he was willing to forgo his own honor for the sake of her honor, and that was why he had these six descendants who were *tzaddikim,* each of whom had six exceptional qualities, as mentioned by *Rashi* in verse 15 (as found in *Yeshayahu* 11:2), "a spirit of wisdom and understanding, a spirit of counsel and strength, a spirit of knowledge and fear of Hashem."

❧ ❧ ❧

One can also say that the six hours of Boaz parallel the 6,000 years of exile until we are all finally redeemed by *Mashiach* the son of David, the descendant of Boaz. R' David Luzzatto quotes the Midrash from the *Zohar* in *Parshas Vayeira,* which states that the ultimate redemption will be through the "secret of *vav,*" etc. That is why all the verses of Ruth begin with the letter *vav,* except for eight verses, as stated by *Yalkut Shimoni.* Thus, when Boaz told Ruth, "Lie down until the morning" (3:13), *Rashi* explains this as "Lie down without any man." Some of the commentators ask why Boaz had to tell Ruth, "Lie down until the morning."After all, everyone lies down at night to sleep. Furthermore, if anything, he should have told her, "Lie down during the night," as Balaam said to Barak's officers (*Bamidbar* 22:8), "Lie down here tonight." It appears, though, that he hinted to her that by the test of "Lie down without any man" she would merit through her descendant "the morning will come" (*vehaya boker*), where the word "*vehaya*"implies joy, referring here to the true morning of the future redemption.

It also appears that Boaz used the word "*ga'al*" six times in addressing Ruth, which seems to be very repetitious, to hint to her about the future redemption which will come at the end of 6,000 years by her descendant, *Mashiach,* the descendant of David.

15. וַיֹּאמֶר הָבִי הַמִּטְפַּחַת אֲשֶׁר עָלַיִךְ וְאֶחֳזִי בָהּ וַתֹּאחֶז בָּהּ וַיָּמָד שֵׁשׁ שְׂעֹרִים וַיָּשֶׁת עָלֶיהָ וַיָּבֹא הָעִיר — And he said, "Hold out the shawl you are wearing

for he said, "Let it not be known that the woman came to the threshing floor." [15] *And he said, "Hold out the shawl you are wearing and grasp it." She held it, and he measured out six measures of barley, and set it upon her; then he went into the city.*

---

and grasp it." She held it, and he measured out six measures of barley, and set it upon her; then he went into the city.

We need to explain why he gave her the gift at this time to bring to the city. In an earlier verse (2:17) we read, "She gleaned in the field until evening, and she beat out what she had gleaned; it was about an *ephah* of barley." On the latter verse, *Shoresh Yishai* states that this verse was meant to praise Ruth, in that even though she had seen how generous Boaz was, she did not want to glean between the sheaves or between the plants left over after plowing, but only gleaned in a field which was ownerless, and which was "Hashem's gift to the poor." That was why she had to glean until the evening — something she would not have had to do if she had gleaned and taken from what Boaz had prepared for her. The question, then, is why was she now willing to take that which Boaz offered her.

On the verse "He said, 'Let it not be known that the woman came to the threshing floor'" (3:14), *Ruth Rabbah* (7:1) asks, "To whom did he say this? . . . R' Chunya and R' Yirmiyahu said in the name of R' Shmuel bar Yitzchak: 'That entire night Boaz lay stretched out on his face in prayer and said, "Lord of the Universe! You know that I did not touch her. May it be Your will that it should not be known that the woman came to the threshing floor, so that the Name of Heaven not be profaned." ' " Indeed, the reason why we are not told that Boaz arose that morning is because that whole night he went sleepless, for he wept and pleaded to Hashem that there should not be a profanation of Hashem's Name through him.

We can see how righteous Boaz was, for even though he was afraid of a profanation of Hashem's Name, he nevertheless told Ruth, "Lie down until the morning" (3:13), in that he did not want to send her away that late at night, lest she be assaulted. Nor would it be appropriate to escort her at that time (see above on 3:13).

The next morning, being afraid of profaning Hashem's Name, Boaz gave her the measures of grain as *tzedakah,* with the hope that the *mitzvah* of *tzedakah* would protect them from such a profanation. Indeed, we are told (*Sotah* 21) that performing a *mitzvah* protects one. Ruth, on her part, agreed to take it so that she might be a *shaliach mitzvah* (a person sent on a *mitzvah* errand) to bring the grain to her mother-in-law, and this *mitzvah* would protect her and Boaz from a profanation of Hashem's Name.

Rashi states that he hinted to her that she would give birth to a son (i.e., *Mashiach*) who would be blessed with six outstanding attributes *(Yeshayahu* 11:2), "a spirit of wisdom and understanding, a spirit of counsel and strength, a spirit of knowledge and fear of Hashem."

It would appear that he hinted this to her after he saw her acting regally, in that one of the symbols of authority of a king is that he has the power to destroy ("*poreitz*") fences, and no one has the right to protest (*Pesachim* 110b). Even though the first time he had seen her he had seen how very modest she was,[1] here he saw conduct which was the exact opposite of modesty, in that she had come to lie down next to him and had "destroyed" the limits of modesty. Boaz thus realized that what she was doing was for the sake of Heaven, to aid the soul of her dead husband — behavior that would have been appropriate for his ancestor Peretz. In this regard, we are told in *Yevamos* 76b that when Shaul asked about the ancestry of David, he said, "If you are from Peretz, you will be the king, because a king has the power to destroy ("*poreitz*") fences, and no one has the right to protest."

Then, when Boaz saw this attribute in Ruth, he understood that the monarchy of the House of David would be descended from Ruth, and that from her would come the *Mashiach,* who would destroy all the fences of the world in terms of the way it had been run until then, until (*Yeshayahu* 25:8), "He will eliminate death forever, and my Lord Hashem/Elokim will erase tears from all faces; He will remove the shame of His nation from upon the entire earth." Upon seeing this Boaz then gave her the six measures as a sign of the eventual advent of the *Mashiach.*

וַיָּמָד שֵׁשׁ שְׂעֹרִים — He measured out six measures of barley.

Rashi states that he hinted to her that she would give birth to a son (i.e., *Mashiach*) who would be blessed with six outstanding attributes *(Yeshayahu* 11:2), "a spirit of wisdom and understanding, a spirit of counsel and strength, a spirit of knowledge and fear of Hashem." This list, of course, hints at the fact that she would be the Mother of Royalty of the Jewish people. The Brisker Rav notes that this was the blessing of the elders (*Ruth* 4:11), "Like Rachel and like Leah, both of whom built up the House of Israel." Just as there is a class of our Mothers, so too is there a class of the Mother of the Monarchy, as it states (*I Melachim* 2:19), "He placed a chair for the king's (i.e., Shlomo's) mother," that being Ruth. The

1. See *Rashi* on 2:5, where *Rashi* asks: "Was it then Boaz's way to ask about women? [The reason he did so was] that he saw in her *tznius* and wisdom; she would glean two stalks but not three; she would glean standing stalks while standing and lying stalks while seated, in order not to uncover herself."

reason Ruth merited becoming the Mother of Royalty was because she bore the burden with Naomi to find her a place to rest and a living, which is the king's duty — as we see in *Berachos* 3a where David HaMelech's day is described: "As soon as dawn arose, the Sages of Israel would come in to him and would say, 'Our master, the king, your people Israel need sustenance,' " etc. As a payment of "measure for measure," she was rewarded with the monarchy.

וַיָּמָד שֵׁשׁ שְׂעֹרִים וַיָּשֶׁת עָלֶיהָ — He measured out six barleys, and set it upon her.

Rashi here states that it is impossible to say that this was six *se'ahs* (a *se'ah* is a unit of dry measure), because it would not be normal for a woman to carry so heavy a load, but rather this was six stalks of barley. Boaz hinted to Ruth that in the future she would have descendants who would be blessed with six outstanding attributes *(Yeshayahu* 11:2): "a spirit of wisdom and understanding, a spirit of counsel and strength, a spirit of knowledge and fear of Hashem."

One can explain that what forces *Rashi* to explain the simple text in terms of *remez* (an indirect allusion) is because *Rashi* found difficulty with the verse (3:17): "She said, 'He gave me these six barleys for he said to me, "Do not go empty-handed to your mother-in-law." ' " Now, where do we find Boaz saying anything like that? Rather, as he hinted to her that in the future she would have a descendant who would be blessed with six outstanding attributes, her comment about not coming empty-handed to her mother-in-law related to these attributes, because Naomi's intention in sending Ruth to the threshing floor was that she would have a descendant who would become the Redeemer of Israel. Thus, Boaz sent Ruth to her mother-in-law to show her by these six stalks of barley that her heart's desire would be fulfilled, and that Ruth had not come back empty-handed to Naomi. Thus, when Naomi asked Ruth (3:16), "Who are you my daughter?" Ruth answered that Boaz had sent these six stalks of barley to show that Naomi's wishes would be fulfilled.

וַיָּמָד שֵׁשׁ שְׂעֹרִים וַיָּשֶׁת עָלֶיהָ וַיָּבֹא הָעִיר — He measured out six barleys, and set it upon her; then he went into the city.

The Midrash (7:2) states, "R' Yehudah ben R' Shimon says: As a reward for 'He measured out six barleys, and set it upon her,' he merited that six righteous men would arise from him, and each of these would have six outstanding attributes. The six men were David, Chizkiyahu, Yoshiyahu, Chananiyah, Mishael, and Azaryah."

Shem MiShmuel (*Shavuos* 5670) writes that Boaz, who gave Ruth six stalks of barley out of the goodness of his heart, was rewarded by having six *tzaddikim* (righteous men) descend from her. As explained by *Ari,* the

ג/יז־יח אֶל־חֲמוֹתָהּ וַתֹּאמֶר מִי־אַתְּ בִּתִּי וַתַּגֶּד־לָהּ אֵת
יז כָּל־אֲשֶׁר עָשָׂה־לָהּ הָאִישׁ: וַתֹּאמֶר שֵׁשׁ־
הַשְּׂעֹרִים הָאֵלֶּה נָתַן לִי כִּי אָמַר [°אֵלַי קרי ולא כתיב]
יח אַל־תָּבוֹאִי רֵיקָם אֶל־חֲמוֹתֵךְ: וַתֹּאמֶר

---

name "Boaz" is "*bo oz* — in him is strength," referring to these six righteous men. Even though when Boaz gave her the barley he did not even know if he would marry her, because he was still unsure whether the redeemer would wish to marry her, yet in spite of that uncertainty he granted her the privilege of having David and the *Mashiach* descend from her.

Shem MiShmuel explains there that Boaz did what he did because he knew that it is better for the monarchy to have come from Ammon and Moab, because if all the Jews are together as one whole it is impossible for one to assume a leadership role over the others, just like in the human body no single organ can be the ruler of the others. That was why the monarchy had to come from a foreign nation. Moab was chosen because of its characteristic of haughtiness, as we see in (*Yeshayahu* 16:6), "We have heard of Moab's pride — exceedingly proud." Thus, David's soul had a part within it of Moab's pride and it was his task to remove that pride from within its negative setting and to cause it to become holy. Thus David would be proud and would take the leadership helm for the sake of Heaven.

Shem MiShmuel concludes by saying that it was an extremely righteous act on the part of Boaz, who was totally unconcerned about himself, even though this could mean that he would not be the founder of the monarchical dynasty and the monarchy would come out of a different person, if this would be the best way. Indeed, from this act itself the House of David was based, for David was always willing to nullify himself where it was important for the Jewish people, as we see throughout *Tehillim.*

We can bring proof as to the pride of Moab, for it states in *Vayeira* (*Bereishis* 19:31), that after S'dom was eradicated, "The older one [Lot's daughter, from whom came Moab] said to the younger, 'Our father is old, and there is no man in the land to marry us in the usual manner.' " On this, *Rashi* quotes *Bereishis Rabbah* (51:8) which states that Lot's daughters believed that, just as with the Flood, everyone had been destroyed. It was indeed conceit on their part to think that they had been spared while Avraham had perished. And it was this conceit which brought about the birth of Moab, from which would eventually come the House of David and the *Mashiach.*

[16] *She came to her mother-in-law who said, "Who are you, my daughter?" So she told her all that the man had done for her,* [17] *and she said, "He gave me these six measures of barley for he said to me, 'Do not go empty-handed to your mother-in-law.' "*

The Midrash notes that the older one stated (*Bereishis* 19:32), "We will preserve the seed of our father" rather than stating "We will preserve a child of our father," where "seed" implies descendants from a different source as well, namely that of the *Mashiach.* On this *Matnos Kehunah* states that when she referred to "seed," "*zera*" in Hebrew, it was an allusion to "*zeirus,*" namely foreignness, in that the *Mashiach* will come from an illicit family relationship, namely that of Moab.

Another way this can be explained is to say that Boaz saw in Ruth unbelievable generosity, in that she was willing to totally forgo any benefit to herself in order to have her mother-in-law benefit. That was why Boaz gave her the great privilege that six great men would be descended from her. Thus, he said to her (3:10), "Be blessed of Hashem, my daughter; you have made your latest act of kindness greater than the first, in that you have not gone after the younger men, be they poor or rich." For all of her intentions were for the good of Naomi and of Machlon, her deceased husband, to help his soul. It is that quality which is needed for someone to be king of Israel — to sacrifice one's own good for that of the whole nation, as David said to Hashem (see *Berachos* 4a), "Lord of the Universe! Am I not pious? All the kings of East and West sit in their glory among their company, while my hands are soiled with blood and with fetus and placenta to permit a woman to her husband" (i.e., David would issue *halachic* rulings in cases such as these). As Boaz saw this attribute in Ruth, he realized that it was fitting and proper for such great men to be descended from her, and they would acquire this attribute from her.

Now that Boaz had performed this very saintly act in totally ignoring his own personal desire, in order to have the monarchical dynasty come about in the best possible manner for the Jewish people, he acted in exactly the same way that Ruth had acted, and for that he merited his true union with her. Indeed, we are told in *Sotah* 2a that when a man marries for a second time, his second wife is paired to him based on his deeds, and here the deeds of both Ruth and Boaz were equal, in that they were both willing to sacrifice their own needs for the benefit of another. That is why both merited having the House of David and of the *Mashiach* descend from them.

ד/א שְׁבִי בִתִּי עַד אֲשֶׁר תֵּדְעִין אֵיךְ יִפֹּל דָּבָר כִּי לֹא יִשְׁקֹט
א הָאִישׁ כִּי אִם־כִּלָּה הַדָּבָר הַיּוֹם׃ וּבֹעַז עָלָה
הַשַּׁעַר וַיֵּשֶׁב שָׁם וְהִנֵּה הַגֹּאֵל עֹבֵר אֲשֶׁר דִּבֶּר־בֹּעַז
וַיֹּאמֶר סוּרָה שְׁבָה־פֹּה פְּלֹנִי אַלְמֹנִי וַיָּסַר וַיֵּשֵׁב׃

---

18. וַתֹּאמֶר שְׁבִי בִתִּי עַד אֲשֶׁר תֵּדְעִין אֵיךְ יִפֹּל דָּבָר — She said, "Sit [patiently], my daughter, until you know how the matter will turn out."

In other words, Naomi wanted Ruth to continue to act like a poor woman who was gathering grain in others' fields. We find a similar case with Mordechai — for even though he saw signs of deliverance beginning, in that Haman had clothed him in the king's clothes and had led him through the streets while calling before him (*Esther* 6:9), "This is what shall be done for the man whom the king desires to honor" — nevertheless we are told (*Esther* 6:12): "Mordechai returned to the king's gate," upon which *Rashi* comments, "to his sackcloth and fasting," because when is it time to say (*Tehillim* 13:6), "I will sing to Hashem"? It is only *after* "He has dealt kindly with me." Until the kindness had been completed, Ruth felt she had to act humbly, and as a result Hashem would take pity on her.

Naomi, though, said to her, "Sit [patiently], my daughter" and do not go out to glean, unlike the case of Mordechai, where the trouble was one which affected all of the Jewish people, and he thus needed to continue in his efforts to awaken Hashem's pity. In Ruth's case, on the other hand, the problem was one that affected only her personally, and once Naomi saw that matters were progressing properly, she had to act with trust in Hashem and was not to go out to glean. It is also commonly said in the name of R' Yisrael Salanter that in questions concerning oneself one must act with full *bitachon* (trust) in Hashem, but when it comes to the needs of others one must act like a heretic and do everything possible to help the other and not rely on Hashem to help him.[1]

IV

1. וּבֹעַז עָלָה הַשַּׁעַר וַיֵּשֶׁב שָׁם וְהִנֵּה הַגֹּאֵל עֹבֵר אֲשֶׁר דִּבֶּר בֹּעַז — Boaz, meanwhile, had gone up to the gate, and sat down there. Just then, the redeemer of whom Boaz had spoken passed by.

Meishiv Nefesh, by *Bach,* notes that the verse should have stated "*va'ya'al*

---

1. It said in the name of the Kotzker Rebbe that all one's attributes were created in order to serve Hashem, and the attribute of heresy was created so that one should attempt to help others, for in such a case one may not say, "Hashem will help," but must work with all one's strength to help others.

[18] *She said, "Sit [patiently], my daughter, until you know how the matter will turn out, for the man will not rest unless he settles the matter today."*

[1] ***B**oaz, meanwhile, had gone up to the gate, and sat down there. Just then, the redeemer of whom Boaz had spoken passed by. He said, "Come over, sit down here, Ploni Almoni," and he came over and sat down.*

Boaz" — the customary way of writing — rather than "*u'Boaz alah,*" as we find in our text, even though both mean the same thing, namely that Boaz went up. One can also ask why Boaz, instead of sitting there, did not go out to look for *Ploni Almoni,* the closer redeemer, in order to know if he would be interested in being the redeemer or not. The *Targum* explains that Boaz was the head of the *Sanhedrin* and was sitting in judgment of any cases that might be brought to it each day. However, as he had already sworn to Ruth that he would take care of the matter and Naomi had said (3:18), "The man will not rest unless he settles the matter today," why didn't Boaz seek out the redeemer immediately?

So too do we need to explain why we do not find that Boaz prayed to Hashem to help him succeed in his mission, for we know that Hashem desires greatly the prayers of the *tzaddikim* (see *Yevamos* 64). Thus, we see that even though Hashem had promised Avraham a wife for Yitzchak — as stated in *Bereishis Rabbah* 57:3, and as quoted by *Rashi* on *Bereishis* 22:20,23, "It came to pass after these things, that Avraham was told, saying . . . Besuel begot Rivkah," Avraham nevertheless prayed and said (*Bereishis* 24:7), "Hashem, God of heaven, Who took me from the house of my father and from the land of my birth . . . you will take a wife for my son from there." Similarly, we have the prayer of Eliezer, Avraham's servant, when he came to Charan, prayed in the merit of Avraham (24:12). Yet here we do not seen any prayer by Boaz that his mission should be successful and that he should be the forefather of the monarchy.

It would appear that since Hashem informed Boaz that the monarchy of the House of David and that of the entire Kingdom of Yehudah would come out of Ruth — as we see on the verse, "He measured out six measures of barley" (3:15), on which *Rashi* states that he hinted to her that she would give birth to a son (i.e., *Mashiach*) who would be blessed with six outstanding attributes — Boaz knew that there was no possibility here of any different choice, and everything was going to happen exactly as Hashem wanted regardless of any human action. Thus Boaz was prevented from praying, because prayer can only be used to try to change matters over which one has discretion (see *Meshech Chochmah,* the end of *Parshas Noach*). So was he prevented from making any effort of any kind. Thus, on the words, "Just then, the redeemer of whom Boaz had spoken passed by" (4:1), our Sages tell us that "Even if he had been at the end of the earth the Holy One, Blessed is He, would have made him fly and brought him there." That is why we are told, "Boaz, meanwhile, had gone up to the gate, and sat down there" (4:1), in that he had no choice, and that neither any prayer nor any effort on his part would make any difference. He understood that at this juncture it was a situation of (*Shemos* 14:13), "Stand fast and see the salvation of Hashem that He will perform for you today," for Hashem had determined the exact course of the actions which would take place.

The source of our words above is *Makkos* 23b: "R' Elazar said: The Holy Spirit appeared in three places: in the *beis din* of Shem, in the *beis din* of Shmuel at Ramah, and in the *beis din* of Shlomo. In the *beis din* of Shem, as it states (*Bereishis* 38:26), 'She is right; it is from me.' How, then, did [Yehudah] know this was indeed so? A *bas kol* (a voice from On High) came forth and said, 'This came from Me.'" On this, *Rashi* comments, "These concealed events came from Me. Yehudah was a king and [Tamar] merited having kings descended from her because she had been modest in her father-in-law's house. I have therefore issued a decree that the two of them should have offspring." It would appear that the decree of "These concealed events came from Me" refers to all the events governing the advent of the *Mashiach* and the End of Days, and that the marriage of Boaz and Ruth was also included in that same decree.

וּבֹעַז עָלָה הַשַּׁעַר וַיֵּשֶׁב שָׁם — Boaz, meanwhile, had gone up to the gate, and sat down there.

Meishiv Nefesh, by *Bach,* notes that the verse should have stated "*va'ya'al Boaz*" — the customary way of writing — rather than "*u'Boaz alah,*" as we find in our text, even though both mean the same thing, namely that Boaz went up. It appears that the reason the verse begins with the name "Boaz" is that he was "*ba oz*" — one who girded himself with strength. In other words, as soon as he promised Ruth that he would seek to marry her, he girded himself with the strength of holiness, and with that he went up to the gate. After all, it is man's responsibility to serve Hashem and to choose to do good deeds, and when a person chooses to do a good deed in the proper way and with the proper intent, he is granted a spirit from on High to help him to carry out his good deed.

If one reads what *Chovas HaLevavos* states in *Sha'ar HaBitachon* Ch. 4, one will see that man only has the choice and power of decision to decide to do a certain thing, but he has no choice about the actual carrying out of that decision, and the actual execution of any decision is ordained in Heaven. As *Chovas HaLevavos* puts it: "The actual deed or sin will not be executed by the person until three factors are involved: first, the person's decision; second, his conscience and his willingness to do as decided; and third, the actual action taken by his body, which executes it." *Chovas HaLevavos* adds that "the Creator, may He be blessed, left in our power the choice of serving Him or rebelling against Him, as it states (*Devarim* 30:19, 'You shall choose life,' but did not give us the power to perform the good deed or sin. Rather, there are factors which are outside the person which on some occasions permit this and on other occasions prevent it." Thus we see from *Chovas HaLevavos* that man's choice is limited to what he wants to do, in that he chooses the way he wants to lead his life, either through serving Hashem or *chas veshalom* through sinning. Each person attempts to do that which he has chosen, but since in the final analysis the actual execution of his actions is dictated by Heaven and the person has no control of his deeds, there is a separate reckoning as to whether he will be given the opportunity to carry out that which he sought, whether for the good or *chas veshalom* for the bad.

Chovas HaLevavos concludes by stating that if the circumstances are such that the person was able to carry out the good deed which he had planned to do, he will receive the largest reward for having chosen to do the deed and for actually having carried it out. If, however, his body is prevented from carrying out the good deed he had planned, he will only receive a reward for his choice.[1] Now we can understand why the verse stated "*u'Boaz alah*" rather than "*va'ya'al Boaz,*" for once Boaz chose the good path, Heaven carried it out.

וַיֵּשֶׁב שָׁם וְהִנֵּה הַגֹּאֵל עֹבֵר אֲשֶׁר דִּבֶּר בֹּעַז — [He] sat down there. Just then, the redeemer of whom Boaz had spoken passed by.

The *Targum* explains that Boaz was the head of the *Sanhedrin* and was sitting in judgment of any cases that would be brought to it. One can ask why Boaz, instead of sitting there, did not go out to look for *Ploni Almoni,* the closer redeemer, in order to know if he would be interested in being the redeemer or not. Why, then, did Boaz just sit there as if this day was the same as every other day?

The answer to this is to be found in accordance with what we noted in *Chovas HaLevavos* above, for the carrying out of Boaz's wishes was dependent on Heaven, while no person has any control over what will actually happen. In regard to whether the person will be permitted to carry out that which he wishes to do, that depends on an entirely different

1. See the *Kovetz Sichos* of my grandfather, R' Yechezkel Levenstein, 5719, *Parshas Vayeishev.*

ב וַיִּקַּח עֲשָׂרָה אֲנָשִׁים מִזִּקְנֵי הָעִיר וַיֹּאמֶר שְׁבוּ־פֹה
ג וַיֵּשֵׁבוּ׃ וַיֹּאמֶר לַגֹּאֵל חֶלְקַת הַשָּׂדֶה אֲשֶׁר
לְאָחִינוּ לֶאֱלִימֶלֶךְ מָכְרָה נָעֳמִי הַשָּׁבָה מִשְּׂדֵה
ד מוֹאָב׃ וַאֲנִי אָמַרְתִּי אֶגְלֶה אָזְנְךָ לֵאמֹר קְנֵה
נֶגֶד הַיֹּשְׁבִים וְנֶגֶד זִקְנֵי עַמִּי אִם־תִּגְאַל גְּאָל
וְאִם־לֹא יִגְאַל הַגִּידָה לִּי °ואדע [°וְאֵדְעָה ק׳]

---

reckoning. Boaz was thus sitting in judgment as on any other day, in order to help others and to thereby increase his own merits. So too was he involved in the *mitzvah* of *bitachon* (faith in Hashem) with the full belief that Hashem would find a redeemer for Ruth. As *Maharal* (*Nesivos Olam* Ch. 1) states, a person who has full *bitachon* in Hashem believes with all his heart that everything is for the best, as we see with R' Akiva and with Nachum Ish Gamzu, and as they had full *bitachon* that Hashem would save them, Hashem had to save them.

And it was through the *bitachon* of Boaz that the redeemer passed by right then, and, as the Midrash (7:7) tells us, "R' Shmuel bar Nachmani said: Even if he had been at the end of the earth the Holy One, Blessed is He, would have made him fly and brought him there so that that *tzaddik* (i.e., Boaz) would not have to sit and be distressed as he waited." Thus the redeemer was there immediately in order to conclude the issue.

וַיֹּאמֶר סוּרָה שְׁבָה פֹּה פְּלֹנִי אַלְמֹנִי — He said, "Come over, sit down here, Ploni Almoni."

Rashi notes that the reason the man's name is not mentioned, but instead the verse uses the derogatory "Ploni Almoni" (something like "Mr. So-and-So") is because the man refused to be the redeemer. I find it hard to understand that comment, because at the time that Boaz asked him to sit down he was still a righteous person, and only later (in verse 6) are we told, "I cannot redeem it for myself, lest I imperil my own inheritance." There, in fact, he is mentioned with the honorable title of "the redeemer." Why then here, before he said anything, is he referred to as "Ploni Almoni," an anonymous person without name and without Torah learning?

We are told in *Pesachim* 66b: "R' Mani bar Pattish said: One who becomes angry, even if in Heaven greatness had been decreed for him, is brought down. From where do we know this? From Eliav (the oldest of David's brothers), where it states (*I Shmuel* 17:28), 'Eliav became angry

[2] He then took ten men of the elders of the city, and said,
"Sit here," and they sat down.
[3] Then he said to the redeemer, "The parcel of land
which belonged to our brother, Elimelech, is being offered
for sale by Naomi who has returned from the fields of
Moab. [4] I resolved that I should inform you to this effect:
Buy it in the presence of those sitting here and in the
presence of the elders of my people. If you are willing to
redeem, redeem! But if it will not be redeemed, tell me,

---

with David' for leaving his sheep. When Shmuel came to anoint one of Yishai's sons, in each case Shmuel said, 'Hashem has not chosen this one either,' but in the case of Eliav we are told that Hashem told Shmuel, 'Do not look at his appearance or at his tall stature, for I have rejected him.' " From the fact that Eliav was rejected, we can see that before that he had been the chosen one. *Rashi* there (beginning with "*lo bachar*") states that even though Shmuel's anointing preceded Eliav's angry outburst, there is no mention anywhere of any other fault of Eliav's, and as it was apparent to Hashem that he had a temper, Hashem rejected him. *Rashash* asks how *Rashi* can say this, when we have a principle that a person is only judged on his deeds. Indeed, we see in *Rosh Hashanah* 16b that this is true even though Hashem knows what will occur in the future, as we find in the case of Yishmael.[1]

I once heard R' Chaim Shmulevitz say that we are forced to state that Eliav had a tendency to become angry, although this only became apparent when they went to war. Since he had that tendency, he was rejected. Along these same lines, we can say that the redeemer already had implanted in him that he would not redeem Ruth, except that this tendency had not become apparent yet, and since he already had the tendency of not helping Naomi and Machlon the verse immediately refers to him as Ploni Almoni. This in accordance with what *Chovas HaLevavos* wrote, as mentioned before, that he had already chosen not to do the good deed which Boaz wanted to ask him to do, and it was for that decision that he was punished. The evil action which he now performed was based on an evil decision which he had reached earlier.

---

1. R' Yitzchak said: A person is judged only for his action of that moment, as it is stated regarding Yishmael, "For God has heeded the cry of the youth as he is there." Even though in the future his descendants would kill the Jews, God judged him only as of that moment.

4. וְאֵדְעָה כִּי אֵין זוּלָתְךָ לִגְאוֹל וְאָנֹכִי אַחֲרֶיךָ — "That I may know; for there is no one else to redeem it but you, and I am after you."

Rashi states that there was no one closer to be the redeemer. Chasam Sofer (*Derashos* 303) explains that Boaz hinted to the redeemer that whether the redeemer wanted to or not, Boaz would ultimately marry her, and that if the redeemer did indeed marry Ruth at this time, this would simply hasten the redeemer's death, so that Boaz would then be free to marry her. That is what is meant by, "and I am after you."[1] The words of Chasam Sofer need to be explained, for how could Boaz marry her after the death of the redeemer, for at that point she would be considered to be a "*katlanis*" (a "murderous woman") as by then she would have had two of her husbands die while married to her. And, as stated in *Yevamos* 64, a *katlanis* may not be married. One can possibly say that as Machlon died before Ruth became Jewish, that death was not counted toward making her a *katlanis,* for a person who converts to Judaism is considered to be like a newborn infant. Even though in regard to the law of *peru u'revu* ("be fruitful and multiply") a convert is not considered like a newborn infant and according to R' Yochanan (*Yevamos* 62) children that he had before his conversion are considered sufficient in terms of fulfilling the commandment to be fruitful and multiply, the reason for this is that non-Jews, too, are included in "be fruitful and multiply." As far as *katlanis,* though, is concerned, since a convert is considered to be like a newborn infant, a woman is not considered to be a *katlanis* until she has had two husbands die on her after her conversion.

It also occurred to me that *Maharsha* on *Yevamos* 77 states that the redemption here, in the case of Ruth, was in accordance with the law of *yibum* (levirate marriage) and *Maharsha* bases himself on what *Ramban* in his Torah commentary writes in regard to Yehudah and Tamar. *Ramban* thus states that "the ancient wise men of Israel made this apply whenever anyone inherits any property, wherever there is no prohibition in terms of marriage, and they referred to this as 'redemption.' This was the case with Boaz and Naomi and her women neighbors."[2]

In the writings of R' Yitzchak Ze'ev HaLevi Soloveitchik, the Brisker Rav, on the Torah, he asks: Yehudah said to Tamar his daughter-in-law

1. Similarly, in *Bava Metzia* 12b, we are told that Rav Chisda's daughter was sitting with her father and with Rava and Rami bar Chama. Her father asked her, 'Which one would you like to marry?" and she answered, "Both." Rava then said, "And I want to be the later one."

2. See 4:14.

that I may know; for there is no one else to redeem it but you, and I am after you." And he said, "I am willing to redeem."

(*Bereishis* 38:11), "Remain a widow in your father's house until my son Shelah grows up," for he thought, "Lest he also die like his brothers." Now, the second part seems to contradict the first and to say that Tamar would not be given to Shelah. The Brisker Rav explains that Tamar really was considered to be a *katlanis,* because two of her husbands had died. However, as we have a rule that (*Koheles* 8:5), "He who obeys the commandment will know no evil" and the *mitzvah* of *yibum* was involved, the rule of *katlanis* did not concern him. Yehudah thus told Tamar to wait until Shelah grew up and the rule of "He who obeys the commandment will know no evil" would apply to him, and he would be obligated to perform *yibum.* On the other hand, as long as he was a minor and there was no obligation on him to perform *yibum,* Tamar could not be given to Shelah as she was a *katlanis.* One can say the same thing in regard to Ruth, in that even though she would be considered a *katlanis,* Boaz would have been permitted to marry her because of the *mitzvah* of *yibum,* for "He who obeys the commandment will know no evil."

I also saw that *Berachos HaMa'ayan* wanted to deduce from the words of *Ramban* that at the time of Yehudah and Tamar there was no obligation yet of *yibum,* but it was merely a custom then. He deduces this from the fact that *Ramban* writes that "the ancient wise men of Israel made this apply . . ." He then brings the *Maharsha* in *Yevamos,* from which it is clear that this was obligatory, because *Maharsha* writes that the *mitzvah* of *yibum* cancels the prohibition of (*Devarim* 23:4), "An Ammonite or Moabite shall not enter the congregation of Hashem." From this we see that there is a clear obligation of *yibum.* And we find the same in what the Brisker Rav wrote when he stated that only an adult may perform *yibum* but not a minor where the woman is a *katlanis,* because of "He who obeys the commandment will know no evil." Even though the *halachah* is that a minor male may perform *yibum* with an adult female and the act is valid (see *Yevamos* 96), nevertheless there is no obligation for him to perform *yibum* until he becomes an adult. That is why "He who obeys the commandment will know no evil" would not apply if a minor performs *yibum* with a *katlanis.* From this, we see that the Brisker Rav also understood *Ramban* to mean that there was an obligation and *mitzvah* of *yibum,* and not only a custom to perform it.

ה אֶגְאָֽל׃ וַיֹּ֣אמֶר בֹּ֔עַז בְּיוֹם־קְנוֹתְךָ֥ הַשָּׂדֶ֖ה מִיַּ֣ד נָעֳמִ֑י
וּ֠מֵאֵת ר֨וּת הַמּוֹאֲבִיָּ֤ה אֵֽשֶׁת־הַמֵּת֙ °קניתי [°קָנִ֔יתָ ק׳]
ו לְהָקִ֥ים שֵׁם־הַמֵּ֖ת עַל־נַחֲלָתֽוֹ׃ וַיֹּ֣אמֶר הַגֹּאֵ֗ל לֹ֤א
אוּכַל֙ °לגאול־ [°לִגְאָל־ ק׳] לִ֔י פֶּן־אַשְׁחִ֖ית אֶת־
נַחֲלָתִ֑י גְּאַל־לְךָ֤ אַתָּה֙ אֶת־גְּאֻלָּתִ֔י כִּ֥י לֹא־אוּכַ֖ל

---

5. וַיֹּאמֶר בֹּעַז בְּיוֹם קְנוֹתְךָ הַשָּׂדֶה מִיַּד נָעֳמִי וּמֵאֵת רוּת הַמּוֹאֲבִיָּה אֵשֶׁת הַמֵּת — Then Boaz said, "The day you buy the field from Naomi, you must also buy it from Ruth the Moabite, wife of the deceased."

We need to explain what right Ruth had in the fields of Elimelech. We can understand that Naomi had a right to them, even though women do not inherit their husbands, because this right had no doubt been granted to her in her *kesubah.* Ruth, on the other hand, as can be seen from the simple meaning of the text and from the Midrash, had not been converted before she married Machlon, so that there was no *halachic* marriage tie between them and she accordingly should not have had a *kesubah.* Why, then, did Ruth have any rights to Elimelech's fields?

Ruth Rabbah (2:14), on the verse (1:8), "May Hashem deal kindly with you, as you have dealt kindly with the dead and with me," states that "you have dealt kindly with the dead" refers to how the two daughters-in-law dealt with the shrouds of their husbands, while "and with me" refers to how they relinquished their *kesubah* rights. *Matnos Kehunah* explains that Naomi might have been the guarantor for Ruth's *kesubah,* because they were in a distant land and neither Machlon nor Kilion had any possessions upon which they could rely. Thus we see clearly from this that Machlon and Kilion were obligated by a *kesubah,* and their lands were mortgaged to Ruth's *kesubah.* We still need to understand this issue, because there seems to be no such thing as a *kesubah* for a non-Jewish woman.

One can answer this based on that which we see in *Parshas Lech Lecha* (*Bereishis* 25:2), "But to the concubine-children who were Avraham's, Avraham gave gifts." *Rashi* there states that the difference between wives and concubines is that wives have a *kesubah* while concubines do not. Thus already in Avraham's day there was a *kesubah.* So too do we find that on the verse (ibid. 48:9), "And Yosef said to his father, 'They are my sons whom God has given me here,' " *Rashi* comments that Yosef showed his father his *eirusin* (marriage) contract and his *kesubah.* Thus we see that there was a *kesubah* even with a non-Jewish woman. We can thus say that what Machlon and Kilion did when they married their non-Jewish wives was to obligate themselves through a *kesubah,* and these fields were mortgaged to Ruth in terms of her *kesubah.*

[5] *Then Boaz said, "The day you buy the field from Naomi, you must also buy it from Ruth the Moabite, wife of the deceased, to perpetuate the name of the deceased on his inheritance."* [6] *The redeemer said, "I cannot redeem it for myself, lest I imperil my own inheritance. Take over my redemption responsibility on yourself for I am unable to redeem."*

---

6. וַיֹּאמֶר הַגֹּאֵל לֹא אוּכַל לִגְאָל־לִי פֶּן־אַשְׁחִית אֶת־נַחֲלָתִי גְּאַל־לְךָ אַתָּה אֶת־גְּאֻלָּתִי כִּי לֹא־אוּכַל לִגְאֹל — The redeemer said, "I cannot redeem it for myself, lest I imperil my own inheritance. Take over my redemption responsibility on yourself for I am unable to redeem."

Rashi says on "lest I imperil my own inheritance," that "inheritance" refers to his children, because by redeeming he might cast a blot on his children, in terms of (*Devarim* 23:4), "An Ammonite or Moabite shall not enter the congregation of Hashem," and in this the redeemer erred, because the prohibition is against the Ammonite males but not the females.

Chasam Sofer in his *Derashos* (303) asks how the redeemer could have said, "Take over my redemption responsibility on yourself for I am unable to redeem." If the redeemer believed that one was forbidden to marry a Moabite woman, how could he tell Boaz to do so? Furthermore, if the redeemer thought this was forbidden, why was he concerned only about his children, and not about himself as well?

The Brisker Rav comments on *Yevamos* 76b, which discusses how we know that Ammonites and Moabites are forbidden for all generations. R' Yochanan says we deduce this from a verse (*I Shmuel* 17:55), "When Shaul had seen David going forth towards the Philistine, he said to Avner, the minister of the army, 'Avner, whose son is this lad?' And Avner replied, 'By your life, O king, I do not know.' " On this, the *gemara* comments: "Doeg the Edomite then said to him, 'Instead of asking about whether he is fit to be king or not, you should inquire whether he is even fit to enter the congregation, for he is descended from Ruth the Moabite.' Avner said to him, 'We have learned: An Ammonite male but not an Ammonite female' . . . Doeg answered, 'Then [following your logic] only a male *mamzer* (the child of an incestuous or adulterous union) should be forbidden, but not a female *mamzer*!' [Avner] remained silent . . . [Shaul] said to him, 'You have forgotten the *halachah.* Go and ask in the *beis midrash* . . .' Doeg asked him all these questions and he remained silent. [Doeg] then wanted to make a public announcement against [David]. Immediately there was the incident of (*II Shmuel* 17:25), 'Amasa was the son of a man named Yisra the Israelite, who consorted with Avigayil

ד/ז ז לִגְאֹל: וְזֹאת לְפָנִים בְּיִשְׂרָאֵל עַל־הַגְּאוּלָּה
וְעַל־הַתְּמוּרָה לְקַיֵּם כָּל־דָּבָר שָׁלַף אִישׁ
נַעֲלוֹ וְנָתַן לְרֵעֵהוּ וְזֹאת הַתְּעוּדָה בְּיִשְׂרָאֵל:

---

daughter of Nachas . . .' Rava said that [Amasa] girded his sword like Yishmael and said, 'Whoever does not accept this *halachah* will be stabbed by the sword. Thus I have a tradition from the *beis din* of Shmuel of Ramah: Ammonite male and not Ammonite female; Moabite male and not Moabite female.' "

In explaining this topic, the Brisker Rav said that the *halachah* had already been determined by Boaz and the elders that the rule applied to Moabite males but not females, and that was what Avner quoted. Doeg nevertheless wanted to argue with this, claiming that whatever ruling one *beis din* made may be annulled by a later *beis din,* as explained by *Rambam* (*Hilchos Mamrim* 2:1). However, since Avner told him that the deduction from the Torah is "Ammonite male and not Ammonite female," Doeg asked him a whole series of questions, until Amasa came and told him, "Thus I have a tradition from the *beis din* of Shmuel of Ramah: Ammonite male and not Ammonite female; Moabite male and not Moabite female." What he meant by "I have a tradition" was that this *halachah* was not based on interpretation, but rather was a *Halachah LeMoshe MiSinai* — a law handed down orally by Moshe from Sinai, and that being the case, one cannot argue against it.

This also explains the words of the redeemer, who said to Boaz, "I cannot redeem it for myself, lest I imperil my own inheritance." In other words, the redeemer was afraid that another *beis din* might come later and disagree with Boaz and the elders and rule that a Moabite female is also forbidden. This would then make all of his descendants forbidden to marry into the congregation of Israel, as indeed what might have happened when Doeg attempted to forbid David from being part of the congregation, until Amasa's announcement. This, then, was what the redeemer meant when he said, "lest I imperil my own inheritance" if a later *beis din* would change the ruling. At the time, though, there was no prohibition, because the ruling had been given about "Ammonite male but not Ammonite female." The mistake made by the redeemer was that he did not realize that this was a *Halachah LeMoshe MiSinai* and that no *beis din* could ever annul the ruling.

Now we can also understand the comment by the Chasam Sofer as to how the redeemer could tell Boaz to redeem rather than doing so himself and that his entire concern related to his children. We are told in *Midrash Talpi'os* ("Boaz") that at this time Boaz was already a very old man, and in

[7] *Formerly this was done in Israel in cases of redemption and exchange transactions to validate all matters: One would draw off his shoe, and give it to the other. This was the process of ratification in Israel.*

---

fact he died that very night. The redeemer thus assumed that Boaz would not have any children from Ruth, and therefore he felt that there was no reason for Boaz to fear "lest I imperil my own inheritance," whereas he felt that if he took Ruth, she might have children and they would be imperiled at a later time.

7. וְזֹאת לְפָנִים בְּיִשְׂרָאֵל עַל הַגְּאוּלָּה וְעַל הַתְּמוּרָה לְקַיֵּם כָּל דָּבָר שָׁלַף אִישׁ נַעֲלוֹ וְנָתַן לְרֵעֵהוּ — Formerly this was done in Israel in cases of redemption and exchange transactions to validate all matters: One would draw off his shoe, and give it to the other.

Rashi writes that this was an act of acquisition as we do now with a scarf rather than a shoe. The main act of the acquisition consists of giving something to the other person, like one's shoe or one's scarf, as an example. Why, then, does the verse specify that it was a shoe in this case, as we see in the next verse, "When the redeemer said to Boaz, 'Buy it for yourself,' he drew off his shoe"? Also, why does it specify that he "drew off" his shoe, when the act of acquisition takes place when one gives a shoe and not when one draws off a shoe?

Based on *Ramban* we brought above (on verse 4:4), we can understand this, because *Ramban* writes on *Bereishis* 38:8, "The ancients before the Torah knew of the great value in *yibum* (levirate marriage) with one's brother's wife, and that it was proper for a brother to take precedence in this, and after him another relative, because there would be great value in this with any relative of his family who would inherit from him . . . It would be considered extreme cruelty for a brother not to want to do this, and he would be referred to as 'the house of the loosened shoe,' for now this (*mitzvah*) had been removed from them."[1] (*Ramban* goes on, "The ancients Sages of Israel, knowing the importance of this matter, instituted in ancient times among the Jewish people that this action be taken among all those who were inheritors, i.e., those for whom there would not be any prohibition of marriage, and they referred to this as 'redemption.' ")[2]

---

1. Recanati explains this concept along Kabbalistic lines.

2. Also see the explanation of *Pnei Yerushalayim,* that by this deed they would redeem the soul of the departed one which was wandering about in another body, and that was the whole case of Boaz and the views of Naomi and her neighbors. The wise person will understand this.

In our case, then, when the man drew off his shoe, it was akin to the drawing off of the shoe that takes place during *chalitzah* (the alternate ceremony when the brother refuses to go through with *yibum*), and that is why the verse made a point of stating that he drew off the shoe, even though the act of acquisition took place in the giving of the shoe and not in the drawing off of the shoe. According to *Ramban* one can also explain the verse, "Formerly this was done in Israel," to mean that in former times in Israel the Sages instituted this action for all the inheritors. "In cases of redemption" then refers to the act of *yibum,* while "and exchange transactions" refers to the sale of property, while "one would draw off his shoe" referred to both *yibum* and *chalitzah,* while "and give it to the other" referred to the acquisition of the fields.

We can also see this in a previous verse (3:13), where Boaz said to Ruth "Stay the night, then in the morning, if he will redeem you, fine! let him redeem. But if he *does not want* ("*lo yachpotz*") to redeem you, then I will redeem you." After all, the verse could merely have stated, "If he does not redeem you, I will redeem you." Rather, there is a hint here at *chalitzah,* for in the Torah it states (*Devarim* 24:7,9), "If the man *does not want* ("*lo yachpotz*") to marry his sister-in-law . . . she shall remove his shoe from on his foot." Thus what we have hinted at over here is that the drawing off of the shoe by Boaz was like an act of *chalitzah* which the woman who was refused levirate marriage must perform to the man who refuses her.

It would also appear that when the verse states, "Formerly this was done in Israel," it is referring specifically to the tribe of Yehudah, which was specially careful to observe the *mitzvah* of *yibum.* Thus *Ramban* states, "In *Bereishis Rabbah* it is said that Yehudah was the first one to perform the *mitzvah* of *yibum,* for when he received the hidden meaning of it from his forefathers he hastened to fulfill it. Then, when the Torah came and forbade the wives of some relatives, the Holy One, Blessed is He, wished to permit the brother's wife because of *yibum.* The tribe of Yehudah were eager to fulfill this *mitzvah,* because their forefather Yehudah, the son of Yaakov, was the first one to perform it."

And the reason, possibly, why Yehudah was more eager than the other tribes to perform this *mitzvah* was because the tribe of Yehudah had been chosen to be the fighters for the Jewish people, as it states in *Shoftim* (1:1-2), "The Children of Israel inquired of Hashem, saying, 'Who should go up for us first against the Canaanite to wage war against him?' Hashem said, 'Yehudah should go up.' " So too did David say (*II Shmuel* 1:18), "To

[8] *When the redeemer said to Boaz, "Buy it for yourself," he drew off his shoe.*

---

teach the children of Yehudah the archer's bow, behold this is written in the book of righteousness. "

Meshech Chochmah on *Lech Lecha* notes that after Avraham fought and vanquished the four kings, he said (*Bereishis* 14:23), "If so much as a thread to a bootstrap." On this *Midrash Rabbah* states that as a reward for his declaration, Hashem gave Avraham the *mitzvah* of *yibum* and of *chalitzah,* as we see in the verse, "she shall remove his shoe." Thus the main part of the *mitzvah* of *chalitzah* is the untying of the shoelace. From this we see that Avraham was given the *mitzvah* of *yibum* as a result of the war against the four kings. That was why Yehudah, the tribe which would in the future be warriors for Israel, was so careful with the *mitzvah* of *yibum* and of *chalitzah.*

8. וַיֹּאמֶר הַגֹּאֵל לְבֹעַז קְנֵה לָךְ וַיִּשְׁלֹף נַעֲלוֹ — When the redeemer said to Boaz, "Buy it for yourself," he drew off his shoe.

Even though the redeemer had already said, "I cannot redeem it for myself, lest I imperil my own inheritance. Take over my redemption responsibility on yourself for I am unable to redeem," (4:6) he now repeated, "Buy it for yourself" as he drew off the shoe, for as we explained above, the drawing off of the shoe was not only an act of *kinyan* (acquisition) but also an act like that of *chalitzah.* That is why the verse states that he drew off his shoe and does not state that he drew off his shoe and gave it to him, which would have been only an act of *kinyan.* Thus *Rambam* rules (*Hilchos Yibum VeChalitzah* 4:9), that as part of the ceremony of *chalitzah,* the man has to declare, "I do not wish to take her," and afterwards she draws off his shoe. Therefore we see that saying "I do not want her" is an integral part of the *chalitzah.* That is why at that time the redeemer said, "Buy it yourself," and then he drew off the shoe.

This also explains a previous verse, "He then took ten men of the elders of the city, and said, 'Sit here,' and they sat down" (4:2), because *Rambam* (*Hilchos Yibum VeChalitzah* 4:2) writes that the judges must set aside a place where they will sit, and afterwards the woman must perform *chalitzah* in their presence, as it states (*Devarim* 25:7), "His sister-in-law shall ascend to the gate, to the elders." On this, Rava states (*Yevamos* 101b) that the judges must appoint a place. So too did Boaz choose elders, because, on the verse, "His sister-in-law shall ascend to the gate, to the elders," *Sifrei* states that this teaches us that the *beis din* for *chalitzah* must consist of elders.

ד/ט-י ט וַיֹּאמֶר בֹּעַז לַזְּקֵנִים וְכָל־הָעָם עֵדִים אַתֶּם הַיּוֹם
כִּי קָנִיתִי אֶת־כָּל־אֲשֶׁר לֶאֱלִימֶלֶךְ וְאֵת כָּל־
י אֲשֶׁר לְכִלְיוֹן וּמַחְלוֹן מִיַּד נָעֳמִי׃ וְגַם אֶת־
רוּת הַמֹּאֲבִיָּה אֵשֶׁת מַחְלוֹן קָנִיתִי לִי לְאִשָּׁה
לְהָקִים שֵׁם־הַמֵּת עַל־נַחֲלָתוֹ וְלֹא־יִכָּרֵת שֵׁם־
הַמֵּת מֵעִם אֶחָיו וּמִשַּׁעַר מְקוֹמוֹ עֵדִים אַתֶּם הַיּוֹם׃

9-10. וַיֹּאמֶר בֹּעַז לַזְּקֵנִים וְכָל הָעָם עֵדִים אַתֶּם הַיּוֹם כִּי קָנִיתִי אֶת כָּל אֲשֶׁר לֶאֱלִימֶלֶךְ וְאֵת כָּל אֲשֶׁר לְכִלְיוֹן וּמַחְלוֹן מִיַּד נָעֳמִי וְגַם אֶת רוּת הַמֹּאֲבִיָּה אֵשֶׁת מַחְלוֹן קָנִיתִי לִי לְאִשָּׁה לְהָקִים שֵׁם הַמֵּת עַל נַחֲלָתוֹ וְלֹא יִכָּרֵת שֵׁם הַמֵּת מֵעִם אֶחָיו וּמִשַּׁעַר מְקוֹמוֹ עֵדִים אַתֶּם הַיּוֹם — And Boaz said to the elders, and to all the people, "You are witnesses today, that I have bought all that was Elimelech's and all that was Kilion's and Machlon's from Naomi. And, what is more important, I have also acquired for myself Ruth the Moabite, the wife of Machlon, as my wife, to perpetuate the name of the deceased on his inheritance, that the name of the deceased not be cut off from among his brethren, and from the gate of his place. You are witnesses today."

We can ask why it was necessary for Boaz to state twice, "You are witnesses today." Also, why does the first verse state, "I have bought all that was Elimelech's," while the second verse states "I have acquired for myself" — why does the second verse add "for myself"?

Tosefes Berachah explains that Verse 9 refers to Elimelech acquiring the fields, and it is to that fact that we have the statement, "You are witnesses today." As to the second such statement in Verse 10, that refers to them being witnesses to Boaz's marriage to Ruth. That is also why the second verse adds, "I have acquired *for myself.*" This is in accordance with what *Rambam* writes (*Hilchos Kiddushin* 3:1): "How is a woman consecrated in marriage? . . . [the man] says to [the woman], 'Behold you are consecrated *to me.*' " *Maggid Mishneh* adds, quoting *Ramban,* that if the man left out "to me" there is no consecration and they are not married. Thus, when Boaz said "I have 'acquired' for myself" that was a reference to marriage.

We also have further proof that the first statement referred to acquiring Elimelech's land and the second to marriage from the fact that the first verse specified that Boaz addressed himself "to all the people" when he said "you are witnesses today," while the second verse has no reference to "all the people." This is in accordance with what *Ritva* states on *Kiddushin* 43, regarding the difference between witnesses to financial matters and witnesses to *kiddushin.* According to *Ritva,* if there are present at a

9 *And Boaz said to the elders, and to all the people,*
"You are witnesses today, that I have bought all that
was Elimelech's and all that was Kilion's and Machlon's
from Naomi. 10 *And, what is more important, I have*
also acquired for myself Ruth the Moabite, the wife of
Machlon, as my wife, to perpetuate the name of the
deceased on his inheritance, that the name of the
deceased not be cut off from among his brethren, and
from the gate of his place. You are witnesses today."

---

marriage some people who would be acceptable as witnesses and others who would be disqualified to serve as witnesses because they are related to the bride or groom, unless the groom specified in advance who his witnesses will be (as opposed to not making any such specification) the marriage is not valid. Since by Torah decree one requires witnesses for a marriage ceremony to be valid, if there was no specification it is as if everyone present is considered a witness, and if in any group of witnesses one or more are found to be non-valid, the entire group is considered to be non-valid, so that there are no valid witnesses. In monetary matters, on the other hand, one does not need to set aside witnesses in advance. Rather, if a case ever goes to the *beis din* for a decision, only the valid witnesses present at the original transaction may come to give testimony. From the above, *Ketzos HaChoshen* states that it is proper to clearly appoint two valid witnesses to a wedding, who will hear the groom's declaration.

Now we can understand why the verses here state, "You are witness today" twice, as the laws of the two are different, for one referred to Boaz acquiring Elimelech's fields and the second to Boaz taking Ruth as his wife.

10. וְגַם אֶת רוּת הַמֹּאֲבִיָּה אֵשֶׁת מַחְלוֹן קָנִיתִי לִי לְאִשָּׁה לְהָקִים שֵׁם הַמֵּת עַל נַחֲלָתוֹ וְלֹא יִכָּרֵת שֵׁם הַמֵּת מֵעִם אֶחָיו — "And, what is more important, I have also acquired for myself Ruth the Moabite, the wife of Machlon, as my wife, to perpetuate the name of the deceased on his inheritance, that the name of the deceased not be cut off from among his brethren."

We need to understand why the verse goes into such detail about Ruth: "Ruth the Moabite, the wife of Machlon." It would appear that this comes to teach us that whenever one makes a *kinyan* (an act of acquisition) it is important to specify exactly what is involved, so that there should be no doubt whatsoever. Thus, here Boaz made it clear that he knew that Ruth was a Moabite and that she had been Machlon's wife, and that he nevertheless wanted to marry her. His statement made this absolutely clear.

ד/יא יא וַיֹּ֨אמְר֜וּ כָּל־הָעָ֧ם אֲשֶׁר־בַּשַּׁ֛עַר וְהַזְּקֵנִ֖ים עֵדִ֑ים
יִתֵּן֩ יהוה אֶֽת־הָאִשָּׁ֨ה הַבָּאָ֜ה אֶל־בֵּיתֶ֗ךָ כְּרָחֵ֤ל ׀
וּכְלֵאָה֙ אֲשֶׁ֨ר בָּנ֤וּ שְׁתֵּיהֶם֙ אֶת־בֵּ֣ית יִשְׂרָאֵ֔ל

וְגַם אֶת רוּת הַמֹּאֲבִיָּה אֵשֶׁת מַחְלוֹן קָנִיתִי לִי — "I have also acquired for myself Ruth the Moabite, the wife of Machlon."

Machlon had married Ruth, while Kilion had married Orpah. We may find a hint in the names of the two men as to their fates, as I found in *Midrash Lekach Tov,* p. 66. Thus, Machlon would imply that Hashem had forgiven ("*mochal*") his sins. We see a similar idea on the verse (*Bereishis* 28:9), "So Eisav went to Yishmael and took Machalas the daughter of Yishmael," where R' Yehoshua ben Levi states that Eisav desired to convert, and the name "Machalas" indicates that Hashem forgave him all his sins. On the other hand, in the case of Kilion, who took the wicked Orpah as a wife and who did not manage to perpetuate his name, he was doomed to destruction ("*keliyah*") by Hashem.

11. וַיֹּאמְרוּ כָּל הָעָם אֲשֶׁר בַּשַּׁעַר וְהַזְּקֵנִים עֵדִים יִתֵּן יהוה אֶת הָאִשָּׁה הַבָּאָה אֶל בֵּיתֶךָ כְּרָחֵל וּכְלֵאָה אֲשֶׁר בָּנוּ שְׁתֵּיהֶם אֶת בֵּית יִשְׂרָאֵל — Then all the people who were at the gate, and the elders, said, "We are witnesses! May Hashem make the woman who is coming into your house like Rachel and like Leah, both of whom built up the House of Israel."

We need to understand how the common people spoke before the elders, for earlier it states, "And Boaz said to the elders," and afterwards "to all the people," for that is the proper manner.

It is possible that something is permitted according to the *halachah,* and may still be forbidden because of (*Mishlei* 4:24) "Remove from yourself distortion of the mouth, and distance perversity of lips from yourself." Thus we are told in *Yevamos* 24b, "If a man is suspected of intercourse with a heathen who subsequently became a proselyte he may not marry her, but if he did marry her he need not divorce her." The reason why he should not marry is because of the suspicion, in terms of "Remove from yourself distortion of the mouth, and distance perversity of lips from yourself." That was what Boaz feared, and he was not content to merely say, "You are witnesses" to the elders. Instead he addressed everyone gathered at the gate, as it states, "And Boaz said to the elders, and to all the people, 'You are witnesses today.' " What he wanted to do by this was to see if anyone would protest, because even if the elders understood, this might not be true for the simple folk, and the latter might not agree. That is why the verse mentioned the simple folk first when it states, "Then all the people who were at the gate, and the elders, said,"

[11]*Then all the people who were at the gate, and the elders, said, "We are witnesses! May* HASHEM *make the woman who is coming into your house like Rachel and like Leah, both of whom built up the House of Israel.*

---

from which we see that even the simple folk realized that this was from Hashem, and that this was a proper match. Since it was the attitude of the simple folk of which he was most afraid, their agreement is mentioned first.

יִתֵּן יהוה אֶת הָאִשָּׁה הַבָּאָה אֶל בֵּיתֶךָ כְּרָחֵל וּכְלֵאָה אֲשֶׁר בָּנוּ שְׁתֵּיהֶם אֶת בֵּית יִשְׂרָאֵל — "May Hashem make the woman who is coming into your house like Rachel and like Leah, both of whom built up the House of Israel."

It is not customary among Jews to pronounce such a blessing. It would appear that this blessing applied specifically to this marriage. Thus, on the verse (*Devarim* 33:28), "Thus Israel shall dwell secure, solitary, in the likeness of Yaakov," *Netziv* comments that "solitary" means without any excessive involvement in this world, but separate and alone by itself. This is "the likeness of Yaakov," namely Yaakov's *middah* (his underlying nature) and his desire that his children would remain "alone," and this is also the desire of Hashem, as we find in *Sanhedrin* 104, on the verse (*Eichah* 1:1), "Alas — she sits in solitude!" Rabbah said in the name of R' Yochanan: "The Holy One, Blessed is He, said, 'Thus Israel shall dwell secure, solitary. . .,' but now 'she sits in solitude.' " Thus, it was Hashem's desire that the Jewish people remain alone and uninvolved in this world, but now that they sinned and did not maintain their identity but mingled with the other nations they became solitary in a different way, namely that the other nations kept away from them. That is the meaning of "Alas — she sits in solitude!"

I once heard from the author of *Pachad Yitzchak,* R' Yitzchak Hutner, that it was our Matriarchs who made sure to keep the children of Avraham, Yitzchak and Yaakov away from the other nations. Thus, in the case of Sarah it states (*Bereishis* 21:10), "Drive out this slave woman with her son." With Rivkah we are told (ibid. 25:28), "Rivka loved Yaakov," even though she also had Eisav. And with Rachel and Leah it states (ibid. 31:15), "Are we not considered as strangers? . . . All the wealth that Hashem has taken away from our father belongs to us and to our children," and by saying so they cut off all ties with their father, Lavan, and no longer had any connection with him.

Thus, the blessing to Boaz and Ruth was, "May Hashem make the

וַעֲשֵׂה־חַיִל בְּאֶפְרָתָה וּקְרָא־שֵׁם בְּבֵית לָחֶם׃
יב וִיהִי בֵיתְךָ כְּבֵית פֶּרֶץ אֲשֶׁר־יָלְדָה תָמָר לִיהוּדָה
מִן־הַזֶּרַע אֲשֶׁר יִתֵּן יהוה לְךָ מִן־הַנַּעֲרָה
יג הַזֹּאת׃ וַיִּקַּח בֹּעַז אֶת־רוּת וַתְּהִי־לוֹ לְאִשָּׁה

---

woman who is coming into your house like Rachel and like Leah, both of whom built up the House of Israel" (4:11), and just as Rachel and Leah had cut off all ties with their father Lavan, so too should Ruth cut off all ties with Moab, and should enter totally into the Jewish people just like Rachel and Leah, both of whom built up the House of Israel.

The question we can ask is why Rachel is mentioned before Leah, when Boaz was from the tribe of Yehudah, which was descended from Leah. *Rashi* states that the reason for this was that even though they were descended from Leah, they all agreed that Rachel was the cornerstone of the Jewish people. Given what we discussed above, that the blessing was meant to be an allusion to the statement the two women made to Yaakov, where the verse reads, (*Bereishis* 31:14), "Then Rachel and Leah replied and said to him, 'Have we then still a share and an inheritance in our father's house?' " and in that verse we see that Rachel's name is mentioned first, which would imply that she led in the cutting off of all ties with Lavan, and that is why we find that order in our verse.

וַעֲשֵׂה חַיִל בְּאֶפְרָתָה וּקְרָא שֵׁם בְּבֵית לָחֶם — "May you prosper in Ephrat and be famous in Bethlehem."

We must understand why Ephrat and Bethlehem were mentioned in the blessing. The fact is that the exile and redemption are linked to one another. The exile from Eretz Yisrael came about directly through Yosef, in that Yosef went down to Egypt and led the way for Yaakov and his sons to follow, and it is Rachel, his mother, who weeps for her children when they go into exile, as we are told that Yaakov said (*Bereishis* 48:7), "I buried her on the road to Ephrat, which is Bethlehem," and our Sages commented that the reason she was buried there was so that she might help her descendants when they were exiled by Nevuzadran. Thus, when the Jews were exiled and had to pass by Rachel's tomb, she cried and implored Hashem for mercy, because exile begins on the road of Ephrat, which is Bethlehem.

So too is the source of our redemption in Ephrat, which is Bethlehem, and that will come through the House of David. The blessing, "May you prosper in Ephrat and be famous in Bethlehem," thus refers to

May you prosper in Ephrat and be famous in Bethle-
hem; 12 *and may your house be like the house of Peretz,*
whom Tamar bore to Yehudah, through the offspring
which HASHEM *will give you by this young woman."*
13 *And so, Boaz took Ruth and she became his wife;*

Mashiach, who will arise from Bethlehem via the House of David.[1]

12. וִיהִי בֵיתְךָ כְּבֵית פֶּרֶץ אֲשֶׁר יָלְדָה תָמָר לִיהוּדָה — "And may your house be like the house of Peretz, whom Tamar bore to Yehudah."

All saw the comparison between the first offspring — namely the child Peretz, born to Yehudah and Tamar, leading many generations later to the House of David — and that of Boaz and Ruth, which led directly to the House of David. The sons of Yehudah were guilty of spilling their seed, and so were Machlon and Kilion guilty of spilling their seed, in that by marrying non-Jewish women their children would not be considered to be descended from them. That, too, was considered to be spilling their seed. Just as in the case of Yehudah and Tamar Hashem ensured that Tamar would have a child from Yehudah, that child being Peretz, Ruth was enabled by Hashem to have a child with Boaz, from whom would eventually come David HaMelech.

We also need to mention how great was the *bitachon* (trust in Hashem) of that generation. After all, Boaz was an extremely old man (*Midrash Talpi'os,* "Boaz") and our Sages say that the same night that Boaz was married he died, and the next day all went to his funeral (*Yalkut Ruth* 608). Also, according to *Ruth Rabbah* 7:13, Ruth was a barren woman. Nevertheless, everyone blessed the couple that (4:12),"May your house be like the house of Peretz, whom Tamar bore to Yehudah, through the offspring which Hashem will give you by this young woman." Thus we see that all were confident that this union would produce a viable child who would be worthy of being a progenitor of the House of David. They all saw that — just as in the case of Yehudah and Tamar, where Hashem had so arranged things so that Peretz was born — here too this union would produce a viable child from whom would come the Kingdom of David. Furthermore, the name "Peretz" was mentioned because the name itself implied royalty, in that one of the symbols of authority of a king is that he has the power to destroy ("*poreitz*") fences. Here, this union would "break fences" in destroying all the conventional wisdom, and would certainly lead to the Kingdom of David.

---

1. See also what I wrote on v. 4:14 below, "May his name be famous in Israel."

וַיָּבֹא אֵלֶיהָ וַיִּתֵּן יהוה לָהּ הֵרָיוֹן וַתֵּלֶד בֵּן׃
יד וַתֹּאמַרְנָה הַנָּשִׁים אֶל־נָעֳמִי בָּרוּךְ יהוה אֲשֶׁר
לֹא הִשְׁבִּית לָךְ גֹּאֵל הַיּוֹם וְיִקָּרֵא שְׁמוֹ בְּיִשְׂרָאֵל׃

---

13. וַיִּקַּח בֹּעַז אֶת רוּת וַתְּהִי לוֹ לְאִשָּׁה וַיָּבֹא אֵלֶיהָ וַיִּתֵּן יהוה לָהּ הֵרָיוֹן וַתֵּלֶד בֵּן — And so, Boaz took Ruth and she became his wife; and he came to her. Hashem let her conceive, and she bore a son.

In this one verse, we are told five separate facts: "Boaz took Ruth," that being *eirusin,* i.e., their "betrothal"; "she became his wife," which was *nisuin;* "he came to her," namely intercourse; "Hashem let her conceive," that very night; "and she bore a son," nine months later. The reason why all five are mentioned in a single verse is that these five events had their counterpart in five events which took place at Mount Sinai, about which Shlomo HaMelech said in *Shir HaShirim* (3:11), "on the day of his wedding," which was the day of the giving of the Torah. Regarding this, we are told in *Shabbos* 86b: "On the first day of Sivan the Jewish people came to Sinai; on the second, Hashem said to them (*Shemos* 19:6), 'You shall be to me a kingdom of ministers'; on the third day He warned them not to approach the mountain; on the fourth they kept away from their wives; and on the sixth they were given the Torah and through it became Children of the Almighty." Now, as the act of Boaz and Ruth was performed only in order to aid the soul of Machlon and to gladden him and to fulfill the wishes of the Holy One, Blessed is He, this action was considered on High as equivalent to the receiving of the Torah at Mount Sinai, which gladdens the hearts of all those who labor in it.

This explains *Berachos* 6b, where R' Chelbo said in the name of R' Huna that whoever enjoys the wedding meal of a bridegroom and gladdens him merits the Torah, which was given with five voices, for each voice corresponds to one of the five events listed in *Maseches Shabbos* in the giving of the Torah. When one gladdens a bride and groom with the proper intention, namely that he rejoices in the building up of the Jewish people — since the Jewish people are as beloved to Hashem and are equivalent to the Five Books of the Torah, as stated by *Rashi* in *Parshas Beha'alosecha* (*Bamidbar* 8:19), on the verse, "I assigned the *Leviim* to be presented to Aharon and his sons" — it is like the receiving of the Torah, which was given with five voices.

וַיִּקַּח בֹּעַז אֶת רוּת — So Boaz took Ruth.

This was *eirusin,* the first stage of the marriage ritual; "and she became his wife," this was *nisu'in,* the final stage of the marriage ritual; "and he came to her," that was the fulfillment of the act of the *mitzvah* of being

and he came to her. Hashem let her conceive, and
she bore a son. [14] *And the women said to Naomi,*
"Blessed is Hashem Who has not left you without a
redeemer today! May his name be famous in Israel.

---

fruitful and multiplying; "and Hashem let her conceive, and she bore a son," that was the fulfillment of the *mitzvah* to be fruitful and multiply. In other words, Boaz fulfilled the *mitzvah* fully and with great alacrity, for our Sages tell us that he died that very night.

The verse makes a point of noting that Hashem let her conceive. This is in accordance with the words of *S'forno* on the verse (*Bereishis* 41:14), "So Pharaoh sent and summoned Yosef, and they rushed him from the dungeon." On this *S'forno* comments, "All deliverance by Hashem comes about in an instant. That was what occurred in Egypt, as it states (*Shemos* 12:39), 'for they were driven out of Egypt,' and they took unleavened cakes 'for they could not be leavened.' So too did Hashem promise for the future, as we see in (*Malachi* 3:1), 'Suddenly the Lord Whom you seek will come to His Sanctuary.' " Similarly, Ruth's conceiving was achieved very speedily, as is all succor from Hashem.

It also appears that this was payment to Boaz measure for measure, in that once Boaz began to arrange his marriage with Ruth, he did so without any delay whatsoever. Indeed, the actions of the righteous are all carried out speedily (see *Bamidbar Rabbah* 10:17). Had Boaz *chas veshalom* been lax in carrying out his words and his promise to Ruth, he would not have merited having the House of David descend from him, for he died right after his wedding night.

וַיִּתֵּן יהוה לָהּ הֵרָיוֹן וַתֵּלֶד בֵּן — Hashem let her conceive, and she bore a son.

As the verse does not say that she bore a son *to him,* this is a hint to that which we find in *Yalkut Ruth* 608, that the night that Boaz took Ruth was his last night on earth, and the next morning everyone woke earlier to go to his funeral. Thus the verse states that she bore a son, but Boaz did not merit seeing his son.

14. וַתֹּאמַרְנָה הַנָּשִׁים אֶל נָעֳמִי בָּרוּךְ יהוה אֲשֶׁר לֹא הִשְׁבִּית לָךְ גֹּאֵל הַיּוֹם — And the women said to Naomi, "Blessed is Hashem who has not left you without a redeemer today."

Sefer HaToda'ah asks how it is that all the sages and elders who had blessed Boaz earlier did not bless Naomi now, and that only Naomi's friends came with a blessing.

To this question, he gives a remarkable answer. According to him, the elders had second thoughts, and were afraid that they might have erred in ruling that Boaz was permitted to marry Ruth. They were afraid that just as

טו וְהָיָה לָךְ לְמֵשִׁיב נֶפֶשׁ וּלְכַלְכֵּל אֶת־שֵׂיבָתֵךְ
כִּי כַלָּתֵךְ אֲשֶׁר־אֲהֵבַתֶךְ יְלָדַתּוּ אֲשֶׁר־הִיא

Elimelech and his sons had died because of their improper actions, their ruling might have led to Boaz's death, as mentioned before. The women, though, who knew Naomi and Ruth, and who were aware that Ruth was indeed worthy of being the mother of royalty, had no doubts whatsoever, and had no hesitation in saying, "Blessed is Hashem Who has not left you without a redeemer today" (4:14).

We are also told (*Yalkut Shimoni Ruth,* 608): "R' Huna said: It was through this blessing of the women that David's family was never obliterated at the time of Ataliah, who killed everyone of the monarchical line except Yo'ash — who was saved by a miracle — and thus was preserved the eternity of the monarchy of the House of David." In other words, what these women's blessings added to that of the sages was that the Davidic line would never come to an end. Our redemption is not apparent to the naked eye, and it will come suddenly when we don't anticipate it. Here, the women saw that the entire method whereby Ruth eventually married Boaz and had a child was the start of the ultimate redemption. Just as the present is a time filled with a great lack of clarity, so too did they understand that the final redemption would be the same. They thus blessed Ruth that regardless of what would happen, the redeemer would eventually arrive.

It also appears that just as we saw with the redemption from Egypt, (*Sotah* 11b), for R' Avira said that as a reward for the righteous women of that generation the Jewish people were redeemed from Egypt — because righteous women have special faith and trust regarding the redemption — the same was true with these women, Naomi's neighbors, who saw and felt what the elders did not see or feel, and who understood from what had happened here that this was the basis for the ultimate redemption. Thus they got up and exclaimed, "Blessed is Hashem Who has not left you without a redeemer today" (4:14).

וְיִקָּרֵא שְׁמוֹ בְּיִשְׂרָאֵל — "May his name be famous in Israel."

This was a special blessing, as he was a "miracle child," in that his father was very old and his mother was barren. Now, there is a general rule that miracles do not persist over time, and there was therefore need for a special blessing that the child should remain alive. "May his name be famous in Israel" was meant to indicate that he should live a long life.

We find a similar idea in *Shemos Rabbah* 48:3-4, on the verse (*Shemos* 31:2), "See, I have called by the name: Betzalel son of Uri, son of Chur," where the Midrash asks why Chur is mentioned in the verse, and answers that when the Jewish people wanted to become involved in idolatry with

15 *He will become your life-restorer, to sustain your old age;*
for your daughter-in-law, who loves you, has borne him,

---

the Golden Calf, Chur gave his life for Hashem. When Chur did not permit the people to worship the calf, they arose and killed him. Hashem said to him, "By your life! All those children who are your issue — I will make a great name for them in the world," as it states, "See, I have called by the name: Betzalel son of Uri, son of Chur." The explanation of this is as follows: Part of the punishment of one who dies young is that his name is forgotten, because he left the world before he was able to accomplish much in the world. Hashem, however, paid Chur measure for measure by having him remembered through his grandson Betzalel.

The Midrash there concludes, "Through what did he (i.e., Betzalel) acquire this distinction? It was because he was of the tribe of Yehudah. And through what did he acquire this great wisdom? It was because of Miriam, as it states (*Shemos* 1:21), 'He made them houses.' . . . Aharon became the *Kohen Gadol* (High Priest), Moshe became a king, and Miriam took wisdom. Betzalel was descended from her, and from him eventually came David, who was the king, as it states (*I Divrei HaYamim* 2:19), 'Calev married Ephrat, who bore him Chur, and Chur begot Uri, and Uri begot Betzalel.' It also states (*I Shmuel* 17:12), 'David was the son of a certain Ephrathite,' who was descended from Miriam, who was called Ephrat." We see from the Midrash that there were two blessings, that of a good name which Betzalel received through the merits of Chur, and that of wisdom, through the merits of Miriam. Thus, the blessing in verse 4:11, that the elders and the people at the gate said, "May you prosper in Ephrat," refers to wisdom derived from Miriam, and that of verse 4:14, "May his name be famous in Israel," refers to the blessing of Betzalel, which he had received from Chur, of a good name.

15. וְהָיָה לָךְ לְמֵשִׁיב נֶפֶשׁ — "He will become your life-restorer."

As we are told in *Berachos* 17a, women merit the World to Come by bringing their sons to the synagogue and their husbands to the *beis midrash,* and that is what is meant by "your life-restorer." Through this child, Naomi could bring her son to the synagogue, that being a "life-restorer."

וּלְכַלְכֵּל אֶת שֵׂיבָתֵךְ כִּי כַלָּתֵךְ אֲשֶׁר אֲהֵבָתֶךְ יְלָדַתּוּ — "To sustain your old age; for your daughter-in-law, who loves you, has borne him."

Iggeres Shmuel explains that Naomi could be sure that this child would support her in her old age, just as her daughter-in-law had done by going from field to field to glean grain, because he would certainly follow in his mother's footsteps.

טו טוֹבָה לָךְ מִשִּׁבְעָה בָּנִים: וַתִּקַּח נָעֳמִי אֶת־הַיֶּלֶד
יז וַתְּשִׁתֵהוּ בְחֵיקָהּ וַתְּהִי־לוֹ לְאֹמֶנֶת: וַתִּקְרֶאנָה לוֹ

כִּי כַלָּתֵךְ אֲשֶׁר אֲהֵבַתֶךְ יְלָדַתּוּ אֲשֶׁר הִיא טוֹבָה לָךְ מִשִּׁבְעָה בָּנִים — "For your daughter-in-law, who loves you, has borne him, and she is better to you than seven sons."

When Naomi returned from Moab to Bethlehem, she told the women of the town, (1:21), "I was full when I went away, but Hashem has brought me back empty," even though she had Ruth to look after her and to aid her. However, Naomi was ashamed of Ruth. This we see in *Yalkut* 601 on the verse (1:12), Naomi said, "Turn back my daughters," where *Yalkut* states that the reason she asked them to return was so that she would not be embarrassed by them. Indeed, we are told that there were different markets in Jerusalem, each with its own clientele. Thus there was the market of royalty, that of the prophets, that of the *Kohanim,* that of the *levi'im* and that of the plain folk. Each group was distinctive in terms of its clothing and its own market, and what one group wore was not worn by the other groups. Coming back with Ruth, a Moabite, changed Naomi's status. In the present verse, then, the women told Naomi that Hashem had indeed returned her full and not empty, because her daughter-in-law was better for her than seven sons.

It would also appear that the women of Bethlehem finally took back what they had said when Naomi first returned, when they had said (1:19), "Could this be Naomi?" We are told in verse 1:19 that "it came to pass, when they arrived in Bethlehem, the entire city was tumultuous over them. " On this, *Shoresh Yishai* asks how it is that when the city was tumultuous over both the women, there is no mention of Ruth, but only "Could this be Naomi?" If we say that they did not know who Ruth was, why was the city tumultuous over both women?

However, the fact that they only mentioned Naomi and not Ruth was in itself a rebuke to Naomi, in that she had taken for her son a Moabite daughter-in-law. In our present verse, though, we see that Hashem so arranged it that in the end the women, too, had to agree with Naomi that her daughter-in-law was better than seven sons.

אֲשֶׁר הִיא טוֹבָה לָךְ מִשִּׁבְעָה בָּנִים — "She is better to you than seven sons."

In the case of Channah, Elkanah said (*I Shmuel* 1:8), "Am I not better to you than ten sons?" Why the discrepancy in numbers? *Me'am Lo'ez* notes that Boaz was the seventh generation from Peretz, while David was the

and she is better to you than seven sons."
[16] *Naomi took the child, and held it in her bosom, and*
she became his nurse. [17] *The neighborhood women gave*

---

tenth. Thus, what the women who were Naomi's neighbors said was that Ruth would become the mother of royalty, whereas Boaz would not be considered to be the progenitor of royalty. Even though Naomi's son-in-law, Boaz, was the seventh generation from Peretz, Ruth was privileged to receive what Boaz was not. What Elkanah told Channah was that he was better to her than Shmuel, who had the privilege of anointing David, the tenth generation.

16. וַתִּקַּח נָעֳמִי אֶת הַיֶּלֶד וַתְּשִׁתֵהוּ בְחֵיקָהּ — Naomi took the child, and held it in her bosom.

The child was so associated with Naomi that the neighborhood women said, "A son is born to Naomi" rather than to Ruth. From this we can see how great was Ruth's forbearance, that at first she was willing to forgo all the wealth and honor of her father's house — for she was the daughter of the king of Moab — and went to glean in the fields to support and sustain Naomi. Finally, when she had a son, she was content to leave him with Naomi so that Naomi could raise him.

My grandfather, author of *Or Yechezkel,* R' Yechezkel Levenstein, explained that giving something to someone does not in itself show that the person is kindly by nature, because sometimes a person gives something to have the action reflect well on himself. When can one know that such an action comes from a pure thought? When a person is willing to forgo his own desires for the benefit of another. This is what Ruth showed at the very beginning and at the end, for at the very end she was willing to give up her son for Naomi's benefit.

Through this action she earned the right to be the Mother of Royalty. Indeed, that is the way that she is referred to in *Bava Basra* 91. That was the level Ruth attained by her forbearance, to the extent that she gave up the right to raise her own child. Through the principle of "measure for measure" she became the mother of royalty.

How pleasant, then, are the words of our Sages, as brought in *Yalkut Shimoni* (601): "R' Zeira said: This *Megillah* (i.e., the Book of *Ruth*) has nothing about ritual purity or ritual impurity, nothing about what is permitted and what is forbidden, and why was it written? To teach us the reward for those who help others, for Ruth became the mother of royalty because of her kindliness to others."

ד/יז הַשְּׁכֵנוֹת שֵׁם לֵאמֹר יֻלַּד־בֵּן לְנָעֳמִי וַתִּקְרֶאנָה שְׁמוֹ
עוֹבֵד הוּא אֲבִי־יִשַׁי אֲבִי דָוִד׃

16-17. וַתִּקַּח נָעֳמִי אֶת הַיֶּלֶד וַתְּשִׁתֵהוּ בְחֵיקָהּ וַתְּהִי לוֹ לְאֹמֶנֶת וַתִּקְרֶאנָה לוֹ הַשְּׁכֵנוֹת שֵׁם לֵאמֹר יֻלַּד בֵּן לְנָעֳמִי וַתִּקְרֶאנָה שְׁמוֹ עוֹבֵד הוּא אֲבִי יִשַׁי אֲבִי דָוִד — Naomi took the child, and held it in her bosom, and she became his nurse. The neighborhood women gave him a name, saying, "A son is born to Naomi." They named him Oved; he was the father of Yishai, the father of David.

As Ruth was his mother, why did Naomi take him to herself to be his nurse? Also, why does the second verse here mention that Oved was the father of Yishai, who was the father of David, when immediately afterwards we are told the entire genealogy from Peretz to David?

Alshich states that Elimelech was aware that from his family would come the monarchy and the *Mashiach,* but as *Yalkut* points out, he erred in thinking that, based on his name, "Eli-Melech" ("To me belongs the kingship") the dynasty would come from him, whereas in reality it came from his daughter-in-law. One of the reasons for this mistake by Elimelech was that he himself was fit to be the king, and he knew how to act regally, so this led to his confusion. So too was Naomi worthy of being a queen. Therefore, when Ruth had a son, Naomi understood that the monarchy of the House of David would descend from him. Naomi therefore took it upon herself to be the child's nurse, and to teach him the proper royal bearing. Thus, when the verse concludes by mentioning the genealogy from Oved to David, it explains why Naomi chose to be the child's nurse and to teach him the proper regal behavior.

One can also add that one of the requirements for royalty is that the king must be (*Devarim* 17:15) "from among your brethren," which we are told in *Bava Kamma* means "among the select of your brethren." Naomi wanted to have the child trace his lineage to her, so that no one would claim later that he was not from "among the select of your brethren," in that he came from Ruth the Moabite. By raising him, she fulfilled the rule that one who raises an orphan is considered as if he had given birth to the child, just as we are told that Serach was the daughter of Asher, even though he only raised her, as stated by *Ramban* on *Bamidbar* 26:46.

17. וַתִּקְרֶאנָה לוֹ הַשְּׁכֵנוֹת שֵׁם לֵאמֹר יֻלַּד בֵּן לְנָעֳמִי וַתִּקְרֶאנָה שְׁמוֹ עוֹבֵד — The neighborhood women gave him a name, saying: "A son is born to Naomi." They named him Oved.

Why does this verse mention his being given a name ("*vatikrenah*") two times? It is possible that when he was small, they simply called him "Naomi's son," but later, when he grew up and they saw how he served *him a name, saying, "A son is born to Naomi." They named him Oved; he was the father of Yishai, the father of David.*

Hashem, they called him "Oved — the one who serves." Indeed, as the *Targum* explains it, he was named thus because of the way he served Hashem with a perfect heart. He was worthy of the blessing of "May his name be famous in Israel" (4:14), for he became famous in his generation.

וַתִּקְרֶאנָה שְׁמוֹ עוֹבֵד הוּא אֲבִי יִשַׁי אֲבִי דָוִד — They named him Oved; he was the father of Yishai, the father of David.

Regarding *yibum* (levirate marriage) the Torah states (*Devarim* 35:6), "It will be the firstborn — if she can bear — who shall succeed to the name of his dead brother, so that his name not be blotted out from Israel." *Rashi* and *Ramban* both comment that the verse does not mean literally that the firstborn should be named after the dead brother, but rather that the brother who performs *yibum* with his dead brother's wife is entitled to take his brother's inheritance from the dead man's father. *Ramban* adds proof that the verse is not meant to be understood literally, namely that the first son must be named after the dead brother, in that when Ruth's son was born he was named Oved, rather than having been named Machlon.

Ibn Ezra, though, states that the firstborn should indeed be given the same name as the deceased brother, so that the brother's name should not be obliterated. According to *Ibn Ezra,* then, we need to understand why the child was not named Machlon. One can answer this in terms of verse 14 above, "And the women said to Naomi, 'Blessed is Hashem Who has not left you without a redeemer today. May his name be famous in Israel" (4:14), from which *Ibn Ezra* deduces that originally the child was indeed called Machlon. Later, in verse 17, when the neighbors saw the remarkable attributes of the child, who, according to the *Targum,* prayed to Hashem with a perfect heart, the neighbors started calling him Oved. The verse then goes on to mention that he was the father of Yishai, the father of David, because that new name, "Oved," remained with him forever. Indeed, the primary name a person has is that which he acquires through his deeds.

הוּא אֲבִי יִשַׁי אֲבִי דָוִד — He was the father of Yishai, the father of David.

The way this verse is constructed, it would seem to indicate that Oved was the father of Yishai and of David. Shouldn't it have stated that Oved was the father of Yishai and Yishai was the father of David? It appears, though, that it was through the merit of Oved that David became so great, because he inherited a combination of the traits of Oved and Yishai. Oved, as we saw, was known for his excellence in prayer, and it was from him that David derived his powers of prayer. The name "Yishai," on the other hand, is related to "*yeishus*" ("being") in that he was so righteous that he would have remained alive forever had it not been for the fact that the sin of the Tree of Knowledge brought death to the world. And it was this fear of sin of Yishai's which David also inherited.

One can also answer this along different lines. In the verses (*II Shmuel* 20:1), "We have no part in David and we have no heritage in the son of Yishai" and (*I Melachim* 12:16), "What share have we in [the House of] David?" and (*I Divrei HaYamim* 12:19), "[We] are yours David, and [we] are with you, son of Yishai," David is mentioned with Yishai. The Brisker Rav explains that there were two selections, in that the House of Yishai was chosen and David was chosen. We see this clearly in (ibid. 28:4), "He chose Yehudah to be the ruler, and of the House of Yehudah [He chose] my father's house, and of the sons of my father it was me that He saw fit to make king over all Israel." Thus, the first choice was of the House of Yishai, and only afterwards was David chosen from the House of Yishai to become king. Similarly, (*II Shmuel* 20:1), "We have no part in David and we have no heritage in the son of Yishai" meant that they wanted no part of either selection, neither that of David nor that of the House of Yishai. And we have the contrary in (*I Divrei HaYamim* 12:19), "[We] are yours David, and [we] are with you, son of Yishai," in that they accepted the choice of both David and of the House of Yishai.

Using this understanding, one can explain the verse (4:17), "They named him Oved; he was the father of Yishai, the father of David," in that Oved was assured of being part of both choices — that of the House of Yishai and that of David. It also explains why it states that he was the father of Yishai and the father of David, even though immediately afterwards we are told the lineage of the House of David (vs. 18-22), "Now these are the generations of Peretz . . . and Yishai begot David." According to what we wrote, though, this is understandable, because the meaning of our present verse is that Oved was elected in two separate choices, from whom came the choice of the House of Yishai and the choice of David as king. Then, the next verse gives the lineage of David, traced forward from Peretz.

Furthermore, the explanation of the Brisker Rav also clarifies the verse (*I Shmuel* 16:1), "Hashem said to Shmuel, '. . . fill your horn with oil and go forth — I shall send you to Yishai of Bethlehem, for I have seen a king for Myself among his sons.' " We would have thought that Hashem was sending Shmuel to anoint David as king, so why was he sent to Yishai of Bethlehem? However, in accordance with the Brisker Rav's explanation, the first choice was that of the House of Yishai, and that was contained in the words, "I shall send you to Yishai of Bethlehem," indicating that Hashem had

18 *Now these are the generations of Peretz: Peretz begot*

---

chosen the House of Yishai. *Yalkut* also points out, on the verse (*Devarim* 33:5), "He became king over Yeshurun when the numbers of the nation gathered — the tribes of Israel in unity," that the initial Hebrew letters of the phrase, "the tribes of Israel in unity" — "*Yachad shivtei Yisra'el*" — are *yud, shin, yud,* which spells out the name "Yishai," thus hinting at the choice in the future of the House of Yishai, from which would come the monarchy.

18. וְאֵלֶּה תּוֹלְדוֹת פָּרֶץ פֶּרֶץ הוֹלִיד אֶת חֶצְרוֹן — Now these are the generations of Peretz: Peretz begot Chetzron.

Rashi states that as David's lineage was traced back to Ruth the Moabite, the verse now traces it back to Yehudah. *Rashi* seeks by this to explain why this verse again describes David's lineage, after the previous verse already stated that (4:17), "They named him Oved; he was the father of Yishai, the father of David." Furthermore, by this *Rashi* explains why the present verse begins with "*ve'eileh*" ("now these") rather than simply with "*eileh*" ("these"), where the additional letter *vav* in "*ve'eileh*" implies that this is a continuation of the previous verse. Whereas the previous verse gave us David's lineage through Ruth, this one gives us his lineage through Yehudah.

This, too, needs clarification, because the verse does not trace David's lineage back to Yehudah, but only back to Peretz. Why, indeed, did the prophet Shmuel, who composed the Book of *Ruth,* not carry the lineage back until Yehudah himself? Furthermore, we know that the monarchy was meant for Yehudah, as *Ramban* tells us on the verse (*Bereishis* 49:10), "The scepter shall not depart from Yehudah, " where *Ramban* writes: "Yaakov bequeathed the monarchy over his brothers to Yehudah, and bequeathed to Yehudah the rule over Israel, as stated by David in (*I Divrei HaYamim* 28:4), 'Hashem, God of Israel, chose me from all my father's family to be king over Israel forever,' because He chose Yehudah to be the leader, and of the House of Yehudah he chose my father's house, and of all my father's sons He chose me to anoint over all of Israel." So too do we find that *Da'as Zekeinim MiBa'alei HaTosfos* notes that the *gematria* value of the word "Yehudah" is thirty, corresponding to the thirty attributes of royalty, as stated in *Avos* 6:6, where it staes that there are thirty attributes of royalty. So too does *Ba'al HaTurim* bring a number of hints in Yaakov's blessing to Yehudah to David, being that the prime plan for Yehudah was to be the progenitor of David. Thus we return to the question of why the prophet Shmuel begins the lineage with Peretz rather than with Yehudah.

Bach, in his introduction to his *Meishiv Nefesh* on the Book of *Ruth,* writes: "Most commentators on the *Megillah* of *Ruth* noted their agreement that it was written by the prophet Shmuel as a *halachic* ruling after Doeg raised doubts about David, of blessed memory, and attempted to prevent him from being part of the community, and wished to announce this, had it not been for Amasa who girded himself with his sword like Yishmael and said, 'Whoever does not accept this *halachah* will be stabbed by my sword: thus I received the ruling from the *beis din* of Shmuel of Ramah: Ammonite male and not Ammonite female; Moabite male and not Moabite female.' Thus, it states in *Yevamos* 76b-77, that they then sent to Shmuel and asked for his ruling, and he wrote the Book [of *Ruth*] as a *halachic* ruling, based on the tradition which he had received, that a Moabite female is permitted, for Shmuel was still alive, as stated there."

According to this, the entire basis for the Book is to show that David HaMelech was part of the community of Israel, and not to tell us the lineage of the monarchy. Now, whenever a *halachic* decision is written, it is customary at the very end to give a summation of the ruling. Thus Shmuel, after having written the decision to prove that Ruth could be a member of the community and that Ruth had all the good qualities of the Jewish people — in that she was modest and bashful, merciful, and one who helped her mother-in-law throughout her life, and was worthy of being a member of the community — concluded his ruling and then added a list of ten generations from Peretz to David, to hint at the statement (*Vayikra* 27:32) that "the tenth one will be holy," because the question had been whether David could be a member of the community of Israel, and this lineage showed that not only did he belong to it, but that as the tenth generation he was holy.

Now we can understand the letter *vav,* which marks a continuation of the previous statement, in that "Now these are the generations of Peretz" tells us that not only was David permitted in the community — and he certainly belonged there in terms of the three qualities of Israel — but that he was holy and was part of the holy assembly of Israel, and entitled to the title of "holy nation" which we received at Sinai. Indeed, while when we left Egypt we became the Nation of Israel, it was only through the giving of the Torah at Sinai that we entered into Hashem's covenant, as stated by *Rambam* (*Hilchos Issurei Bi'ah* 13), that through three elements the Jewish people entered into Hashem's covenant: *bris milah,* the immersion in a *mikveh,* and the bringing of sacrifices, and that sanctified them with the sanctification of the people of Israel. David, too, was sanctified by being "the tenth one will be holy," and that refers to the ten generations from Peretz to David.

Beis HaLevi (*Drush* 18, *She'eilos U'Teshuvos Beis HaLevi,* Part II) writes that in the Tablets which Moshe received at Sinai everything was in writing, including every future insight of the Torah thought that a great *talmid chacham* would come up with in future generations. Just as the letters *mem* and *samech,* which have a central section which is entirely detached from the outer perimeter and where the central section miraculously remained in place in the first Tablets, by the same token the entire Torah, including all future Torah thoughts, was miraculously included on the first two Tablets. Only afterwards, after the people had sinned and Hashem decreed that if they would sin in the future they would go into exile, was the Oral Torah given to them, including the Mishnah, Talmud and Aggadah, these being the principal differences between the Written and Oral Torahs. Thus, even if the other nations would enslave the Jewish people and take the written Torah from them, they would remain with the Oral Torah. When the second Tablets were given to the Jewish people, along with the Oral Torah, they ascended to an even higher level. Prior thereto all the Torah was contained within the Tablets, and the Jewish people had two functions — to observe the laws of the Torah and to preserve the Torah. At that time they were only like a vessel into which the Torah was placed, just like the Ark of the Torah in which the *Sefer Torah* is placed, where the Ark is considered to be an appurtenance of a ritual object but not a ritual object in itself. Afterwards, when the Oral Torah was given to them, the Jewish people were considered to be like the parchment of the Oral Torah, as we read, "Write them on the tablets of your heart." Just as the parchment of a *Sefer Torah* is the actual ritual object and not an appurtenance, for the parchment and the writing on it are both together the Torah scroll, similarly the Torah and the Jewish people are one entity.

Now the Written Torah states (*Devarim* 23:4), "An Ammonite or Moabite shall not enter the congregation of Hashem," and the Oral Torah explains that that only applies to their males, but their females may enter the congregation of Hashem. Shmuel then came and wrote the Book of *Ruth* and translated the Oral Torah statement of "Moabite male but not Moabite female" into written Torah, which has the sanctity of the Holy Books, thereby reverting to the situation of the original time of the first Tablets, where everything was in writing. That is why we read the Book of *Ruth* on *Shavuos,* the time when the first Tablets were given by Hashem, to show that in the first Tablets even the Oral Torah was given in writing.

We can also say, based on this, that just as David, King of Israel, was able to be part of the Congregation of Israel through the Oral Torah, i.e., through the oral teaching of "Moabite male but not Moabite female," so are the Jewish people able to suffer the bitter exile and be here today through the Oral Torah which was written and sealed on their hearts. Thus we see in *Gittin* 60b, "R' Yochanan said: The Holy One, Blessed is He, only made a covenant with Israel for the sake of the Oral Torah, as it states (*Shemos* 34:27), 'According to these words have I sealed a covenant with you and with Israel,' " because this is what keeps us alive in each generation. Indeed, David represents all of Israel, as stated in *Rambam*, *Hilchos Melachim,* that he was the heart of all Israel. We therefore read the Book of *Ruth* on *Shavuos* in order to strengthen ourselves with reading and reviewing how Hashem protected the seeds that led to the birth of David, King of Israel, *chai ve'kayam.*

ד/יט־כב

יט וְחֶצְרוֹן֙ הוֹלִ֣יד אֶת־רָ֔ם וְרָ֖ם הוֹלִ֥יד אֶת־עַמִּֽינָדָֽב׃
כ וְעַמִּֽינָדָב֙ הוֹלִ֣יד אֶת־נַחְשׁ֔וֹן וְנַחְשׁ֖וֹן הוֹלִ֥יד אֶת־
כא שַׂלְמָֽה׃ וְשַׂלְמוֹן֙ הוֹלִ֣יד אֶת־בֹּ֔עַז וּבֹ֖עַז הוֹלִ֥יד
כב אֶת־עוֹבֵֽד׃ וְעֹבֵד֙ הוֹלִ֣יד אֶת־יִשָׁ֔י וְיִשַׁ֖י הוֹלִ֥יד
אֶת־דָּוִֽד׃

סכום הפסוקים של ספר רות שמונים וחמשה. וסימנו **ובעז** הוליד את עובד.
וסימנו סורה שבה **פה** פלוני אלמני.

4/19-22 *Chetzron;* 19 *and Chetzron begot Ram, and Ram begot*
Amminadav; 20 *and Amminadav begot Nachshon, and*
Nachshon begot Salmah; 21 *and Salmon begot Boaz,*
and Boaz begot Oved; 22 *and Oved begot Yishai, and*
Yishai begot David.

⁂ Regarding the Receiving of the Torah

We learn in *Shabbos* 88a, "Chizkiyah said: What is meant by (*Tehillim* 76:9), 'From heaven You made judgment heard; the earth feared, and was silent'? If it feared, why was it silent? And if it was silent, why did it fear? At first it feared, and then was silent. Why did it fear? This is in accordance with Reish Lakish, as Reish Lakish expounded: 'The Holy One, Blessed is He, made a condition with Creation, and said to it, "If Israel accepts the Torah, you will continue to exist and if not, I will return you to emptiness and void ("*tohu vavohu*")." ' "

Shem MiShmuel asks (*Shavuos* 5682) that since Hashem made this condition with Creation itself, it must have included everything created in the Six Days of Creation, including the heavens. If so, why was it only the earth that feared, and not the heavens? He also brings another question from his father, the *Avnei Nezer,* that since *tohu* and *bohu* were among Hashem's creations and were also created by the power of Hashem looking in the Torah, they, too, should have disappeared if Israel had not accepted the Torah. Reish Lakish, then, should have said that Hashem would return everything to nothingness rather than to *tohu vavohu.*

Shem MiShmuel then explains that *tohu vavohu* means that everything is mixed together in utter confusion, while the Torah arranges everything in orderly fashion. Indeed, everything was created on the first day of Creation but it was all mixed together. Each day, the various elements were separated from one another. Thus, the failure to accept the Torah, which is what makes everything orderly, would have caused the world to revert to confusion.

Now, the verse itself states that (*Bereishis* 1:2) "The earth was *tohu vavohu,* with darkness upon the face of the deep." From this we see that only on the earth — where there is earthiness — is there *tohu vavohu.* Indeed, the earth is full of lies and deceit, and it even appears as if the forces of evil control everything and are succeeding, while truth and justice seem to be missing. In the heavens, on the other hand, there is no *tohu vavohu,* because that is a World of Truth and everything there is clear (see *Bava Basra* 10b). That is why the heavens did not fear.

On the verse (*Bereishis* 1:31), "And there was evening and there was morning, the sixth day," *Rashi* comments: "Another interpretation: 'The sixth day' — the sixth day upon which everything was dependent, namely the sixth day [of the month] of Sivan, which was set aside for the giving of the Torah." We need to explain why everything was dependent on "the sixth day." Wasn't it dependent on the accepting of the Torah, which just happened to be on the sixth day of Sivan?

However, based on what we wrote above, this is answered. When the world was created, it needed to be improved, and its improvement ("*tikkun*") came about when the Torah was given and when the *mitzvos* of the Torah were observed. As long as the Torah had not been given to improve the world, it kept degenerating. As with anything which degenerates, in the earlier stages it is much easier to rectify matters, but if the thing degenerates too far, no amount of rectification will help. The same was true with the world, and if Israel had not accepted the Torah on the sixth day of Sivan, the world would have degenerated to such an extent that it could no longer be rectified. That is what is meant when we are told, "the sixth day upon which everyone was dependent," for without the acceptance of the Torah on the sixth day of Sivan the world would have passed the point where it could be rectified, and would have returned once again to *tohu vavohu.*

This also answers the question as to why, as our Sages tell us, it was necessary at Sinai for Hashem to place the mountain over the Jewish people and to say to them, "If you accept the Torah, all will be well, but if not, this will be your burial place" (*Shabbos* 88). If their not accepting the Torah would have meant that the world would in any event return to a state of *tohu vavohu,* why was it necessary to place the mountain over them? However, based on what we noted before, the world would not return to the *tohu vavohu* state that preceded the Creation, where there was absolutely nothing, but to a state of the mixing of the bad and the good to the extent that it could not be rectified. That, though, would only be in regard to the world as a whole, which would return to *tohu vavohu,* but as far as the Jewish people are concerned, Hashem showed them that if they didn't accept the Torah, that would literally be their grave.

❧ ❧ ❧

One can also add here that in general the body is only awakened by what it actually experiences with its senses, and if a person physically sees something himself he can be moved to rouse himself to better his ways. On the other hand, only a person with great wisdom can understand something intellectually without seeing it. Even in the case of a very wise person, understanding something intellectually does not make as great an impact as actual experiencing it with one's senses. As the *Alter* of Kelm explained in his *Chochmah U'Mussar* I:27, on what we learn in *Megillah* 14, "The removal of [Achashverosh's] ring [and the giving of it to Haman] had a more pronounced impact than forty-eight male and seven female prophets, all of whom prophesied in Israel and did not bring the people to repent, whereas the removal of the ring brought them to repent." From this, the *Alter* said, we can learn that the most wise person in the world, like the Jewish people at the time of the prophets, will not be as affected by his intellect as he will by what he experiences with his senses, as in the days of Mordechai and Esther. That being the case, a person should try to experience the ideas of reward and punishment as much as possible through his senses, as we saw in the quote from *Megillah* earlier. This was what Hashem did when he held the mountain over the Jewish people and told them, "If not, this will be your burial place." By placing the mountain above them, He made sure that they would feel with their senses the consequence if they refused to accept the Torah. This was necessary, even though intellectually they knew that if they did not accept the Torah the world would cease to exist.

I heard from my grandfather, the author of *Or Yechezkel,* that the founder of the Rothschild dynasty, Meyer Anshel, would go to a specific place each day, where he would sequester himself away from everyone. One day, one of his servants followed him to see where he was going and what he was doing. The servant saw that he went into a hidden room, took out shrouds and wrapped them about himself and then went to lie down in a coffin. This was his way of reminding himself of the fact that everyone must die, regardless of how great or how lowly he is.

◆§ More on This Topic

We learn in *Shabbos* 88a, "Chizkiyah said: What is meant by (*Tehillim* 76:9), 'From heaven You made judgment heard; the earth feared, and was silent'? If it feared, why was it silent? And if it was silent, why did it fear? At first it feared, and then was silent. Why did it fear? This is in accordance with Reish Lakish . . . Why does it state (*Bereishis* 1:31), 'And there was evening and there was morning, the sixth day,' " with the extra word "the" (unlike all the other days, where the Torah merely states "a" second, third, etc., day)? This teaches us that The Holy One, Blessed is He, made a condition with Creation, and said to it, "If Israel accepts the Torah, you will continue to exist and if not, I will return you to emptiness and void ("*tohu vavohu*")."

Sefas Emes regarding Shavuos (5635, *"Eretz"*) notes that *Chiddushei Harim* asks that it seems from the above quotation that the earth feared when Hashem gave the Torah to the Jewish people, as it states, "From heaven You made judgment heard," which refers to the giving of the Torah. It was at that time the earth feared. However, if the earth feared about whether Israel would accept the Torah or not, this fear should have begun from the moment of Creation, and not only just before the giving of the Torah.

It would appear that the fear of the earth as to whether Israel would accept the Torah was whether Israel was worthy of receiving the Torah. Earlier, the earth had had no such fears, because it assumed that Hashem would not create the heavens and earth in vain, and that as time went on the Jewish people would reach the heights of being able to receive and observe the Torah. Hashem would then give them the Torah at the proper time. Now that the actual time had come for receiving the Torah, in that "from heaven You made judgment heard," the earth looked at the generation which was meant to receive the Torah, the generation which had left Egypt but fifty days earlier, at which time it had been at the lowest level spiritually, and in that short time had raised itself to the level of receiving the Torah. The earth feared that the people might not be worthy of receiving the Torah after all, and without Torah study for even an instant, the world would return to its *tohu vavohu* state. That the absence of learning for even a moment would lead inexorably to the *tohu vavohu* state is true even today, as *Nefesh HaChaim* writes.

Then the earth was silent. *Midrash Tanhuma* (*Yisro* 11) states, "R' Shmuel bar Nachmani said in the name of R' Yonasan: What is meant by (*Tehillim* 29:4), 'The voice of Hashem [comes] in power'? How can we say that, when [even the voice of] a single angel is something which no one can withstand, as it states (*Daniel* 10:6), '[The angel's] body was like rock crystal, his face like the appearance of lightning, his eyes like flaming torches, and his arms and legs like the color of burnished copper; the sound of his words [loud] as the sound of a multitude'? If that is true for angels, then the voice of the Holy One, Blessed is He, about Whom it states (*Yirmiyahu* 23:24), 'Do I not fill the heaven and the earth?' is all the more so. What the verse means, though, is that while Hashem did indeed speak with great power, it was a power that Moshe could tolerate." In other words, Hashem only asks of a person whatever that person has the capability of doing — Moshe according to his capability and the rest of us according to our capability. Thus, the earth became silent when it realized the principle that the observance of the Torah must be based on the capabilities of every person, and not in accordance with the capabilities and abilities of the angels.

I heard from R' Yaakov Galinski that when the other nations of the world were offered the Torah and they asked, "What is written in it?" they did not understand that a person is only required to observe the Torah based on his ability. That is also the meaning of the blessing that the other nations blessed when they heard from Bilam (*Zevachim* 116a) that Hashem wanted to give the Torah to His people. Thus when the other nations heard that (*Tehillim* 29:11), "Hashem will give might (i.e., the Torah) to His nation," they exclaimed [completing the verse], "Hashem will bless His nation with peace ("*bashalom*")." What they meant to convey was that they had rejected the Torah because they felt one needed to perform the *mitzvos* perfectly ("*bishleimus*"), not realizing that perfection is relative to the abilities of the person.

Nor did the other nations know the principle (*Shir HaShirim Rabbah* 5:2): "Open for Me an opening of repentance the size of the eye of a needle, and I will widen it to form openings as large as the *ulam* (the hall leading to the interior of the *Beis HaMikdash*)"; namely, that if a person strives for perfection, Hashem will help him. This is also what we see from what our Sages commented regarding the blessing which Bilam blessed the Jewish people (*Bamidbar* 24:5), "How goodly are your tents, O Yaakov, your dwelling places, O Yisrael." On this *Rashi* says that Bilam saw that the openings of their tents did not face one another. Homiletically, however, this verse can be understood to mean that the opening the Jews had to open — an opening the size of the eye of a needle — is not the same as the wide opening that Hashem opens. The other nations did not believe in the goodness of Hashem, Who does not come with complaints against His creatures and only asks from each person to open an opening the size of the eye of a needle.

That, also, is what Hashem said to Moshe (see *Shabbos* 88b), when He said to him, "Take hold of the Throne of My Glory and answer [the angels" — who had complained that man was not worthy of receiving the Torah], for the angels had claimed (*Tehillim* 8:5), "What is frail man that You should remember him, and the son of mortal man that You should be mindful of him?" The angels complained that mortals cannot fulfill the Torah perfectly. Hashem told Moshe to take hold of the Throne of Glory and answer them, namely that simply by taking hold of the Throne of Glory, Man has assistance from Hashem to perfect himself. Indeed, we have seen how our great Sages — the *gedolim* — opened up an opening but the size of the eye of a needle, and through that small opening, through assistance from Hashem, were able to fulfill the entire Torah.

This also explains the text of the blessing of the Torah that precedes the saying of the *Shema,* where we say, "Our Father, Our King, because of our fathers who trusted in you and whom You taught the statutes of life, so too favor us and teach us." Only through the *bitachon* (faith) that our fathers had when they left Egypt and received the Torah — that Hashem would help them observe and fulfill the entire Torah — did they accept the yoke of Torah upon themselves, and proclaimed (*Shemos* 24:7) "*Na'aseh venishma* — we will do and we will obey." It was because of that *bitachon* that they merited receiving the Torah, and it is that *bitachon* which we mention in our prayers every day.

☙ The Acceptance of *Na'aseh Venishma*

We learn in *Shabbos* 88a, "R' Elazar said: When Israel said *na'aseh* ("we will do") before saying *venishma* ("we will hear"), a *bas kol* (a voice from On High) came forth and said, 'Who revealed to My children this exalted secret, which is used by the Ministering Angels?' " Later (88b), the *gemara* goes on to tell how a certain *Tzeduki* (Sadducee) told Rava that the Jewish people should not have been impetuous in saying *na'aseh* before saying *venishma,* for obeying the Torah might cause a person troubles, and they should first have known what was in the Torah before accepting it. Rava answered that one who follows the Torah properly has nothing to fear: "For, us, who walked in uprightness, it states (*Mishlei* 11:3), 'The innocence of the just will guide them.' " On this, *Rashi* comments, "We walked with Him in uprightness as one does out of love, and we relied upon Him not to lead us astray in a way which we would be unable to resist."

I wondered whether for us to receive the Torah we needed to state *na'aseh venishma,* and whether, if we had asked — as the other nations did (see *Sifrei* beginning of *Vezos Haberachah*) — "What is in it?" we might not have received it. Alternately, would it have been enough for us accept the Torah without saying *na'aseh venishma,* except that since we did say it, that saying elevated us to a higher level spiritually, to the level of the Ministering Angels, and was it because of that fact that all of Israel merited receiving crowns, as stated there in the *gemara*? According to the second view, then, when Hashem made the creation of the world conditional on the Jewish people accepting the Torah, any acceptance would have been sufficient, without specifically requiring *na'aseh venishma.*

It would appear to me that as far as the condition which Hashem made at the time of the Creation, any acceptance of the Torah by the Jewish people would have been sufficient, even without *na'aseh venishma.* However, without the acceptance of *na'aseh venishma* they would not have been able to receive the Torah in such a way as to be able to say, "It is not in heaven." Thus, *Beis HaLevi* (*Yisro,* beginning "*lehavin ha'inyan*") comments on the *gemara* (*Shabbos* 88b) where the Ministering Angels argued that "the secret treasure which has been hidden for 974 generations before the world was created — would You now give it to flesh and blood? (*Tehillim* 8:5), 'What is frail man that You should remember him, and the son of mortal man that You should be mindful of him?' (*Tehillim* 8:2), 'Hashem, our Master, how mighty is Your Name throughout the earth, who places Your majesty on the heavens.' " After all, the Torah was given to us in order for us to make *halachic* inferences from it, based on the different *halachic* principles, and whatever is inferred using these principles is the truth. Thus we are told in *Bava Metzia* 86 that the *halachah* is not in the heavens but is as the *beis din* in this world decides. Now, what the angels wanted was to have the Torah given to them and not to man, and the truth would then be whatever the angels decided. This is what the angels meant when they quoted, "who places Your majesty on the heavens," namely that those in the heavens would have the "majesty," i.e., dominion, over the Torah. The Jewish people, though, because of their acceptance with *na'aseh venishma,* received this dominion over the Torah.

Similarly, had the Torah remained "from heaven," the Jewish people would have had to be like the angels, adapting themselves to the natural heavenly habitat of the Torah, in order to understand it. Now, though, by accepting the Torah with *na'aseh venishma,* which is the way it was accepted by the angels, the Torah was brought down to earth and could flourish in a normal human habitat.

☙ The Attributes of the Jewish People Which Made Them Worthy of Receiving the Torah

We are told (*Bamidbar* 1:18), "They established their genealogy according to their families." On this *Yalkut Shimoni* (684) comments: "When Israel received the Torah, the [other] nations of the world envied them, and asked, 'Why did [Hashem] bring them closer than the other nations?' The Holy One, Blessed is He, set aside their arguments and said to them, 'Bring me your genealogical trees,' as it states (*Tehillim* 96:7), 'Render unto Hashem, O families of the peoples,' namely bring in your family records — your genealogical trees — just as My sons did, as it states, 'They established their genealogy according to their families.' "

On the verse (*Devarim* 33:2), "He said: Hashem came from Sinai — having shone forth to them from Seir, having appeared from Mount Paran," we are told in *Avodah Zarah* 2b, "Why is Seir mentioned? Why is Paran mentioned? R' Yochanan said: This teaches us that the Holy One, Blessed is He, brought [the Torah] to every nation and tongue and they did not accept it, until He came to Israel and they accepted it." How, then, do the other nations now come and demand that they be given the Torah?

On the verse (*Shemos* 18:1), "Yisro, the minister of Midian, the father-in-law of Moshe, heard everything that God did to Moshe and to Israel, His people," the *gemara* in *Zevachim* (116a) tells us that R' Elazar Hamoda'i said: "What Yisro heard about was the giving of the Torah, for when the Torah was given to Israel the sound was heard from one end of the world to the other. All the kings of the pagan nations trembled in their castles, and recited praise of Hashem, as it states (*Tehillim* 29:9), 'In his castle all will proclaim, Glory!' " From this we see that the giving of the Torah affected the entire world, and that all recognized the need for Torah in the world. Even in the kings' castles and temples, where all their idols were kept, they praised the Glory of Hashem, for they realized that the only good in the world is the Torah. At that time, they all sought to draw closer to the Jewish people. We also see this idea in what we are told by our Sages regarding the giving of the Torah by Hashem, in that as each of the Ten Commandments was uttered the entire world remained silent and no other sound was heard. In other words, it was totally clear that there is nothing in the world except for the Torah, with no one in the entire world as much as uttering a sound to deny it. Then, all the other nations came and asked, "Why did [Hashem] bring them closer than the other nations?" for had they known what they now knew, they would have wanted to receive the Torah.

Hashem silenced them and said to them, "Bring me your genealogical trees," for only the Jewish people has its genealogical records because it lives with its past, namely with the merits of its forefathers. The Jewish people relates everything to those who came before, for only through the power of our forefathers can we be faithful to Hashem and His Torah. That is why the blessings before the *Shema* mention the previous generations when we recite, "Our Father and King, for the sake of our forefathers who trusted in You, and whom you taught the laws of life, so too favor us and teach us." The other nations, on the other hand, do not have any genealogical tree, for they do not live with the past but only in the present, and think that they are better than their ancestors. They do not link themselves to the merits of their forefathers, and are simply unable to remain faithful to Hashem and His Torah.

❦ ❦ ❦

One can explain the words of our Sages which we brought above in a different way. At first, when Hashem asked for those who would be willing to be guardians of the great treasure of the Torah — one that would not depart from their mouths and the mouths of their descendants forever — a nation which would be willing to carry the yoke of the Torah on its back throughout all its trials and tribulations and through all kinds of suffering and to go through fire and water, and to have its blood shed just for the Torah, He did not find a single one of the seventy nations which was willing to accept this guardianship, except for the Jewish people, the descendants of Avraham, Yitzchak, and Yaakov. All the other nations said that they were not interested in receiving it. However, after Hashem finally brought the Torah down to the earth the other nations asked that they, too, should be commanded to fulfill it, and were willing to do so.

When He heard this request by the other nations, Hashem asked them to bring their own genealogical tree, for to be suitable to observe the Torah one must be extremely holy. As the Midrash brought by *Tosfos* in *Kesubos* (104, "*lo neheneisi*") says, rather than have a person pray to have the Torah enter his body, he should pray that delicacies do not enter his body. Thus we see in *Yoma* 82b, "A certain pregnant woman who smelled food on Yom Kippur had a tremendous craving for it. They came to Rebbi [to ask him what to do]. He said, 'Whisper to her that today is Yom Kippur.' They whispered this to her, and she accepted their suggestion. To her was applied the verse (*Yirmiyahu* 1:5), 'Before I formed you in the belly I knew you, and before you left the womb I sanctified you.' From her came forth R' Yochanan. A certain pregnant woman smelled food on Yom Kippur and had a tremendous craving for it. They came to R' Chanina [to ask him what to do]. He said, 'Whisper to her that today is Yom Kippur.' She did not accept their suggestion. To her was applied the verse (*Tehillim* 58:4), 'The wicked are estranged from the womb.' From her came forth Shabsai, who hoarded provisions." Now, since the other nations do not maintain their holiness, they cannot be entitled to keep the Torah.

◆§ The Qualities One Needs to Receive the Torah

Bamidbar Rabbah (1:7), on the verse (*Bamidbar* 1:1), "Hashem spoke to Moshe in the wilderness of Sinai," asks why this took place in the wilderness of Sinai. "Our Sages learned: The Torah was given in association with three things: fire, water, and the wilderness. How do we know fire? From (*Shemos* 19:18), 'All of Mount Sinai was smoking, because Hashem had descended upon it in the fire.' How do we know water? From (*Shoftim* 5:4), 'Hashem, as You left Seir, as You strode from the fields of Edom, the earth quaked and even the heavens trickled; even the clouds dripped water.' How do we know in the wilderness? From (*Bamidbar* 1:1), 'Hashem spoke to Moshe in the wilderness of Sinai.' "

The Kotzker Rebbi explained why the festival of Shavuos is known as "the day of the giving of the Torah" rather than "the day of the receiving of the Torah." The reason is that the giving of the Torah was an act which was the same for every person, regardless of whether it was Moshe himself or the smallest and youngest of Israel. All were given the Torah. As to receiving the Torah, on the other hand, it depended on the person's capacity, in terms of how much he was able to absorb.

It would appear that the purpose of the Midrash was to explain that the capacity to receive the Torah depends on these three factors: fire, water, and wilderness: the ability to act like water, to have within oneself a fire, and to act like the wilderness, as will be explained below. The Torah is compared to water, and indeed, we are told in *Taanis* 7a, "Why are Torah thoughts compared to water? Because just as water always flows from a higher place to a lower place, so too, Torah thoughts exist within a person who is humble." On this, *Nefesh HaChaim* says that "Had there been alive a person who was as humble as Moshe, he certainly would have merited knowing the entire Torah perfectly. As an example, in a vessel, the thinner its walls are, the greater its capacity as the walls take less space, to the extent that if its walls were as thin as a garlic skin the vessel would hold almost its entire outer capacity. Similarly with a person — the more humble he is, the greater his capacity to absorb a correspondingly larger amount of Torah."

Similarly with fire, just as fire warms others and has the power to melt two pieces of metal and fuse them into one, so too in receiving the Torah one needs the power of fire to warm the heart to have a greater desire to study Torah and to have the Torah cleave to the person's heart. In this, Torah is different from any other body of knowledge, for while all the other bodies of knowledge require the head, the Torah requires the heart. Thus we learn in *Sanhedrin* 61a that R' Eliezer said about those of his students who had not come to study Torah with him, "I will be amazed if they will die a natural death." R' Akiva asked him, "What about my death?" He answered, "Your death will be more cruel than theirs." *Rashi* there explains that R' Akiva's fate would be such because his heart was as large as an auditorium, and had he but served R' Eliezer, he would have learned a great deal. Thus we see that it is the heart which is the seat of Torah study. We also see that the first letter of the Torah is a *beis* while the last letter is a *lamed,* where the two together (in reverse order) form the Hebrew word, "*leiv,*" or a heart. Now, the only way that the Torah, which is from heaven, can be joined to the human body, which is coarse and of the earth, is through the power of fire. Thus *Nefesh HaChaim* writes in one of his letters that the main factor in acquiring Torah is how much one desires it. Indeed, he says, one hour of Torah study with desire can accomplish much more than a number of hours of Torah study without desire. The power to desire is the power of fire within the person.

Finally, the power of the wilderness also affects the Torah, in that the wilderness is not populated. Similarly, one needs the power of acting alone to receive the Torah, in that Torah study is not related to the masses and is not affected by masses, and one does not have to take particular actions only because others take them. That was the difference between Avraham and Haran, even though both opposed the entire world. The difference was that Avraham did so as a single individual — as an *Ivri* — where the whole world was on one side and he was on the other. Haran, on the other hand, was willing to go along with Avraham only if he saw that Avraham had emerged victorious. Thus it was from Avraham that there emerged an entire nation which has the power of the wilderness — of doing things alone. When Hashem approached every single nation in the world and offered it the Torah, each one said it was not interested, while the Jewish people said *na'aseh venishma.* That was through the power of the wilderness, which is independent of any other and is not linked to the overall population of the world.

I heard in the name of *Pachad Yitzchak* that once, when the *Sefas Emes* was a young child, he went into the room of his grandfather, the *Chiddushei Harim.* The *Chiddushei Harim* asked him what he had learned in *cheder* that day. He answered that he had learned the verse (*Shemos* 19:2), "Israel encamped there, opposite the mountain." On this, the *rebbi* had said that this meant that all faced the mountain, because they all awaited expectantly the giving of the Torah. "And I," said the young lad, "wanted to add that they had had their backs to the people. In receiving the Torah, it is not enough to have one's face to the mountain. One must also have one's back to the people, to be able to be alone and not follow everyone else's ways." His grandfather kissed him on the head, and said, "This one is worthy of becoming a great Torah leader." *Pachad Yitzchak* concluded by stating that it is not enough for yeshivah students to have their faces toward the mountain. They must also have their backs to the masses.

◆§ The Unity of the Jewish People at the Time of the Giving of the Torah

"Israel encamped there, opposite the mountain" (*Shemos* 19:2). *Rashi* notes, "like a single person, with a single heart." The simple explanation of this is that in order to receive the Torah it was necessary for the Jewish people to be unified, to fulfill "Torah, the Jewish people and the Holy One, Blessed is He, are one." However, in order to have all three as one, the Jewish people first had to be unified. It occurred to me, though, that there is another reason why it was necessary for the people to be unified at the giving of the Torah at Sinai. At that time, the Jewish people received the Torah under oath and made a covenant with Hashem, as it states (*Vayikra* 26:46), "These are the decrees, the ordinances, and the teachings that Hashem gave, between Himself and the Children of

Israel, at Mount Sinai, through Moshe." On this, *Ibn Ezra*[1] states that the words "between Himself and the Children of Israel" seem strange. Shouldn't the Torah have said, "that He gave to the Children of Israel"? Rather, this is an allusion to the creation of a covenant, and every covenant needs the agreement of both parties, the giver and the taker. That is what is meant by, "between Himself and the Children of Israel" — the two sides to the covenant. We see this in the *Shabbos zemiros,* where it says, "They all came together in a single covenant; they said *na'aseh venishma* in unison," namely that just as they were all in agreement about the acceptance of the Torah and all said *na'aseh venishma,* there was also agreement by all about making a covenant with Hashem.

We find that there was a difference between this covenant and the one made in the plains of Moab. While in the first covenant all were unified, in the latter we are told (*Devarim* 29:9-10), "You are standing all of you, before Hashem, your God: the heads of your tribes, your elders, and your officers — all the men of Israel; your small children, your women, and your proselyte who is in the midst of your camp." In the latter case it was impossible to unify their hearts, and there were differences between the various people. Thus, *Pachad Yitzchak* writes that they did not accept the covenant of the plains of Moab until they arrived in Eretz Yisrael, at Mount Gerizim and Mount Eival, for it was Eretz Yisrael that unified them. This is stated by *Maharal.* This covenant was unlike the covenant of Mount Sinai, where they reached the greatest heights, and where there was unity even without Eretz Yisrael. That is why at Sinai there was no division into heads of tribes, elders, etc.; they all accepted the covenant as one.

This high level that the Jewish people reached at Sinai was only for the time of the giving of the Torah. That is why there is a view that the Jewish people did not become guarantors for one another at Sinai, but only in the plains of Moab. As *Maharal* (*Nesivos Olam, Nesiv HaTzedakah* Ch.10) explains it, to become guarantors of one another they needed to be unified, and Eretz Yisrael unified them. The unity which they attained at Sinai, on the other hand, could not require them to be guarantors for one another, as that unity was only for that limited time.

We find this clearly in the *Minchah* prayer of *Shabbos,* where it states, "You are One and Your name is One, and who is like Your people Israel, one nation *in the land,*" in that only in Eretz Yisrael did the Jewish people become a unified nation permanently. At Sinai, the unity was not permanent, and dissipated soon after the giving of the Torah.

---

1. I saw the same thought in the memorial volume of *Pachad Yitzchak,* p. 363, who quotes it in the name of *Ramban.*

◆§ The Advantages of the Oral Torah

We are told (*Menachos* 29b) that Hashem showed Moshe the Torah learning of R' Akiva. Moshe said to Hashem, "Lord of the Universe! You have shown me his Torah. Now show me his reward." Hashem said, "Turn around." He turned around and saw that they were weighing R' Akiva's flesh on a scale. Moshe said, "Lord of the Universe! Is that the Torah and its reward?" Hashem said to him, "Remain silent! That was My intention." This passage seems puzzling, because while Moshe asked to see R' Akiva's reward, Hashem showed him R' Akiva's torment and did not answer his question.

We see in the above account that Hashem showed Moshe how they weighed the flesh of R' Akiva on a scale, but did not show him (as related in *Berachos* 61a) R' Akiva's death *al kiddush Hashem* (in sanctification of Hashem's Name) in that they combed his flesh with metal combs, and how he died as he completed saying the word "*echad*" of the *Shema* verse. Let us explain this matter more fully.

The Holy Books tell us that Moshe was the source of the Written Torah, while R' Akiva was the source of the Oral Torah. *Beis HaLevi* (*Drush* 18) writes that in the first Tablets, all of the Torah was written down, including every single Torah thought that every Torah scholar throughout the ages would ever innovate. All of this was there miraculously on the Tablets, just as the centers of the letters *mem* and *samech* remained in place miraculously, even though they were totally unattached to the rest of the letter.

However, when the first Tablets were broken and the second Tablets were given to Moshe, Hashem gave Moshe the Oral Torah (the *Mishnah, Talmud,* and *Aggadah*) separately, orally. *Beis HaLevi* quotes the Midrash (*Shemos Rabbah* 47:1) that Moshe said to Hashem, "Let me write it down for the Jewish people," but Hashem refused to allow this, because He foresaw a time when the heathens would rule the Jewish people and take the Torah away from them. This we saw in the days of Ptolemy, who copied the Written Torah. Had the Oral Torah also been written, the heathens would also been able to take away the Oral Torah from them.

Beis HaLevi (*Drush* 18, *She'eilos U'Teshuvos Beis HaLevi,* Part II) also notes that when the second Tablets were given to the Jewish people along with the Oral Torah, they ascended to an even higher level. Prior thereto all the Torah was contained within the Tablets, and the Jewish people had two functions — to observe the laws of the Torah and to preserve the Torah. At that time they were only like a vessel into which the Torah was placed, just like the Ark of the Torah in which the *Sefer Torah* is placed, where the Ark is considered to be an appurtenance of a ritual object but not a ritual object in itself. Afterwards, when the second Tablets were given, the Oral Torah was given to them, and the Jewish people were considered to be like the parchment of the Oral Torah, as we read, "Write them on the tablets of your heart." Just as the parchment of a *Sefer Torah* is the actual ritual object and not an appurtenance, for the parchment and the writing on it are both together the Torah scroll, similarly the Torah and the Jewish people are one entity.

Now that R' Akiva was the source of the Oral Torah, whatever happened to him was a paradigm for what happened to the Oral Torah in *galus* (exile). Just as the parchment and the writing on a Torah scroll are two separate entities which together are the Torah scroll, so too was the flesh of R' Akiva considered like the parchment of the Oral Torah, while the Oral Torah which he had acquired was a separate entity. When he was killed, it was only his body — the "parchment," as it were — that was controlled by the non-Jews, who weighed his flesh with a scale. The non-Jews, though, did not control his Oral Torah, and we are thus guaranteed that the Oral Torah will never be forgotten by us or our descendants forever.

Now we can understand that Hashem indeed showed Moshe the reward of R' Akiva, who merited having the Torah become his own. Even though the non-Jews totally controlled his body when they weighed his flesh, that was only the "parchment," while they were unable to control his Torah learning. This was Hashem's plan: to have the Oral Torah remain exactly that, so that the other nations would not be able to control it and change it throughout the bitter *galus*.

We are told in *Eruvin* 54a that had the first Tablets not been smashed, no nation or tongue would have been able to rule the Jewish people. The *gemara* also adds there that had the first Tablets not been smashed, there would have been no such thing as forgetfulness in the world. Both of these happened in the time of R' Akiva, in that non-Jews ruled the Jewish people and destroyed the Temple, and it was in his generation that Torah was forgotten. Both of these resulted from the smashing of the first Tablets. As stated in *Yevamos* 62b, R' Akiva had 12,000 pairs of students, and all died in one time period because they did not show respect to one another, leaving the world desolate. *Rashi* there explains that the world was desolate because the Torah was forgotten. The *gemara* there ends by telling us that R' Akiva came to the rabbis in the south and taught them, and they reestablished the Torah. Thus we see that whatever happened to R' Akiva happened to the entire Jewish people, for R' Akiva was the source of the Oral Torah, and just as R' Akiva reestablished himself, so too the Jewish people reestablished itself. That was R' Akiva's reward that Hashem showed to Moshe.

☙ The Greatness of Action in a World of Action

Magen Avraham 494:1 explains that the reason for the custom of staying up the whole night of Shavuos is to rectify the actions of the Jewish People when they all went to sleep on the night before the receiving of the Torah. My grandfather, R' Yechezkel Levenstein, asked how they could possibly have gone to sleep after all the days of preparation until they reached the spiritual level of *na'aseh venishma.* After all, they had been waiting with such great anticipation that time and again Hashem had to warn them not to approach the mountain, as it states (*Shemos* 19:12), "You shall set boundaries for the people roundabout, saying, 'Beware of ascending the mountain or touching its edge; whoever touches the mountain shall surely die.' " This was later repeated, because one warns a person in advance and then warns him again as the time approaches. *Chiddushei Harim* explains that just as the other nations were tested by being told of *mitzvos* which were against their nature — Eisav about the prohibition against murder, Yishmael about the prohibition of committing adultery — thus the Jewish people, which has a tremendous desire to come close to Hashem, was tested by the prohibition against coming close to the mountain. How then, after all their preparations, did they go to sleep that night?

I heard in the name of the late R' Schwab (the *Mashgiach* of Gateshead) that they erred in thinking that the Torah would be given through prophecy, for in the giving of the Torah Hashem showed them that there is none but He: "From heaven He caused you to hear His voice in order to teach you, and on earth He showed you His great fire, and you heard His words from the midst of the fire" (*Devarim* 4:36). They thought that the Torah would come to them in a dream as they slept, and they accordingly went to sleep. Hashem, however, wanted to show them everything while they were awake, and in the same way He appeared to Moshe, with (*Bamidbar* 12:8), "Mouth to mouth do I speak to him," and to show them that there is none like Hashem.

The way the events at Sinai and the receiving of the Torah took place served as the source for the words of the Gaon of Vilna, quoted by his student, R' Chaim of Volozhin, in *Sidra d'Tzniusa,* that even though the soul can understand great ideas while a person is asleep — as the soul goes up and studies in the study centers on High — that is not the most important thing. What is most important is that which a person accomplishes while awake, through hard work when he chooses the good and turns to studying Torah. In doing so, he gives pleasure to his

Creator, may His Name be blessed. On the other hand, whatever the soul comprehends during one's sleep is achieved without any effort and without any freewill decision or specific desire on the person's part, and is inferior to what one learns while awake. Thus, the giving of the Torah at Sinai had to be done while they were awake and not asleep, to teach future generations that whatever a person achieves is only through working hard at improving his Torah knowledge and wisdom.

My grandfather would say: "See how far-reaching an action can be! Because the Jewish people went to sleep that night, we need to rectify that deed each year, and for more than 3,000 years, old and young have afflicted themselves and have not gone to sleep. And this is so even though that generation did not go to sleep for their own enjoyment, but in order to experience prophecy. Thus we can see the power of a single action!"

We read in *Sotah* 48b: "R' Elazar asked: What is meant by (*Zechariah* 4:10), 'Who is scornful on the day of small things?' What causes the tables of the righteous to be spoiled (i.e., for them to receive a lesser reward) in the World to Come? It is their limited faith in the Holy One, Blessed is He." The question that we can obviously ask is that if they had only limited faith in Hashem, why should they be called "righteous"? Is the fact that their faith was limited in nature nothing more than a minor problem? *Pachad Yitzchak* answers that here we are obviously speaking of people who had faith in Hashem. Their failing was in not realizing that everything in the world is of great consequence, coming as it does from Hashem, while they felt certain things are small and inconsequential. That is why they spoiled their tables in World to Come.

Ruth Rabbah 6:4 (quoted in *Chochmah U'Mussar* p. 381) notes that Elisha ben Avuyah (who had turned away from the Torah path) became ill. R' Meir was told, "Your rebbi, Elisha, is sick." R' Meir went to visit him and said to him, "Repent!" [Elisha] asked him, "Will they still accept me after what I have done ?" [R' Meir] answered, "We have read (*Tehillim* 90:3), 'You reduce man to pulp and You say, "Repent, O sons of men' " — that even when a man is crushed to pulp [he may repent]." Elisha started to cry and died. R' Meir rejoiced, because he said, "It appears that my teacher died while repenting." From this we see that if a person cries and repents for even but a short time, he can be saved from the torments of *Gehinnom*. This teaches us the power of even a small action in this world. This is true for a small act of repentance and also when one performs a *mitzvah*. Just before his death, the Gaon, as he held his *tzitzis* in his hand, said, "One is able to buy, for pennies, a *mitzvah* which our Sages said is equal to all of the other *mitzvos*. Imagine the gift which we received when we received the Torah."

⁂ The Merit of Receiving the Torah as Opposed to the Sin of the Golden Calf

The *gemara* states in *Shabbos* 88, "R' Simai expounded: When Israel stated *na'aseh* ("we will do") before *venishma* ("we will hear"), 600,000 ministering angels came and placed two crowns on each one's head, one for *na'aseh* and one for *nishma.* When Israel sinned [with the Golden Calf] 1,200,000 destructive angels came down and took them away, as it states (*Shemos* 33:6), 'So the Children of Israel were stripped of their jewelry from Mount Chorev.' "

From the *gemara* it appears that it was the sin of the Golden Calf which made them lose the two crowns they had received when they had said *na'aseh venishma,* and that no other sin would have made them lose these two crowns. This needs clarification. Furthermore, *Avnei Nezer* (brought in *Shem MiShmuel* p. 52) notes that there is a Midrash that says that when the Jewish people sinned with the Golden Calf, Hashem said to them, "You have violated *na'aseh* with the Golden Calf; now be sure not to violate *nishma.*" If by the sin of the Golden Calf they only violated *na'aseh,* why did they lose both crowns, including the crown of *nishma*? Again, had they reversed the order and said *nishma vena'aseh* they would not have received any crown, because that would be the normal sequence of events: first to hear and then to do. The reason they received the crowns was because they pledged to do even before they had heard, thereby using the hidden secret of the Ministering Angels, as stated in the *gemara.* By doing so, they earned the same two crowns which the angels have. However, since by saying *na'aseh venishma* they had simply reversed the normal order, shouldn't they have been entitled to only one crown for that one action of reversing the order?

The *gemara* in *Shabbos* 88a states, "R' Elazar said: When Israel stated *na'aseh* ("we will do") before *nishma* ("we will hear"), a *bas kol* (a voice from On High) came forth and said, 'Who revealed to My children this exalted secret, which is used by the Ministering Angels?' as we see in (*Tehillim* 103:20), 'Bless Hashem, O His angels; the strong warriors who do His bidding, to obey the voice of His word.' " I once heard R' Eliyahu Lopian explain the passage, using an allegory. If a person comes to ask his friend for a favor without specifying what he wants, the friend will say, "Tell me what you want, and I'll see if I'm able to help you. After all, it might be something which is beyond my capability." That only applies to mortals, but when we deal with angels, whose sole purpose in having been created was to fulfill their mission, there is no doubt that they were created with the ability to accomplish whatever task is assigned to them.

Now we can understand better that when the Jewish people accepted the Torah with *na'aseh venishma,* in the words of Rava this shows that the Jewish people went with Hashem in complete trust, like one does with someone he loves. Thus they relied on Hashem not to subject them to anything which they would be unable to withstand. In other words, they believed Hashem would give them the power to observe the Torah which He was giving them, and did not try to make any prior calculations. Rather, they accepted it with full conviction. The reason is that one who adopts this approach has an entirely different *nishma* experience than one who starts with *nishma* and only then adds *na'aseh,* and only does what he does because of the intellectual calculations which he has reached. That was why they merited two crowns, one for *na'aseh* and one for *nishma.* Had they said *nishma vena'aseh* they would not have merited any crown. When they reversed the order and said, *na'aseh venishma,* they merited two crowns — one for *na'aseh* and one for *nishma* — because even the *nishma* had a certain *na'aseh* element in it (see *Shem MiShmuel* p. 90, regarding the *piyut* before *Kedushah*).

Now we can also understand why they lost both crowns at the time of the sin of the Golden Calf, because the sin of the Golden Calf came about because now they made calculations, arguing that Moshe must have died, and who was there to lead them to Eretz Yisrael? Even though they did not actually sin with the Golden Calf, because the only ones who worshiped it were the mixed multitude who had accompanied them from Egypt, they were guilty in that they did not protest, after they, too, had made the same calculations. This sin specifically undermined the entire receiving of the Torah by *na'aseh venishma,* and that was why they lost the two crowns which had come about through their acceptance through *na'aseh venishma.*

❦ ❦ ❦

Let us return to the question of *Avnei Nezer,* that if by the sin of the Golden Calf they only violated *na'aseh,* why did they lose both crowns, including the crown of *nishma*? We can also ask another question: Why is it that when they received the crowns there was one angel for each person, who brought down two crowns for each, but when removing the crowns, there were two angels — one for each crown? I have also seen a question asked on the verse (*Shemos* 33:6), "So the Children of Israel were stripped of their jewelry from Mount Chorev." We are told two verses earlier (v. 4) that "no one donned his jewelry," so why did they have to be stripped of it?

It would appear that v. 4, "no one donned his jewelry," referred to the crown they received for *na'aseh,* but as they had not sinned with *nishma,* they did not lose the second crown immediately, and it remained with them. Later, though, when they heard that Hashem had said to Moshe (ibid. v. 5), "If I ascend among you, I may annihilate you in an instant," it was clear that they still had to repent. Therefore they gave up their second crown, as is the custom of those who repent to cast aside from themselves all types of fancy clothing and dress in simple clothing. This we see in Rabbeinu Yonah (1:29), who writes, "[The one who repents] should not concern himself with fancy clothing and jewelry, as it states (ibid.), 'And now, remove your jewelry from yourself.' "

Now, as there were two separate acts of removal of their crowns, at two different times, they needed a separate angel for each removal, for the rule is that an angel does not undertake two tasks. On the other hand, when the crowns were given out, they needed only a single angel, because it was a single task. The removal of the two crowns was carried out at two different times, and thus there was the need for two separate angels.

◈ The First Tablets and the Second Tablets

In *Shemos* 34:1, we are told, "Carve for yourself two stone Tablets like the first ones, and I shall inscribe on the Tablets the words that were on the first Tablets, that you shattered." *Beis HaLevi* points out (*Drush* 18) that the second Tablets were not meant to replace the first ones, but rather that this was a new giving of a separate set of Tablets. That was why Hashem did not ask Moshe to return the pieces of the broken first Tablets, but instead asked him to carve new ones. *Beis HaLevi* goes on to explain various differences in the actual writing of the two sets of Tablets, beyond that which is stated in the Torah.

Let us explain and list the differences between the way the two sets of Tablets were given and the way they were received.

(A) When the Jewish people received the first set of Tablets, they attained the level of Adam before the sin of the tree of knowledge, in that the defilement brought about by the primeval snake, namely the *yetzer hara* (the Evil Inclination) had terminated. The acceptance of the Torah at that time and its study required a complete freedom from sin, because only someone who is totally free of sin could study the Torah given directly by Hashem.

At the time of the second Tablets, on the other hand, even a sinner was permitted to study the holy Torah, including a person whose heart and mouth were not totally free of sin. One must still know that the more free of sin a person is and the holier he is, the greater the aid he receives from Hashem in absorbing the Torah in his heart and in his brain. That was why our Sages[1] said that a person should not pray that Torah should enter into his body, but should rather pray that excessive food and drink should not enter his body, and thereby have a holier body. We also find in *Midrash Rabbah* (19:2) that at the time of David HaMelech young children who had not yet tasted sin were able to interpret the Torah in forty-nine different ways to declare something *tamei* (ritually impure) and in forty-nine different ways to declare it *tahor* (ritually pure), and David would pray, "May You, Hashem, guard them and guard the Torah in their hearts."

We also find in *Pesachim* 50a that R' Yehudah said in the name of Rav, "A person should always be involved in Torah and *mitzvos* even if it isn't for its own sake, for from (carrying these out) not for their own sake one (comes to carrying them out) for their own sake." That is the power of the second set of Tablets. In the case of the first Tablets, though, the rule was that a person was not to be involved in Torah and *mitzvos* if it wasn't for its own sake, because a person who was not free of the dross of a desire for prestige and other desires had no connection to Torah, and was even forbidden to study Torah.

(B) The first Tablets had the same attributes as the Tree of Life [*Tikkunei Zohar,* end of *Tikkun* 40 and *Avodah Zarah* 5a], in that the Angel of Death ceased to function and it was no longer possible to die. And it is obvious that the abolition of death also meant the abolition of pain, suffering, exile and poverty, because all of these might otherwise cause a disturbance to one's Torah studies. Thus, a person was totally free of any concerns, as stated in *Avos* 6:2, " 'The Tablets were God's handiwork, and the script was the script of God, engraved ("*charus*") on the Tablets' (*Shemos* 32:16). Do not read [the word] as *'charus'* ("engraved") but as *'cheirus'* ("freedom"), for no person is free unless he studies the Torah." However, when the second Tablets were given, we are told in *Yalkut Mishlei,* they were given in conditions of poverty and a world full of worldly cares. With the second Tablets, though, all the Torah one learns — regardless of the external factors — is one's own. One works hard at learning it, learns it and often forgets it, as stated by R' Yitzchak (*Eruvin* 54), "When the [first] Tablets were smashed, the trait of forgetting came down to the world," and only through hard work and exertion does the Torah become one's own. Now there are internal disturbances, such as forgetting the Torah, and external disturbances, such as subjugation to [other] regimes, and it is only in such circumstances that one can truly acquire the Torah. Thus with the second Tablets we are told *(Avos* 6:4), "This is the way of [acquiring the] Torah: You will eat bread with salt and drink water by measure, and sleep on the floor, and you will work hard in Torah study. Only then will it go well for you in this world and in the World to Come."

---

1. *Tosfos, Kesubos* 104a, "*Velo.*"

(C) I saw in *Michtav MeEliyahu* (II:24) that the first Tablets were given more as a gift from heaven than through human powers, whereas the second Tablets were given through human powers. With this, I would like to explain that which our Sages said in *Shabbos* 88b, that at every word which came forth from Hashem, every person's soul departed, as it states (*Shir HaShirim* 5:6), "My soul departed at His decree." Hashem then brought down the dew, which He will use to revive the dead, to revive these people. We need to understand why, if Hashem would in any event revive them, did He need to give them the Torah in a way that would have their souls depart at every word. Why didn't He restrain His might as He did in the *Mishkan*? Rather, this teaches us that the Torah was given through Divine powers greater than the ability of mankind, yet a person must do all that is in his power and ability, and upon doing so he can expect Divine help. [Also see *Michtav MeEliyahu,* who describes the dangers of Divine powers.]

◆§ The Type of Reception Needed for Receiving the Torah

Michtav MeEliyahu quotes R' Tzvi Hirsch Brody that time does not pass one by, but that rather one travels through time. Throughout each year there are a number of "stations," and all the *yamim tovim* are like these. Just as a station remains in the town in which it was built, so too does the holiness of every specific time remain the same throughout history, and Shavuos, the time of the giving of the Torah, has the same sanctity in time now that our forefathers had at the actual time of receiving the Torah. It is our duty — each and every one of us — to each year receive the yoke of the Torah anew on Shavuos, because that is the time of receiving the Torah. I once saw in *Sefas Emes* that to the extent a Jew accepts the Torah on Shavuos, that will be his portion in Torah study in the coming year, for Shavuos is the Rosh Hashanah of the Torah. Thus the obligation on each person on Shavuos is to accept the Torah again.

This day has no other obligation except the acceptance of the Torah, and we have an extended period of time to prepare for it, namely the forty-nine days of *sefirah* leading to this acceptance. Let us explain what is required in order to accept the Torah.

It is quoted in the name of the Gaon of Vilna that each day, when a person gets out of bed, he must accept the Torah anew. The Gaon bases himself on a *Mishnah* in *Avos* (3:5), "Whoever accepts upon himself the yoke of the Torah, there will be removed from him the yoke of the authorities and that of worldly affairs." The Gaon says that anyone who accepts the yoke of the Torah daily in full sincerity is guaranteed not to have any earthly concerns that day that would hinder his Torah study. What, then, is the difference between the daily acceptance of the Torah and that on Shavuos?

It would appear that the difference between the two is that on Shavuos one' s acceptance of the yoke of the Torah must be out of love, to realize and understand that without this day we would be no different than the other billions of people in the world, and therefore it is a day of rejoicing in having received the Torah. However, the acceptance of the Torah on the other days is acceptance out of fear, as in the words of *Avos* (3:5), "Whoever accepts upon himself the yoke of the Torah there will be removed from him the yoke of the authorities and that of worldly affairs, and whoever does not accept upon himself the yoke of the Torah there will be placed on him the yoke of the authorities and that of worldly affairs." We can see this from the verbose manner in which the *Mishnah* here is stated, for after all, shouldn't the second part, regarding one who doesn't accept the yoke of the Torah, be understood in terms of its being the opposite of the first? Rather, what the second part adds is that one who does not accept the yoke of the Torah actually has the other yokes placed on him. Thus the daily acceptance is one of fear of the consequences of non-acceptance, and that acceptance must be renewed daily.

Now, since the acceptance of the Torah on Shavuos must be with joy, in order to attain the level of joy in the Torah one needs a great deal of preparation, and that is given to us in the counting of the *sefirah* and the three days before Shavuos (when the Jewish people were forbidden to approach Mount Sinai). Thus, *Chochmah U'Mussar* (I:104) wrote something which should bring joy to our hearts: "In reality, Hashem should not have given a free gift of His Holy Torah, because He already favored man with knowledge and discernment and all seventy powers needed to understand things, and man was sent to the world to be tested. This way, he can attain the World to Come through his efforts, so that he will not need to be ashamed and embarrassed in the World to Come for the gifts he receives.

"Man was blessed with intelligence to see how the universe, the world and everything in it, was prepared for him, including whatever he needs for food or drink, clothes and medicine. Just as he has the knowledge of how to plant a seed and have it produce a hundredfold, so too does he have the intelligence to understand that the reason he was created is to examine everything and to go in Hashem's ways, like Avraham, Yitzchak, and Yaakov, and to beg and plead to Hashem to show him the path to follow, to prepare his soul for the World which is Only Good, at the time when he returns to the place from which he came. It was only through the merits of our holy forefathers that we merited receiving the Torah, which is broad and deep. Now all we have to do is to prepare ourselves to go in the paths of Torah and the fear of God."

Proof to the words of the *Alter* of Kelm is quite clear from Ruth the Moabite, who was not brought up or educated in the ways of the Torah and fear of Hashem, and was the daughter of the king of Moab. And about Moab we were told (*Devarim* 23:4), "An Ammonite or Moabite shall not enter the congregation of Hashem," because of their corrupt ways, as stated by *Ramban* in *Parshas Ki Seitzei.* Yet, by studying, Ruth discovered the true path of the Jewish people, the Chosen People, to whom it was proper to cling. As a result, she left all the pomp of this world and became a poor woman who needed to glean in other people's fields, just so that she could become a part of the Jewish people and live under the *Shechinah.* As Boaz said to her (*Ruth* 2:11-12), "You left your father and mother and the land of your birth and went to a people you had never known before . . . to the God of Israel, under Whose wings you have come to seek refuge." Ruth came to these conclusions without Torah and only through logical recognition by studying the world.

By studying what *Chochmah U'Mussar* writes and how Ruth acted, the heart of each person should have aroused in him feelings of joy and gratitude for our lot and our destiny, that we merited receiving the Holy Torah which teaches us the path that we must follow in order to merit this world and the World to Come, as we are told in *Sotah* 21, on the verse (*Mishlei* 6:22), "As you go forth, it will guide you; as you recline, it will guard you; and when you awake, it will converse with you." "As you go forth, it will guide you" — that is in this world. "As you recline, it will guard you" — that is when you die. "And when you awake, it will converse with you" — that is in the World to Come.

◆§ The Torah Reading for Shavuos

"They journeyed from Refidim and arrived in the wilderness of Sinai and encamped in the wilderness; and Israel encamped there, opposite the mountain" (*Shemos* 19:2).

Rashi explains that the journey from Refidim was juxtaposed with their arrival in the wilderness of Sinai to teach us that just as they arrived at Sinai in a state of repentance, they left Refidim in a state of repentance. Our Sages tells us that the place was called "Refidim" because "their hands were weakened ("*rafu yedeihem*") in their performance of the *mitzvos*" (see *Ba'al HaTurim* on *Shemos* 17:8). This name is problematic, because we have a rule that when a person repents out of love of Hashem, all his sins become *mitzvos.* Why, then, did the name of the place remain unchanged?

It would appear that it is meritorious for a place when a person draws from it a spiritual benefit. Refidim was a place that offered them a remarkable lesson in the dangers posed to a flesh and blood person, for even after all the positive experiences the people had at the Sea of Reeds, at Marah, with the manna, and the well which followed them, a specific place and time can still lead to a weakening of one's performance of *mitzvos.* [1] Thus the name remained unchanged as an object lesson to all.

We must still explain what they repented of in the desert. We understand that at Refidim they repenting their falling away in their performance of *mitzvos,* but in the wilderness of Sinai they were at the highest level of spirituality, and what should have caused a need to repent?

It appears that there is a hint in the conclusion of the verse as to why they needed to repent, in that we are told, "they encamped in the wilderness, and Israel encamped there, opposite the mountain." First, we need to note the following: It is known that R' Sa'adiah Gaon would repent each day on his previous day's knowledge of Hashem, for each day he refined his knowledge and his closeness to Hashem, in accordance with (*I Divrei HaYamim* 28:9), "Observe and seek out all the commandments of Hashem, your God." And since on each day he was drawing closer to Hashem, he would repent his more limited closeness to Hashem and his less satisfactory observance of the *mitzvos* in the previous days.

It appear that that was the repentance in the wilderness of Sinai, as hinted in "Israel encamped there, opposite the mountain," for they saw there that the service of Hashem is akin to the climbing of a very high mountain, about which we read (*Tehillim* 24:3), "Who may ascend the mountain of Hashem, and who may stand in the place of His sanctity?" Thus, each day one must ascend the mountain and reach a deeper understanding of Hashem, and thereby come closer to Him. They then repented about that which they had lacked the previous day, in that their understanding of Hashem the next day was superior to that of the previous day.

This is also what our Sages meant in *Succah* 52, that in the World to Come the Holy One, Blessed is He, will bring the *yetzer hara* (the Evil Inclination) and slaughter it before the righteous, etc. To the righteous, it will appear as a huge mountain, which they climbed day by day in their getting closer and closer to Hashem, and they will merit thereby that which R' Chiya bar Ashi said in *Berachos* 64, that *talmidei chachamim* (Torah scholars) have no rest, neither in this world nor in the World to Come, as it states (*Tehillim* 84:8), "They advance from strength to strength; each one will appear before God in Zion."

---

1. We must say that the place was instrumental in having them weaken their performance of the *mitzvos,* because otherwise it would not have had its name.

■ *Israel encamped there, opposite the mountain* (19:2).

Rashi brings the *Mechilta,* which explains the word in the verse, "there" ("*sham*"), which would seem to be superfluous. From this we learn that only "there" did the Jewish people camp "like a single person, with a single heart." At every other place there were all types of recriminations and arguments. It would appear that the place itself was conducive to unity, because they camped opposite Mount Sinai, a mountain which our Sages tell us was extremely modest. Thus, on the verse (*Tehillim* 68:17), "Why do you prance, O you mountains of majestic peaks?" we are told (*Megillah* 29a) that a *bas kol* came forth and told the other mountains, "Why do you oppose Mount Sinai? You are full of blemishes when compared to it." Thus, because of the humility of Mount Sinai, the Jewish people were moved to be humble and tolerant of others[1] and that is why there were no arguments there.

This might also be the meaning of *Baba Metzia* 59b, where R' Yehoshua said, "We do not pay attention to a *bas kol,* because You (i.e., Hashem) wrote in the Torah at Mount Sinai (*Shemos* 23:2), 'You are to follow the majority.' " On this we can ask: Why does the R' Yehoshua state "You wrote in the Torah at Mount Sinai"? Why mention Sinai here? Wouldn't it be enough simply to say, "You wrote in the Torah"? The reason is because the entire *halachah* which requires one to follow the majority, even if the individual who opposes them is a greater Torah scholar than all the others, in an act of acquiescence starting at Mount Sinai.

We should also note that the *gematria* value of "Sinai" is the same as "*ani*" — a poor person, and an attribute of Mount Sinai was that it was able to motivate a person who was poor in good attributes and proper actions.

■ *Moshe ascended to God, and Hashem called to him from the mountain* (19:3).

Ibn Ezra asks: It is obvious that Moshe would not ascend the mountain with receiving Hashem's permission in advance. That being the case, shouldn't the order in the verse be reversed, namely that Hashem called to Moshe and then Moshe ascended? *Ramban* and *S'forno* both write that "Moshe ascended" means that Moshe prepared himself to receive prophecy, because he knew that Hashem wanted to speak to him. Hashem had already told him at the burning bush (ibid. 3:12), "You will serve God on this mountain," i.e., that he would receive the Torah, as *Rashi* notes there. That was why, as soon as they arrived at the mountain, Moshe prepared himself with great alacrity for prophecy.

It occurred to me that one can say that Moshe ascended to God by means of prayer, namely that he immediately began to pray to Hashem.

---

1. *Rashi* on *Bamidbar* 12:3 explains that humility includes tolerance of others.

After all, our Sages tell us (*Berachos* 6b) that prayer is of the greatest importance in the world. The *Alter* of Kelm explains that prayer is something which lifts up a person. By praying there, Moshe fulfilled "You will serve God on this mountain." After all, prayer is service of the heart, and as Moshe immediately prayed to Hashem, he merited "Hashem called to him from the mountain" (19:3).

■ *Moshe ascended to God, and Hashem called to him from the mountain saying, "So shall you say to the House of Jacob and relate to the Children of Israel"* (19:3).

Or HaChaim, quoting the verse in which both names of Hashem are mentioned, states that it is commonly known that the word "*Elokim*" refers to God's attribute of strict justice, while "*Hashem*" refers to His attribute of mercy until the Torah was given. As this verse contains both Names of Hashem, Moshe thought that Hashem had combined His attribute of strict justice with that of mercy. Thus, on *Bereishis* 1:1, at the beginning of the *Chumash, Rashi* states that the reason the Torah begins with "*Elokim* created" rather than "Hashem created," was that at first Hashem wanted to make the world according to strict justice. When He saw that the world could not survive with that alone, He added the attribute of mercy to that of strict justice. This we see in the verse (*Bereishis* 2:4), "On the day Hashem *Elokim* made heaven and earth." We are told in *Tehillim* 89:3, "The world will be built on mercy." We also find in *Avodah Zarah* 9a, that the first 2,000 years of the world it was void, in that there was yet no Torah in the world to keep it going, for as we are told in *Nedarim* 32 on *Yirmiyahu* 33:25, "If my covenant (i.e., the Torah) with the night and with the day would not be," then "I would not have set up the laws of heaven and earth." That was why Hashem added the attribute of mercy to that of strict justice. However, after the first 2,000 years had passed and the Torah was given in order to have the world continue to exist through the observance of the Torah and the *mitzvos,* Moshe thought there is no longer the need to have the attribute of strict justice along with that of mercy and the world could exist entirely on strict justice. That is why it states that Moshe ascended to "*Elokim*" rather than to Hashem.

We learn in *Menachos* 29b: "R' Yehudah said in the name of Rav: When Moshe ascended on High, he found the Holy One, Blessed is He, attaching 'crowns' to the different letters in the Torah. Moshe said to Hashem, 'Lord of the Universe! What is missing on these letters that You had to add these crowns?' Hashem answered him, 'There will be a certain person in the future, in a number of generations, whose name will be Akiva ben Yosef, who will expound myriads of *halachos* on each such "crown"' . . . Moshe said to Hashem, 'Lord of the Universe! You have shown me his Torah. Show me his reward.' Hashem said, 'Turn around.' He turned around and saw that they were weighing R' Akiva's flesh on a scale. Moshe said, 'Lord of the Universe! Is that the Torah and its reward?' Hashem said to him, 'Remain silent! That was My intention at the beginning of the Creation of the world.' " *Shelah* explains that what Hashem meant was that He showed Moshe what would have happened had He continued with his original plan of creating the world according to strict justice. From this we see that even after the giving of the Torah there is still very much of Hashem's attribute of mercy present, and without it the world cannot exist. Thus it states that Hashem (and not "*Elokim*") called Moshe to the mountain, to show us that we still need to have Hashem's strict justice tempered with mercy.

■ *You shall be to Me a kingdom of ministers and a holy nation* (19:6).

S'forno states, "'A holy nation,' is as stated in *Yeshayahu* 4:3, 'Of every remnant that will be in Zion and every remaining one in Jerusalem, "Holy" will be said of him.' On this, our Sages said (*Sanhedrin* 92a), 'Just as the Holy One exists forever, these, too, will exist forever.' " In other words, "a holy nation" tells us that the Jewish people will exist forever.

In accordance with this, one can explain what we are told by our Sages (*Sanhedrin* 94b), that King Chizkiyahu planted a sword by the door of the *beis hamidrash* and said, "Whoever does not occupy himself with Torah study will be pierced by the sword." *Netziv* (*She'eilos U'Teshuvos Meishiv Davar* 1:44, "*Ellah*") understood this to be literal, namely that they would kill everyone who did not sit down and study Torah. Using that as his basis, *Netziv* remarks that if people only studied Torah in order not to be killed, that certainly was not studying Torah *lishmah* — for its own sake, which is not the level of Torah which brings *kedushah* (holiness). However, a bigger concern is how it is that they permitted people to be killed for the sin of not studying Torah.

Based on *S'forno* above, we can say that the time of King Chizkiyahu was definitely a time of great danger for the Jewish people, and without the merit of Torah study the Jewish people would not have survived. Only through the merit of Torah study and the promise of "You shall be to Me . . . a holy nation" could they be saved from the hands of Sancheriv. That was why King Chizkiyahu ruled that whoever did not study Torah was considered a *rodef* (a "pursuer" with the aim of harming another) of the Jewish people, and the *halachah* is that "one who comes to kill you, take the initiative and kill him first." Indeed, the law is that a *rodef* should ideally be killed by the sword. Thus, at that very perilous time, when they needed the merits of Torah study to save them, anyone who was lazy and

---

1. A "pursuer" with the aim of harming another.

did not study Torah was considered like a *rodef,* and that was why King Chizkiyahu decreed what he decreed.

As to the question of *Netziv* that this was certainly not studying Torah *lishmah,* one can say that the difference between *lishmah* and not *lishmah* refers to the ideal way to perform the *mitzvah* and to fulfill Hashem's wishes, but when it came to rescuing the Jewish people in a time of great danger, just the very fact that people studied Torah — regardless of their motivation — was enough to bring salvation from their troubles.

■ *These are the words that you shall speak to the Children of Israel* (19:6).

Rashi on "these are the words" comments, "no less and no more." It would appear that what *Rashi* means by this is that even though there are seventy different facets to the Torah, nevertheless the way to come to love of Torah and to clinging to it is only a single one, as described here by Hashem, and that is by thinking of the punishment ("you have seen what I did to Egypt" — v. 4) and of the reward ("I have borne you on the wings of eagles"), and having an appreciation of how much Hashem loves His nation ("and brought you to Me"). If one contemplates these matters, it will bring him to a proper acceptance of the Torah and to cleaving to Hashem and His Torah.

■ *These are the words that you shall speak to the Children of Israel. Moshe came and summoned the elders of the people* (19:6-7).

As Hashem told Moshe to speak to all of Israel, why did he call only the elders at first? From this, we see that Moshe taught them an important lesson in *derech eretz* (proper behavior). Indeed, the rule is that *derech eretz* comes before Torah, and the *derech eretz* Moshe taught the Children of Israel was that one first speaks to the elders.

This also explains why Hashem did not instruct Moshe to first speak to the elders. If this had come from Hashem rather than from Moshe, there would have been no lesson in *derech eretz.* Thus, when Hashem told Moshe to speak to the whole nation and Moshe on his part spoke to the elders first, he taught everyone a lesson in *derech eretz.* Furthermore, since our Sages tell us that *derech eretz* comes before Torah, it is clear that one who practices *derech eretz* is thereby observing the Torah. Along these lines, we find R' Yitzchak Ze'ev HaLevi Soloveitchik, the Brisker Rav, commenting on the saying by our Sages that "had the Torah not been given, we could have learned modesty from a cat," etc. The *gemara* (*Eruvin* 100b) says now that the Torah was indeed given, modesty itself is part of the Torah law, and one must learn the *derech eretz* of modesty from the Torah itself, and only that which the Torah instructs us to be considered modesty is indeed such.

■ "On the third day Hashem shall descend in the sight of the entire people on Mount Sinai" (19:11).

We find in *Shabbos* 89 that the reason the mountain was called "Sinai" is because from there hatred ("*sin'ah*") descended upon the pagans. *Rashi* explains that the other nations were angry because they were not the ones who had received the Torah.[1]

Tosefes Berachah asks why the mountain was named for hatred (i.e., "*sin'ah*"). Why shouldn't its name have been derived from the love which was bestowed on the Jewish people by Hashem when they received the Torah? The reason for the present name may be in order to elicit merit for the Jewish people even when they do not observe the Torah and there is no reason for Hashem to love them — and yet the hatred of the other nations for the Jewish people remains. Indeed, in *galus* (exile) one sees this hatred clearly. It is through this hatred that the love of the giving of the Torah is aroused, for this hatred is a by-product of the receiving of the Torah, and the more the others hate us, the more merits are ascribed to the Jewish people.

This principle also explains a topic in *Berachos* 32b: "[The Jewish people] said to the Holy One, Blessed is He, 'Since there is such a thing as forgetfulness before Your Throne of Glory, could You possibly forget our conduct at Sinai?' Hashem answered, 'I (a reference to the "I" of "I am Hashem your God" — the first of the Ten Commandments) will not forget you.' " On the same topic, we are told that R' Elazar said in the name of R' Oshaya, "What about the verse (*Yeshayahu* 49:15), 'Even these may be forgotten' (implying that God might indeed "forget")? That refers to the [sin of] the Golden Calf, while 'I will not forget you' (in the same verse) refers to the giving of the Torah at Mount Sinai." Thus, even if the Jewish people do not observe the Torah which they received at Sinai because of their being under foreign domination, nevertheless "I will not forget you," because the enmity of the other nations still exists, and that enmity traces back to the giving of the Torah at Sinai. That is why Hashem will never forget our conduct at Mount Sinai.

We also find a similar idea in *Bamidbar Rabbah* (22:2), on the verse (*Bamidbar* 31:3), "to inflict Hashem's vengeance against Midian." Hashem referred to it as the vengeance of the Children of Israel, while Moshe referred to it as Hashem's vengeance. Moshe said, "Lord of the Universe! Had we been uncircumcised or pagans or deniers of the *mitzvos,* they would not have hated us. They have only persecuted us because of the

---

1. I heard from a woman that when she was a child in England, she and her sister were chased by a group of non-Jewish girls. When the girls asked why they were being chased, the others replied, 'Because we are jealous of you." Thus we see that this feeling of jealousy is within their souls, which is a frightening thought.

Torah and the *mitzvos* which you gave us. Therefore vengeance is Yours — 'to inflict Hashem's vengeance against Midian.' "

■ *Hashem said to Moshe, 'Descend, warn the people, lest they break through to Hashem to see, and a multitude of them will fall'* (19:21).

Rashi quotes *Mechilta* (*Parshas Yisro* 14:5), that even if a single one of them falls, he is as important to Me as a multitude.

What this may mean is to be understood from the end of the *Mechilta* passage there, for Hashem said, "Even if a single one of them is lacking, he would be equivalent to the entire Creation," because Hashem made a condition with Creation that the very Creation would be conditional on the acceptance by the Jewish people of the Five Books of the Torah [see *Rashi* on *Bereishis* 1:31]. So too are we told in *Sanhedrin* 91b that the Torah is the inheritance of the entire Jewish people ever since the six days of Creation.[1] For this purpose, "the Jewish people" consisted of the 600,000 who left Egypt, in order to keep Hashem's condition that all 600,000 should accept the Torah. Therefore, if even a single one was missing, the count would not be complete and the condition made by Hashem during the Creation would not have been fulfilled.

We also find that *Mechilta* quotes the prayer of Ya'avetz (*I Divrei HaYamim* 4:10), "Ya'avetz called out to the God of Israel saying, "If You bless me and expand my borders, and Your hand is with me, and You keep me from harm, that I not be saddened . . .' God granted him that which he had requested." *Mechilta* then proceeds to explain the verse: "If You bless me" — in studying the Torah; "and expand my borders" — with students; "and Your hand is with me" — that I do not forget that which I studied; "and You keep me from harm" — that you grant me friends like me; "that I not be saddened" — that the Evil Inclination does not hinder me in my study of the Torah.

The above passage teaches us about how one acquires Torah. First, one must study himself. Thereafter he must teach, because one learns more from his students than from anyone else. There is nevertheless the possibility, *chas veshalom,* of forgetting. Indeed, we find that R' Yosef, who was a leader in his generation and a Torah scholar, forgot all his Torah learning because of illness. One also needs friends like oneself, to show him when he is right and when he has strayed. Yet, even after all of this, the Evil Inclination can come and cause the person to fritter away his time rather than learning Torah. The thought is really frightening.

■ *God ("Elokim") spoke all these statements, saying* (20:1).

This is the first verse of the Ten Commandments. We know that when

1. See *Rashi* on that passage.

the term "*Elokim*" is used, it denotes God's attribute of strict justice, yet in the next verse we are told, "I am Hashem," which denotes God's attribute of mercy. *Or HaChaim* writes that the reason why the word "*Elokim*" is used in regard to the giving of the Torah, in addition to "Hashem," is to teach us that the Torah was given through both of Hashem's attributes — strict justice and mercy.

Tosfos Yomtov on *Mishnah Berachos* (7:3) explains why there are differences in the use of Hashem's Name between the prelude to *birkas hamazon* (Grace After Meals) where, if there are ten males present one adds "*Elokeinu,*" and the blessing when one receives an *aliyah* to the Torah, where the name used is "Hashem." In the case of *birkas hamazon,* he notes, it is with justice that Hashem supports all His creatures [for, having created them, He must support them], but when Hashem gave us the Torah, He did so in His great mercy, as we see in *Yeshayahu* (42:21), "Hashem desired for the sake of [Israel's] righteousness that the Torah be made great and glorious." For the Creator to tell His creatures His ways and His laws is certainly not something which strict justice would require, and indeed Hashem did not do so with the other nations, which are also His creatures. That is why in the blessings of the Torah we use the term "Hashem."

This explanation needs clarification because, on the verse in *Bereishis* (1:31), "the sixth day," *Rashi* explains that "the sixth" refers to the sixth day of Sivan — the day the Torah was ultimately given — where Hashem made the Creation of the world conditional on Israel accepting the Torah, and if they wouldn't, the world would return to a state of *tohu vavohu.* According to this, the Torah was given under the condition of strict justice, for without its acceptance the *tohu vavohu* would return, and it is only proper for the Creator to ensure that His creatures survive. Why, then, does *Tosfos Yomtov* state that the giving of the Torah was an act of mercy?

It would appear that, indeed, the giving of the Torah was an act of justice on Hashem's part, as without it the world could not have survived, as we see in *Yirmiyahu* (33:25), "If My covenant with the night and with the day would not be, [then] I would not have set up the laws (i.e., the Torah) of heaven and earth." Nevertheless, "the fact that the Torah was given to the Jewish people was an act of mercy," in that Hashem chose us above all the other nations on earth. Now we can understand that when the Torah states, "God ("*Elokim*") spoke all these statements, saying" (*Shemos* 20:1), it alludes that under His attribute of strict justice, Hashem gave the Torah to the entire world, but it was "I am Hashem . . . Who has taken you out of the land of Egypt," referring to the Jewish people, to whom Hashem gave the Torah in mercy.

■ *You would have raised your sword over it and desecrated it* (20:22).

Rashi states, "From this we learn that if you raised your sword on it, you have desecrated it, because the Altar is meant to bring about peace between Israel and their Father in Heaven. That is why that which cuts or destroys may not be used on it."

We find something amazing in the verse (*I Shmuel* 17:54), "David took . . . the weapons [of Goliath] and put them in his tent." *Radak* explains that "his tent" means David's home, and that Goliath's weapons included everything except for his sword, for the sword was kept in the *Ohel Mo'ed* (the "Tent of Assembly") in Nov, "wrapped up in a cloth behind the *ephod*" (*I Shmuel* 21:10). The sword was kept there as a remembrance of the great miracle, and whoever came to the *Ohel Mo'ed* in Nov to pray or bring a sacrifice would see it and remember the miracle of Hashem's deliverance and thank Hashem for it, and it would strengthen his faith in Hashem.

We know that a sword, which signifies cutting short one's days on earth, may not be brought into the *Mikdash,* which was deduced from the fact that even stones carved with metal may not be used for the Altar. Thus, we find in *Sanhedrin* 82 that one was forbidden to enter the *Beis HaMikdash* with weapons. Yet, in spite of this law, we see that if by bringing a sword — in this case Goliath's sword — into the *Ohel Mo'ed* it will increase people's faith in Hashem, it is permitted.

Now we may ask why the stone used for killing Goliath was not brought into the *Ohel Mo'ed.* However, the *halachah* is that if a person is hanged, the tree upon which he was hanged is also buried, and the same would apply to the stone which killed Goliath, because it is improper to display a stone which killed a person. From this we can see how careful the Torah was in respect for human beings, for even though Goliath was an evil man and displaying the stone that killed him would foster greater faith among people, they nevertheless did not display a stone that would have shown contempt for Goliath.

Along these lines, we can understand why Hashem killed Bilam's donkey (see *Rashi* on *Bamidbar* 22:33), even though it would have been a glorification of Hashem's Name if one saw the donkey which had rebuked Bilam. Hashem nevertheless wanted to spare the feelings of Bilam and killed his donkey. Thus we see how Hashem cares about the feelings of people, even if this refers to an evil man such as Bilam.